What Professionals and Parents Are Saying About Betsy Brown Braun

Betsy Brown Braun has done it again! *You're Not the Boss of Me* is an essential tool for any parent, filled with deep wisdom and sharp insights. If you hope your child will embody empathy, respect, independence, and creativity, this book's practical tips will help you get there. Based in research and years of clinical experience, this volume is, quite simply, a treasure.

—Ted Mitchell, President, California State Board of Education, President and CEO, New Schools Venture Fund, President Emeritus, Occidental College, and former dean, UCLA Graduate School of Education and Information Studies, Los Angeles, California

Betsy Brown Braun's book, *You're Not the Boss of Me*, which offers very sound advice and guidance, gets to the heart of parenting issues today and provides useful and insightful principles for addressing them in a very accessible format. Synthesizing research and focusing especially on relevant issues . . . it gives you a quick overview and then offers solutions that are quite useful. Betsy also offers a helpful reminder of what matters and how we can make a positive difference in challenging areas as parents.

—Daniel J. Siegel, M.D., author of *Mindsight: The New Science of Personal Transformation*; coauthor, *Parenting from the Inside Out: How a Deeper Self-Understanding Can Help You Raise Children Who Thrive*; and Executive Director, Mindsight Institute

With refreshing clarity and extensive professional experience, Betsy Brown Braun writes directly and meaningfully to parents about their children. She alerts them to the nature of the spontaneous developmental process and offers valuable, very specific pathways for reinforcing the positive emerging behaviors that each child presents.

—Saul L. Brown, M.D., Emeritus Director, Family Child Division, Department of Psychiatry, Cedars-Sinai Medical Center, Los Angeles, California; Emeritus Director, Department of Psychiatry, Cedars-Sinai Medical Center, Los Angeles, California; and Emeritus Clinical Professor, Department of Psychiatry, Child Psychiatry, UCLA School of Medicine, Los Angeles, California

Once again, Betsy Brown Braun hits the nail on the head (so you don't have to hit yours against the wall!) with insightful, clear, and helpful advice for raising your children. If there were a Martha Stewart of parenting, she would be the one, with the "secret sauce" to helping you raise the kind of children we all hope to have.

—Jane Buckingham, founder of Youth Intelligence and author of
The Modern Girl's Guide to Motherhood

Betsy Brown Braun dares to give very specific answers for all the very specific issues that come up in raising a child in today's world. She gives answers, and she gives reasons for her answers. Best of all, her no-nonsense wisdom shines through on every page. I cannot think of a book that I have read about child raising that teaches as much about so much.

—Anthony E. Wolf, Ph.D., bestselling author of *Get Out of My Life, but*
First Could You Drive Me and Cheryl to the Mall?

Betsy Brown Braun is a rare combination of intelligence, experience and humor. . . . she is a remarkable gift to the lives of parents and children.

—Barbara K. Polland, Ph.D., M.F.T., Professor Emeritus,
Child and Adolescent Development, California State University,
Northridge; author of *We Can Work It Out!*

Just open any one of Betsy Brown Braun's books and you will see why she is one of the most sought after parenting consultants out there. Betsy has a great way of making the complex simple and helping parents find the right words when we are at a loss. Having one of Betsy's books in your hand is like having a piece of Betsy's wisdom, experience, and expertise at your fingertips at all times.

—Dr. Jenn Berman, marriage/family/child therapist, mother, and
author of *The A to Z Guide to Raising Happy Confident Kids* and
SuperBaby: 12 Ways to Give Your Child a Head Start in the First 3 Years

---

Betsy Brown Braun offers insight and expertise into one of life's most challenging and rewarding endeavors—parenting. Her direct approach provides support and guidance to navigate these often-uncertain waters and to help facilitate a more joyful parent-child connection.

–Cyndi Sarnoff-Ross, marriage and
family therapist and mother of two girls

Time and again I've referred my clients to the incredibly user-friendly *Just Tell Me What to Say*. After all, parenting is not in and of itself user-friendly—so this book is the most-welcome one in its class!

—Dr. Erica M. Rivera, clinical and consulting psychologist, mother of two girls

---

Betsy's wisdom and wit guides parents in the skills of child rearing. . . . Her influence today may just make a difference in making the world a better place tomorrow.

—Pearl Barlev, rabbi, chaplain

Betsy is an icon in child development. . . . Her "tell it like it is" approach doesn't leave any room for misinterpretations.

—Shadi Bakhtiari, director of Beverly Glen Playgroup and mother of two

---

Betsy's parenting tips are worth their weight in gold. . . . She is the go-to expert for parents at the end of their rope!

—Kristen Muller, parent and network news producer

Now whenever I help my children work through problems, they'll look at me and say, "Where did you hear that, your mommy book?" And I'll say, "That's right, it's in my mommy book, written by my mommy teacher" . . . Thank goodness for Betsy and her "mommy book."

—Lisa Breckenridge, Entertainment Anchor, Fox Morning News; mother of four-year-old twins

---

I often find myself in parenting situations where I ask myself "What would Betsy do?" Her advice and approach to parenting is respectful, straightforward, and real. Her book sits on my bedside table, dog-eared and always within arm's reach.

—Melissa Schrift, TV producer, mother of three children

Betsy's parenting strategies are like nuggets of gold. From dealing with unruly children in the backseat to getting out the door in the morning to answering those dreaded questions about death, sex, and money—her advice works.

—Laura Zimmerman, mother of twin eight-year-old boys

Betsy is our parenting Sherpa. Any time we run into something that is just throwing us off our parenting game, we call Betsy for a tune-up. You know Betsy's good when, after a particularly hard weekend with the kids, your husband says, "I'll call Betsy."

—Amy Glover, mother of two children

Betsy's pragmatic advice has given us the strength to be better parents. . . . She offers the ultimate parenting "tool kit" and a clear understanding of what children are going through every step of the way. No one should have a baby without her!

—Jill Chayet, mother of two boys

To drive a car you need a license. To be a parent, you drive blindly. Betsy is what I would call an expert in parenting advice as to prevent you from having a collision—an insurance policy in a sense.

—David and Deborah Fried, parents of two boys

Betsy is one of the most practical and thoughtful advocates for happy, healthy, and balanced families. At least once a day, I find myself asking "What would Betsy do in this situation?" Her books have made it much easier to answer this question quickly!

—Christine Weller, mother of two children

I find myself regularly reaching to my nightstand for Betsy's book for practical solutions to the day's dramatic parenting challenges.

—Amy Geibelson, mother of two girls

What was life like before Betsy? Betsy Brown Braun and her book have helped me become a better parent. Her attitudes toward parenting and discipline have brought structure and harmony to my home, where we can all enjoy and respect each other. Every mother should have one of her books by her nightstand!

—Carol Wetsman, mother of twin daughters

© Michael Branigan, David Michael Photography

About the Author

BETSY BROWN BRAUN is the bestselling author of *Just Tell Me What to Say*, a renowned child development and behavior specialist, popular parent educator, and mother of adult triplets. She is a frequent speaker at educational and business conferences, has been a guest expert on *Today*, the *Early Show*, *Good Morning America*, and NPR, and has been cited in *USA Today*, the *New York Times*, *Family Circle*, *Parents*, *Parenting*, *Cookie*, and *Woman's Day*, among other publications. As the founder of Parenting Pathways, Inc., Betsy offers private consulting and parent seminars as well. She and her husband live in Pacific Palisades, California.

You're
Not
the Boss
of Me

Also by Betsy Brown Braun

Just Tell Me What to Say

You're Not the Boss of Me

Brat-Proofing Your
Four- to Twelve-Year-Old Child

BETSY BROWN BRAUN

HARPER

NEW YORK · LONDON · TORONTO · SYDNEY

HARPER

HarperCollins books may be purchased for educational, business, or sales
promotional use. For information please write: Special Markets Department,
HarperCollins Publishers, 10 East 53rd Street, New York, NY 10022.

FIRST EDITION

Library of Congress Cataloging-in-Publication Data is available upon
request.

ISBN 978-0-06-134663-7

10 11 12 13 14   OV/RRD   10 9 8 7 6 5 4 3

For Ray,
my partner in parenting our three amazing kids and
my biggest fan, whose patience, flexibility, and
unflappable disposition enabled me to write this book.

Contents

❖

Acknowledgments

❖

As with parenting children, one's second book is completely different from the first. In some ways it's easier because you have more experience; in other ways it's harder because the first one still needs your attention. But in both instances it takes the help and support of family, friends, and in my case, colleagues.

Hope Innelli, my editor at Harper, was a gift to me from Mary Ellen O'Neill. A match made in heaven? I think so. Hope took pains to get to know my voice and guided me with endless patience and kindness. Mindy Werner, editor, word Ninja, and good friend, once again worked her magic with my manuscript. Alison Graham, my indefatigable publicist and cheerleader, sprinkled her optimism over each step of this project. Bob Myman and Jenifer Grega, my attorneys, were my tireless advocates.

Many colleagues have been supportive and enthusiastic, spreading the word about my first book, *Just Tell Me What to Say*, and cheering me on as I wrote this second one. I am so grateful and flattered to have won their confidence. For generously sharing their expertise and time once more, I especially want to thank family therapists Kathy Wexler, Phyllis Rothman, and Ian Russ. My colleagues Tandy Parks and Carol Gelbard shared their perspectives and insights just when they were needed. And Barney Saltzberg, children's book author, explored the importance of humor with me.

Erica Myers and her children, Mari and Delia, must be thanked for allowing me to use their Chore Chart, reproduced in chapter 9. Young Zachary Eisenstadt gets full credit for inventing the word "choosements," which has found its way into my practice and into chapter 9.

"You've got to have friends" is quite an understatement when you are immersed in writing a book. I am so lucky to have an incredible cheerleading squad—Barb, Janie O, Nanci, Jill, and Lucie. Thanks, too, to my sister, Lorna, for her enthusiasm, and to my brother, Jon.

My children, Jessie, Ben, and Lucas, have always been my inspiration, to say nothing of my real teachers. Talk about on-the-job training! Each of them has evolved into a magnificent adult, and they continue to make me and their dad incredibly proud. Thank you for allowing me to share some of our juiciest family tidbits. You make me real.

I feel privileged to work with parents as a consultant, group facilitator, and seminar leader and to share in their lives. Their parenting successes and failures have enhanced my understanding about what works with children and families. For this I am truly grateful.

How to Use This Book

❖

This book is chock-full of information that will help you brat-proof your child. While you *can* read it in one sitting, I don't recommend that, because it may leave you feeling a bit overwhelmed. Instead, I suggest that you focus on one chapter at a time in order to process the material in more manageable sections. You might begin with the chapter whose subject matter interests you the most, or the one that screams, "My child needs me to know this right now!" Read the chapter, absorb the information, and let it be the filter through which you view your child for a while as you practice the tips and scripts I've included. Work on that one trait until you feel comfortable with the suggested techniques. Each of the chapters stands on its own, offering information and a course of action to digest—and that takes time. The messages you want to send take practice, too. You just can't rush the parenting process, nor can you master it all in one sitting.

Regardless of which chapters speak to you, I urge you to begin by reading chapter 1, "Did You Hear Me?: How to Talk to Your Kids." All parents can use a refresher course on how to communicate effectively with their children. Otherwise, all the good stuff you will get out of this book might fall on deaf ears.

The chapters are ordered in the same way a building is built: The foundational character traits come first. But there is some overlap among the chapters. That's because certain techniques are used to develop more than one character trait, and some traits expand on others. To my mind, you can never hear good advice often enough.

The advice in this book is geared toward parents of children roughly between the ages of four and twelve, although parents of younger and older children will find it helpful as well. When I say "young children," I am referring to children in the four- to six-year-old range; the term "elementary-school-age children" includes seven- to ten-year-olds; and "older children" refers to those ages eleven and twelve. In the back of the book you will find an appendix, which contains information to further help you on your parenting journey. For additional resources, including video clips on specific topics and my blog, visit my website: www.betsybrownbraun.com.

Introduction

❖

"Can you believe my son actually said, 'You're not the boss of me!'?" Thus began the litany of complaints this particular dad shared with me about his seven-year-old child. He continued, "I hate to admit it, but my kid is a brat."

I wish I could say this scenario is rare, but I assure you, it isn't. So often parents tell me tales of raising the child they swore they'd never have. But while many a discouraged parent has declared her child a brat, the label has different meanings for different parents. Her brat might be whiney; another's might be irresponsible and lazy, while yet another's is sneaky and unreliable. And though most bratty traits are intolerable at any age, some actually have the potential to be positive attributes later in life. For example, the child who is disrespectful now may have the capacity for the wit and irreverence that so often gives rise to out-of-the-box thinking—traits that may someday serve him well if used appropriately.

The truth is, most kids behave in bratty ways at one time or another in the course of growing up. In some instances it is a necessary part of some stages of development, as the child struggles to be separate from you, become his own person, and test his wings. Being bratty can also be a temporary condition in response to an environmental change such as a new baby, a parent who is working out of town, a relative who has been visiting for too long, a move to a new house. Or bratty behavior can be a cry for help due to unhappiness at school, trouble with peers, or issues with siblings. With some adjustments, these brats can be brought back on course. As different as brats might be, when the behaviors fall within the realm of what is typical for a child's developmental stage, parents can take comfort in knowing that their child—the brat—is not on the way to being a lifelong sociopath. (When this is not the case, however—when the child's challenges are unrelenting and appear to be quite different from those any other parent is encountering—it is a good idea to consult with a mental health professional.)

Essentially, what every parent needs to know is that the brat is a child who doesn't feel significant, who doesn't feel as if he plays a meaningful role, and who needs to feel that he has a purpose in the life of the family. While it may seem that the opposite is true—that he believes the world revolves around him—he is really just trying to find his place in that world. Sometimes being a brat is better than having no place at all. The child who has a loving, trusting, and secure relationship with his parents, who feels connected to his family and feels good about himself, is not a brat.

Brat-proofing your child—that is, cultivating character traits and inculcating him with values—is a tall order indeed. In ages past it wasn't something that parents even had to think about. In the rural cultures that dominated the landscape for centuries, children were apprenticed to their parents, working side by side with them from sunup to sunset. Their participation was essential. Who had time to be a brat? Children developed their parents' character traits because that was exactly what they were exposed to all day long. Extended families lived together, too. Grandma was there to reinforce the message with a clear explanation or a gentle "slap upside the head" and to give an embrace to underscore the lesson. Core values were reiterated by many and passed on from generation to generation.

And it was real life, not a lecture or wagging index finger, that taught the lesson. When a responsibility wasn't met, the system broke down, and everyone suffered. If the eggs weren't collected, there wasn't any breakfast. If the field wasn't watered, the crops died. Meaningful consequences followed irresponsible behavior.

Today, children are no longer needed for their help in the fields. Many are treated more like an acquired accessory than a contributing member of society. Raising a child who shines takes a whole lot more than a little silver polish now and then. It is a twenty-four-hour-a-day job. I don't have to tell you that being a parent is the most difficult role you will ever have. (It will also be the most rewarding, but you may have to wait a while before you get to that part.) And raising a child who is mostly not a brat can be especially hard work.

Over the years, I have been a teacher, a preschool director, and now a child development and behavior specialist, not to mention the mother of triplets! Working with hundreds of families, I have seen that the children who go through their growing years with the least sense of entitlement also have specific character traits such as independence and self-reliance, empathy and gratitude. It is these traits and others that this book teaches you to facilitate and encourage as a means to brat-proofing your child.

Although life is much easier today in many ways, it is much harder in other ways. Families are splintered; each member has a full calendar of daily obligations and events. Not only do we live in a world filled with conveniences and amenities, but there are choices, distractions, and temptations aplenty for parents and children. Today's world often sabotages the very values you want to instill in your child. Missing is a whole range of meaningful interactions with people. Even the family meal has all but disappeared. When and where will these crucial lessons be absorbed? Not out in the fields anymore, that's for sure.

And then there is technology. As amazing and useful as it can be, technology often works against the child's cultivation of anti-brat character traits. As an ever-increasing part of our children's daily existence, iPods, DS, Xboxes, Wii, and computers are robbing our children of the raw contact—the real interactions, feedback, body language, facial expressions, and social cues—that build their social and emotional intelligence. They cut our children off from other people. And it is from experiences with real people—most of all, from *you*—that children absorb valuable and lifelong lessons.

Children learn from living with their parents. That's a lot of responsibility, I know. It is really hard to be the person you want your child to be. In fact, it's really hard to be the person each of us wants to be. Life gets in the way. You are tired, hungry, irritated, stressed, and any number of other normal states that result just from getting through each day. But your children are paying attention and look to you as a model of how to be.

You may be wondering if it is ever too late to start instilling these good qualities in your children. I sure hope not. Even if you don't see the light until your child is in elementary school (much like the dad of the seven-year-old at the start of this introduction), all is not lost. Children as old as eleven can still be turned around. Bear in mind, however, that the older the child, the more difficult the process, both for the child and the parent. He will have had many years of practice being a brat, and you will have developed the habits that allowed that to happen.

Many times my husband shared with our children the story of a buddy who flunked out of college after his first semester of his freshman year. After hearing the news, the young man's father sent his son $600 with the suggestion that he figure out what he wanted to do with his life, anywhere but at home. After six months of renting a bed in a stranger's house on the other side of the country (having gotten there by bus) and washing dishes in a restaurant for a living, he decided to return to college and raise his grade point average, proving the point that lessons can be learned at any age. But as this man's parents would tell you, it's a whole lot harder to close the front door on your almost-adult child than it is to make good on a threat to take away your six-year-old's tech time.

It's no coincidence that we say couples are "expecting" when they are pregnant. Every child comes into this world carrying his parent's expectations, as well as their hopes and dreams. You want your baby boy to grow up to be honest and responsible, independent and self-reliant. If only that were all it took—wanting and expecting! But as you well know, your child is not like a self-basting turkey; he's not going to emerge well-seasoned and having just the right tenderness without some effort. Your child is born with potential, but not with complete abilities. He comes with the capacity to be the kind of person you want him to be, but it is up to you to cultivate in him these character traits and values. Having high expectations means that you believe in his capability. My hope is that this book will help give you the tools you need to teach all of your children how to be active agents in their own lives. It is, after all, your job to make it their job.

CHAPTER ONE

"Did You Hear Me?"

How to Talk to Your Kids

"Do as I say, not as I do." You know that old saying, right? But what in the world was that person thinking? Could he have been more off base? The truth is you cannot rely on words alone. When it comes to brat-proofing your kids by instilling in them the most important character traits, you can't "talk" those traits into your kids. Cross my heart, it's the truth! The most powerful way parents can communicate with their children is by example. As Robert Fulghum, author of *Everything I Need to Know I Learned in Kindergarten,* said, "Don't worry that your children never listen to you; worry that they are always watching you." Your children are observing all of the time; they take in your every move, and they remember each one. When you are on the phone gossiping with a friend and think that your child has been struck deaf, I promise, he is absorbing what you say. When you are having a heated argument with your spouse behind closed doors, he hears that too. When you mumble under your breath about how much you detest your neighbor, your child is picking up that message as well.

My client Lisa confessed that she talks on her cell phone in her car all the time, even though she knows it is illegal here in California. I asked her if she does it when her kids are with her, and she said, "Yes, but they understand that sometimes you have to break the rules." It's those "Yes, but . . . "s that speak the loudest. I can almost promise Lisa that not only will her children rationalize that talking on the cell phone is okay when they're driving (even though she will have told them never to do it), but that excuse-making for rule-breaking is contagious. And Lisa has demonstrated the technique!

Modeling is the most powerful form of communication there is, but it is just one of four ways in which we "teach" our children. *Nonverbal communication* is the second. This includes your posture, stance, and facial expression as well as the way in which you set up the communication. Your proximity to the child and even the height differential between you two sends a message. The third form, *verbal communication*, is the most obvious form of communication, and it includes not only the words you say but also your decibel level and tone of voice. Your tone, in turn, gives your child potent clues about what you are feeling at that moment. Finally, there is the way in which a parent listens to her child. How well you receive your child's communications, verbal and nonverbal, gives your child a strong message.

Tips for Setting Up Communication

What you say, if supported by what you do (and vice versa), will have great impact, especially if you give serious thought not only to your words but also to the communication setup itself. Regardless of the child's age, the setup for the communication sends a message about how much you honor and respect your child.

- **Be deliberate.** The optimal distance for communication between two people is two to four feet, and no more. The space between players will depend upon the age of the child. The very young child often prefers to be right in your face, even sitting on your lap. It's hard to give an objective message when you are nose to nose with your child. And it invades personal space. The older a child is, the farther away from you he will want to be . . . like all the way across the room! Think twice about calling out to your child from across the house, or even from room to room, or couch to computer. Instead, say: *"I know that you can hear me from your room, but I value our conversations. Will you please come in here so we can see and hear each other clearly?"* Then ignore the inevitable grumbles. As your older child will always be busy, you may be more successful if you plan a time for your discussions. Ask: *"What might be a good time for us to talk? I don't want to interrupt what you are doing."*

- **Location, location, location.** Certain places lend themselves to conversations, especially the heavier ones. My particular favorite is the car. Not only are car talks great because you don't actually have to look at one another (sensitive topics and older children can be tricky), but both parties know there is a beginning and an end. You arrive at your destination and the conversation is over. Tuck time is another good time to talk because it is cozy and intimate. But heavy topics shouldn't be addressed before sleep, unless you are interested in a sleepless night for your child or for you. With older children and more serious conversations, sometimes it is helpful to plan them around something else—a walk, a hike, or a meal out.

A client, Janet, carefully planned a conversation she needed to have with her ten-year-old son, knowing that he would likely have an explosive reaction when he learned that previously made plans had been changed. While mother and son were on a bike ride at the beach, Janet explained—using carefully chosen words—that their weekend plans had been cancelled. Daniel was furious, spewed some bad language, and sped off ahead of her. Janet gave him a little time to himself and when she caught up to him, Daniel had calmed down enough for them to talk and not yell. Peddling hard used up a lot of angry energy.

- **Nothing should come between you.** Be aware of the barriers between you and your child when you are talking. Even a coffee table, the laundry you are folding, or the desk at which you are sitting separates you from your child and interrupts the flow of your communication. Tell him: *"I want to hear everything you have to say to me, and I want you to hear me. Let's sit together on the couch so we can talk."*

- **Noise is a barrier.** The television, the radio, and even running water are sensory distractions that can detract from your communication. Clearing the sound space between you gives your child the message that your communication with him is important: You want to focus on and hear him, and you want the same attention from him. *"What you say to me is so important. Because I really want to hear you, I am going to ask you to turn off your music while we talk."*

- **Get down on your child's level . . . or bring your sprouting adolescent down to yours.** Eye-to-eye communication levels out the playing field and takes away the home court (height) advantage. When

I taught sixth grade (at my height of 5' 4"), I began my conversations with the taller kids by saying, *"Have a seat so we can talk."*

- **Do not demand your child's eye contact.** Though your father may have grabbed your face in his hand and yanked it around to get you to look him in the eye, such a gesture will not enhance your communication with your child. In fact, doing so will detract from your child's focus as he thinks to himself, *I hate it when my dad holds my face. I am so mad at him for doing that.* He will not be able to concentrate on your words. In addition, for some children, especially those who may be challenged by sensory integration issues, looking at you takes a tremendous amount of effort. (See the box on sensory integration below.) As he struggles to keep his eyes on you, he won't be able to hear your words. Rest assured, a child can hear you even if he isn't looking at you.

  Looking someone in the eye is a sign of respect and part of the good manners you want your child to learn. It is reasonable to ask a child to do so as he grows; and the older he gets, the easier and more automatic this will become. But for children who are temperamentally more timid or introverted, looking someone in the eye is a real challenge. (See chapter 3, p. 39, for a discussion of temperament.)

SENSORY INTEGRATION

All people, even very young children, integrate in different degrees the information they take in through their senses. This process is known as sensory integration. Some people are particularly sensitive to noise, others to bright light. You might know someone who has a really "good nose," sniffing out a pie baked earlier in the day or a sponge that needs to be washed. There are people whose sense of touch is particularly heightened—seams on socks and tags in shirts are highly irritating to them. There is hypersensitivity (taking in too much information) and hyposensitivity (not taking in enough). The person hyposensitive to touch loves a deep tissue massage while the hypersensitive individual may be able to tolerate no more than a tickle. If you suspect that your child may have issues with sensory integration, consult your pediatrician about having an evaluation by an occupational therapist.

- **Use multiple senses.** Set your child up to receive your communication. Walk over to him, get down (or up) to his level, and put a hand on him . . . somewhere. This is a multisensory approach. He may not be looking at you, but he is hearing you and feeling you. There's no way he can say he didn't know you were talking to him!

- **Relax! Your child is extremely sensitive to you and your moods (even though it often seems that he doesn't care).** If you are tense, nervous, or ill at ease, your child will sense it. Try to be aware of your body language. Your feelings will be evident in your facial expression or in the way your arms are folded across your chest. Try to have an open, available stance, facing the child with your whole body.

  If you need to have a heavy conversation, practice what you want to say, even write it down in advance so you are clear about your agenda and script. And don't let your feelings get the best of you. You may need to make a mid-course correction. *"Hold on. I don't like what I just said. I need a do-over."* Crazy as it sounds, you really can start over. Your child will appreciate your ownership of the direction the conversation is taking. And he will learn he can do the same.

What Your Child Hears

Remember how the adults in the *Peanuts* comics were portrayed: *Waaaaaaohh Waaaohh Waaaohh,* like the noise of a horn, droning on in the background? That's not going to be you. The tone of voice that you use in any communication says as much as the words you choose. It gives a message about your attitude and the emotion behind your words. In fact, your child first hears your feeling before he ever processes your words. That is his first clue about how to interpret the conversation.

Tips and Scripts for Using an Effective Tone of Voice

- **The contagion of tone.** The mirror neurons in a human's brain (see chapter 2, p. 36, for a description of mirror neurons) contribute to our ability to take on the feelings of another person. Have you ever noticed that when someone whispers, you tend to respond in a whisper? When you use a calm tone, there is a greater chance that your child will react in a similar fashion. When you raise your voice, the volume pumps up your child's reaction to your level, thereby sabotaging communication. Making use of your child's mirror neurons can improve communication dramatically.

- **The tone needs to match the message.** Be sure to reserve your most serious tone for the most serious communication. When you want your child to stop poking the baby in the eye, saying *"Now sweetie pie, Stevie doesn't like it when you poke him in the eye,"* is not likely to stop the behavior. You must convey that message like you mean business. But do save your big voice for the big stuff. If used too often, your child will become immune to it.

- **Beware of your anger.** All parents get angry now and then, and at certain stages in child's life, your anger seems more *now* than *then*. Displaying your anger by yelling or using a really big voice signals danger to children. No child likes to feel that his parents are mad at him, and to the young child it is downright scary. Some children even say things like, "Stop yelling at me!" when the parent isn't even yelling at all. In this instance, all of the child's energy goes into defending against the anger, and he doesn't even hear the words his parents are saying. Use your loud, angry voice sparingly and not when you want a lesson to be learned. If you feel an explosion coming, remove yourself by saying, *"I am going to go in my room so I can cool off."* Not only will you be better able to deal appropriately with the situation at hand, but you are modeling what people should do when they are feeling explosive.

- **Consider your own decibel level.** Some people have loud voices (my husband, for example). Some children are particularly sensitive to loud voices, especially the child who may struggle with sensory integration issues. Speaking loudly usually signals anger (that means danger) to the child, and it doesn't guarantee that the child will get your message. Ever notice how an effective teacher gets her class's attention? She begins talking in a very quiet voice, and soon the whole class quiets down to hear her. Take a lesson from that teacher. You are an adult and can control your voice.

Some children use loud voices all the time. It may be genetic or because of a hearing issue—have you asked the pediatrician to check your child's ears and hearing? Might it be a characteristic of his Sensory Integration Dysfunction? Or has it developed just from living in a loud-voice house? Help your child to use a quieter voice by pointing out his use of the voice you want him to use. *"You are speaking to me in the perfect voice. That's a great inside voice."* And when he doesn't, *"That voice is too loud for inside the house. Let me help you take that voice outside, where it is just fine to be as loud as you want."* Don't threaten. Just walk him outside. Remember, it's not a punishment; it's a lesson. No anger, please.

Listening

It seems like listening should be really easy. But there is listening and then there is *listening*. It is one form of communication that sends a powerful message. It says: *What you say is important . . . you are important.* Or it says the opposite.

Tips and Scripts for Listening to Your Child

- **Your days are numbered.** Sad though it is, there will come a time when your child will prefer communicating (texting, IMing, posting on Facebook or tweeting, etc.) with his friends more than talking with you. Somewhere between the ages of eleven and seventeen, it will happen. The communications you have with your child are a gift, so honor them. When your child talks to you, take the time to listen. Stop what you are doing, turn your body to face your child, and look him in the eye. If you are unable to take the time that he deserves, give him a quick listen and say, *"I really want to hear what you have to say, but I can't give you my full attention right this minute. I hope it can wait until I come to a stopping point."* Be sure to get back to him as soon as possible. If you forget, it is a clear message.

- **Don't talk over your child.** It often takes a child longer than an adult to get his story out. Don't interrupt. Be patient and restrain yourself from finishing his sentence, thoughts, or story. It shows that you respect him and welcome his communication. The more patient you are and the more available you are to listening on his terms, the more he will communicate with you.

- **Listening means listening.** Some things a child says do not call for an answer, a solution, or an opinion. Listening can simply be your receipt of the gift your child is giving. An enthusiastic, *"Oh!"* or *"Is that so?"* or *"That must have made you feel happy (sad, mad, proud, etc.)"* followed by *"Thanks for sharing that with me"* is all that is necessary.

Getting Your Child to Talk

At least once a week a parent will ask me how to get her child to talk with her. Seems like a funny question, but I get it. Mom is really eager to hear every tidbit of his day. She asks the child, young or old, what he did at school, and he replies, *"I played."* Or *"Nothing."* There are lots of reasons that children don't offer up their news on a silver platter or don't feel like talking, and there are lots of things parents do that actually sabotage their goal of having a good schmooze with their child.

Tips and Scripts for Encouraging Communication with Your Child

- **A child's day belongs to him.** There aren't a whole lot of things that belong to a child alone, over which the parent has no control. His day is one of them. Sometimes a child needs to have his day all for himself. Painful as it is, he may not want to share it with you. Some children choose to withhold their news because it is a form of control over you.

- **It takes time to process a day.** Greeting your child with *"So, tell me about your day. What did you do at school?"* the moment he gets in the car might actually stop the communication that would have, given time, naturally sprung forth. All people need time to digest the events of the day. Occasionally, at dinner, my husband will ask me about clients, and that is the last thing I want to talk about, having been in the thick of it for nine or so hours. Kids are no different. When your child gets in the car, try telling him about your day. *"So, I'll tell you about my day. Today I had a meeting with a really interesting guy who has ten children. After that I went to the market, and the cleaner, and then I stopped by the hardware store to see if I could find a new soap dish for the shower."* Believe me, after hearing all that, your child is liable to say, *"Well, don't you want to hear about my day?"* And sometimes just being empathetic is enough communication to loosen his tongue. You might identify how he is feeling by saying: *"You look pooped out. It must have been a tiring day for you today."* And leave it at that. Sometimes being together in silence is supportive and loving, too.

- **Don't be intrusive.** Sometimes parents overstep their bounds. This is a tricky one, as you don't really know what the boundaries are. Even though you have cultivated a climate of open, frequent communication, children often become more private as they grow older. Right before your eyes, the operating instructions seem to have changed. Pay attention. Your child lets you know how much is too much to ask. If you have overstepped, it's always good to own your mistake with: *"I am sorry. I didn't mean to be nosey; I was just curious, and you know I love everything you share with me."*

- **Talk about things that don't focus on the child.** It is amazing how willing to talk and listen children can be when they are not the subject matter! Try telling a story, sharing something you saw, something you have been thinking about, even the news. *"I read in the paper that there is some discussion about banning skate boards from the village. I guess an older woman was knocked over and hurt pretty badly. Kind of interesting, yes?"* And then just wait to see what your child says. It may take a while, but he is thinking about it. Allow for the silence and, if nothing comes, try a different topic. Ask your child his opinion, and then listen to his answer.

- **Expand your communications with your child beyond giving directions.** My friend Linda shared the story of her seven-year-old son, Brett, who said to her, "You never talk to me." Horrified, she denied it to the hills, saying, "I talk to you all the time. What are you talking about?" He continued to claim that she did not talk to him, and when she asked him what he meant, he said, "You and Daddy talk all the time. First you say something and then he says something, then you say something and he says something." "Oh," Linda replied, "You mean having a conversation." "Yeah," Brett said, "When we talk you just tell me what to do." Linda hadn't been talking *with* Brett; she had been talking *at* him.

- **Beware of saying too much.** Whether you are giving an explanation or addressing a problem, children can take in only so much at a time. After the first few words or sentences, they stop listening. *"Blah blah blah, Ginger,"* as the famous Gary Larson cartoon goes, when he is admonishing Ginger the dog about getting into the garbage. Use your words sparingly, and make the ones that you do use count. In other words, less is more.

Children's Questions

Children ask questions for all sorts of reasons: Sometimes they are trying to get your attention; sometimes they are stalling before bedtime; and sometimes they really need information. Real questions are good things—good because the child is thinking and gathering new information and good because the child is coming to you for answers. Not only can you filter and shape the knowledge he will gain, but you know he will get correct information and not "street stories." Every time your child comes to you with a question, it is an opportunity for you to deepen your trusting relationship.

Tips and Scripts for Answering Children's Questions

- **Answer questions with great care.** Questions are gifts from your child. In order to welcome your children's questions and get more of the same, the way in which you answer your child's questions should be deliberate.

  All questions are good questions. There is no such thing as a "stupid question." Communicate that message with, *"I am so glad you asked me that question."*

- **Take the time you need to think about your answer and create your script.** *"I want to answer that question in a way that you will understand. I am going to think about it and get right back to you."* Then be sure to get right back; don't wait days. Not answering tells the child a lot about his question.

- **Listen for the question underneath the question.** What is your child really asking? Restate what you have heard. *"Are you asking what happens to a person's body after it is buried?"*

- **Listen for the question that hasn't been asked.** Take a stab by saying, *"I think you are telling me that you are worried that I am going to die. Is that right?"*

- **Correct any misinformation you may uncover**. *"Actually, the stork doesn't bring babies. Would you like to know how babies are made?"*

- **Use the "drip method" and answer a little bit at a time.** If you have not given enough information, your child will tell you. If it is enough, you'll know it; the questions will stop . . . for now, anyway!

- **It takes time for an answer to sink in.** Be patient and tolerant. Your child may continue to talk about the answer or even ask the question over and over, as he processes the information. Be sure to be consistent with your answer and refrain from *"I already told you the answer."*

- **Tell the truth.** Questions should be answered factually and honestly but with the child's age and development in mind. Doing so encourages the child to continue to come to you with his questions and not seek answers elsewhere.

    As yesterday's wild teens are becoming adult parents, I am getting many more questions about whether a parent should reveal her past when it includes "sex and drugs and rock and roll." How interesting it is that the parents who have the most colorful histories feel most strongly the need to lie.

- **Always follow up.** Check in with your child by asking *"Did I give you the answers you needed?"* Or, *"What do you think about the answers to your question?"* Or, *"Do you have any more questions?"* In so doing you will be able to gauge your child's feelings and understanding about what you have just said. With some children it is best to check in as the conversation winds down. With others, you might do a "revisit" a little while later. Different than weighing in with your child as the conversation winds down, a revisit happens twenty minutes to a couple of hours after an event or conversation. It allows the child time to process what has been said or done, and it is usually initiated by you. A revisit can be met with a resolute "I don't want to talk about it" if you are revisiting an unpleasant scene or misbehavior. In this case you can say, *"You don't have to talk about it. I will."* Sometimes parents fear bringing up an issue up all over again, but the revisit cements an experience. It is less emotion-packed, and provides both parties with the distance to be more objective.

- **It's okay not to know an answer.** Not knowing gives you an opportunity to teach the child some of the ways that answers are found. You might say: *"I think we have a book that might have the answer to your question or we can have a look at the library."* Or, *"Why don't we call Uncle Rich and see if he knows the answer,"* or *"Let's Google that question and see if we can find an answer."*

Communication and Technology

Technology is a double-edged sword. While it enhances, expedites, and makes possible communications, it also tends to reduce our interactions to a one-dimensional state: just words. When messages are read or heard in this way, the recipient must infer the rest of the communication. Everyone knows you can't have a meaningful conversation via the Internet. Too much is lost: There's no feeling, no inference, no tone behind the words. The same holds true for texting, IMing, tweeting, and writing on someone's Facebook wall. Recent research has pointed to the importance of face-to-face contact. When humans observe the facial expression of others, the mirror neurons in their brains ensure that both parties will experience the feelings.

While people in the United States accept technology as the norm, its overuse is stacking the odds against meaningful communication. I am not asking that you ban technology from your home. (It would be easier to take away your child's cell phone than to get you to give up your own Black-Berry.) But I am suggesting that you create a balance in your home and in your children's lives.

I am reminded of the three boys, probably aged six, eight, and ten, whom I saw sitting on a bench as they waited for their family's table at a local restaurant. They were together, but they were not at all together, as each was buried in his own iPod. Those boys should have been bugging each other, fighting, laughing—just being together as siblings. But their iPods cut them off from one another. How sad that they didn't even get to hear their parents chew them out for misbehaving!

Too much time with technology deadens people to real, meaningful, feeling-filled communication. Reading tweets is no substitute for reading someone's facial expression and knowing the tone and words to use in response. Face-to-face communication: Use it or lose it? I certainly hope not.

Knowing the components and skills of effective communication is the first step in brat-proofing your child. Now you can use this information as you begin to cultivate the character traits discussed in the rest of the book. On your mark, get set . . .

CHAPTER TWO

"Why Is That Girl Crying?"

Growing an Empathetic Child

"My child is just heartless," a devastated client sobbed to me, incredulous that her five-year-old child could be so "uncaring toward her friend."

Empathy—the ability to experience and understand to some degree the feelings of others, and to respond in helpful ways—is the foundation of many desirable qualities, including kindness, respect, honesty, responsibility, self-reliance, all the traits discussed in this book. Being empathetic is part and parcel of being a moral person. It is at the core of positive social behaviors and is basic to all human relationships. Children who are raised without empathy training grow into adults who are self-centered, callous, and often narcissistic. There are enough of those people in our world today; we don't need any more.

Having empathy is one of the things that keeps a child on the right track as she grows. When she is a preschooler, it helps her to navigate her social world, seasoning her social interactions, and expanding her repertoire of social skills. As the child's circle widens, empathy gives her a point of reference for processing these interactions and making decisions about how she will behave. Focusing on other people's needs and desires forces consideration of oneself, too. As your child watches others respond to certain situations, she is learning how to respond as well. Watching others with sensitivity ultimately helps her develop the inner voice that screams *yes!* or *no!* in the face of peer pressure and hopefully encourages her to make the right choices. (See chapter 6, p. 117, for a discussion of a child's "little voice.") As a child enters the more daunting period of adolescence, having empathy enables her to evaluate all the information coming at her from peers and the media, particularly the kind of information that threatens to pull her off track. The misogynistic lyrics to the rap song she hears will be accompanied by the sound of your voice (and her own inner voice) telling her that those words degrade women. She will recognize that the billboard with the sexually explicit message is inappropriate. Early and ongoing lessons in empathy enable the growing child to make better sense of her world and thus enables her to navigate it more effectively.

The Development of Empathy

Researchers tell us that to some extent human beings are prewired to be empathetic. (Note that this doesn't mean the empathy will actually manifest.) This existence of this prewiring may be hard to believe when you watch your eighteen-month-old walking around saying "mine mine mine!" like the seagull in *Finding Nemo*, as she is grabbing toys from her little friends, or when you try to get your three-year-old to share with her younger sibling. The young child is developmentally focused on herself; she is egocentric. Her worldview is only as big as her reach, so putting herself in someone else's shoes is quite a challenge, except if it means she gets to play with those shoes!

There is even some data that suggests being more or less empathetic is a matter of genetics. When Dr. Mark Brackett of Yale University looked at identical twins, he found that children with the exact same genetic makeup had highly correlated scores on measures for empathy, indicating that genetics plays a role in the development of this trait.

Here is what's interesting: The first buds of empathy can be seen in children as young as a year old. This child can recognize a person in distress and, in addition to demonstrating concern through facial expression, can offer comfort in the ways she knows how. In one experiment, researchers saw repeatedly that fourteen-month-old babies helped a woman retrieve a marker she intentionally dropped and could not reach. Only by her grunting and whining in her effort to reach the pen were the babies aware of her need, and they scaled obstacles in their way to pick up and hand the pen to her, thus exhibiting empathy. Experiments with eighteen-month-olds yielded similar findings.

Many a parent has reported her twelve- to fourteen-month-old baby's attempts to comfort a crying peer. When my own triplets were babies, still very much attached to one another, it was easy to see this in practice. One would cry and another would come to check it out. *What's going on here? Uh oh, someone is sad. This is not good. Should I be sad? Is something bad going on? This crying makes me uncomfortable. I had better soothe him.* And Jessie would run to find her brother Ben's pacifier or blankie. Certainly this was empathy. But from where I stood, the empathy involved Jessie soothing herself as much as it involved her soothing her sibling. *There is sadness here and I am not sure whose it is. Soothing* Ben *will make* me *feel better.* Developmental neuroscientists tell us that experiencing what happens to another as if it is happening to oneself is at the root of empathy.

The way in which Mommy is tuned into her baby is called attunement. Mommy comforts with her voice, her strokes, her pats, her kisses. And those small acts trigger the release of endorphins—the feel-good hormones—in the baby's brain. Baby absorbs those experiences as how one relieves distress. Through her attachment to her parents and experiencing their love and affection, she learns to respond in similar ways to others. One of the baby's primary learning modes is imitation, doing what she has experienced and watched. Such imitation also lays the groundwork for empathy and its expression, which will blossom later on. The capacity for empathy is hard-wired by virtue of the child's innate ability to imitate.

We know that the development of empathy seems to be related to three things:

- The child's age and development
- The child's temperament
- The physical and social setting in which the child finds herself

With the above considerations in mind, a child needs to have cultivated the following in order to demonstrate empathy:

- A strong self-concept, as differentiated from others
- The ability to read other people's faces
- An emotional vocabulary with which to express what she feels and observes
- The ability to understand and relate to why the person feels the way she does

- The ability to regulate her behavior because of her consideration of someone else.

Many of these skills begin to blossom around the age of two-and-a-half. But it is not typically until after the age of three or four, when the child has gained experience in the world and can relate to the woes and experiences of others, that she can understand and respond with empathy. The child needs personal experience as well as cognitive maturity in order to feel empathy for another.

Somewhere around eighteen months, the toddler understands that she is truly separate from her mommy or daddy in a new way and that other children inhabit her world, separate from her. Witness the toddler class full of eighteen-month-old babies and their parents. Each parent sitting on the rug is encircled by a collection of toys that the child has brought to her for protection. No one is going to get her toys! She understands that there are others who also want stuff, the same stuff she wants. That awareness of the other must be in place before a child is capable of true empathy.

When the child is close to three years of age, there is a change. While seeing things from another's point of view is still a challenge, she acknowledges the existence of that other perspective. Bumping up against this, and seemingly out of nowhere, the three-year-old "cops an attitude," folds her arms across her chest, sticks her nose up in the air, and lets loose with: "You are not my friend!" This age child may not be happy about sharing and other demonstrations of empathy, but she has the capacity for it. She can stand in another's shoes.

The four-year-old is able to identify with another person's feelings—not always willingly, but she can. It was not so long ago that she was still an egocentric-me-mine toddler. Looking out only for #1 still plays a role, but the four-year-old is gaining experience, perspective, and the ability to recognize feelings—her own and others'.

Not only can the five-year-old talk about how other people feel, but she can imagine different situations that yield different feelings, for herself and for others. The elementary school years and beyond are ripe with opportunities for cultivating empathy in all its forms—compassion, kindness, manners, emotional literacy (see p. 31), philanthropy—the works. Herein lies the meat of this chapter.

What Gets in the Way of Empathy?

While we know that all children have the capacity for empathy, it's not always that easy for them. Children are egocentric before they are anything else. Falling back into that default, me-first state of being occurs throughout the child's growing years. In fact, I am quite sure you know many adults whose first response is still to look out for #1.

In my parenting groups I hear over and over how the first-born child seems to have less empathy than the second or third—at home, anyway. But when you consider that child's position in the family, it makes sense. She was born first and had Mommy and Daddy, Grandma and Grandpa, and the rest of the doting relatives all to herself, at least for a while. Then along comes #2, and the spotlight shifts. It's hard to consider someone else, to feel empathy, when you believe you've been robbed of that which has been rightfully yours. It will take time, but all is not lost. As the child grows, so does her perspective. She derives satisfaction from people and places other than home and she will be more able to behave in empathetic ways.

Then there is the child who is temperamentally more introverted, timid, or "slow to warm up." You know her, she is the observer, the one who won't say hello, who hides her face in her mom's pant leg, who is a totally different child at home than out in the world. This child is first and foremost protective of herself. All of her energy goes into guarding against anything that might make her feel uncomfortable. How can she demonstrate empathy when she needs to protect herself? It isn't that she doesn't feel compassion; it's that the compassion is being overridden by her temperamental needs.

THE SHY CHILD

The word *shy* has such negative connotations that I make a conscious effort to replace it with words like *introverted, sensitive,* or *reactive.* Children who are labeled shy are burdened with preconceived notions about how they should behave and in many ways are actually given permission to behave that way.

There is much research that points to the role of genetics in these children. Shyness is often a temperamental trait with which the child is born.

However, it does not have to be a lifelong sentence. Many a once-shy child becomes a fully functioning, well-adjusted, and social adult. She may never be the life of the party, but most shy children grow up to be comfortable adults who remember how it felt to be painfully shy.

Some children do pass through periods wherein they behave in shy ways. Know that these are usually circumstantial and temporary.

As children grow, they pass in and out of various states of being. There are times when development, over which they may have no control, gets the best of them. It's a little like *The Invasion of the Body Snatchers*. Whether it's hormones, social pressures, or school workload, there are influences that completely cramp a child's ability to be empathetic. She is simply overwhelmed. As empathetic parents, it is crucial that you temper your expectations for your child at that time. I promise you it will pass, and all your hard work at cultivating empathy will reemerge.

Once in a while we do see a child who seems to be without any empathy at all, not even for family, friends, or pets. It is not dissimilar from seeming to have no conscience at all. This child falls outside the realm of what is typical, and it is important that the parents consult a mental health professional about her.

Do Girls Have More Empathy Than Boys?

There has been a lot of discussion about whether boys and girls feel empathy to the same degree. Neurobiologists have found that boy and girl babies are hardwired differently in their visual cortexes. Boy babies focus on moving objects, looking for where they are and where they are going. Girl babies process color and texture of stationary objects, "asking" what they are. In one study, infants just forty-eight hours old were placed in a seat with a spinning mobile on one side and a face on the other; the boys turned their heads to the spinning mobile, and the girls turned to the face. This is important because it shows that girls pay more attention to faces, which reflect feelings. In so doing, they are getting information that enables the more rapid growth of empathy via their mirror neurons. (See box on p. 36 regarding mirror neurons.) From an evolutionary perspective, this finding makes sense, as it was the females who had to be able to "read" their babies' needs while the menfolk were out hunting.

As children grow, it seems that girls do behave more empathetically than boys. In fact, there is some research showing that girls from elementary school through adolescence score higher on measures of empathy than do boys. While the reasons (beyond the hardwiring of the visual cortex) are unclear, researchers have suggested that the difference may also stem from the girls' earlier ability to regulate their behavior. It is not so much that they feel more empathy than do boys, but that they are better able to control themselves and direct their behavior to express their empathy.

In addition, a child's environment can encourage and amplify these gender tendencies. In *Raising Cain*, Dan Kindlon and Michael Thompson address the ways in which boys are socialized to behave less empathetically than girls, thus calling attention to our collective need to address the emotional life of boys. For example, from an early age some boys are taught that anger is the most acceptable emotion for them to express, sadness being the least acceptable. Comments like "Be Brave!" "Shake it off!" "Tough it out!" "Suck it up!" "Be a man!" and even the very old fashioned "Boys don't cry!" give the clear message that it isn't okay to be anything other than tough and strong.

This research suggests that parents of boys in particular may need to give them an extra dose of experience in reading people—teaching them how to read facial expressions as well as other nonverbal communication and cues. Our boys could benefit from extra patience and help in learning to regulate themselves, as it is not in their biology.

Both boys and girls need to become familiar with the full palette of their feelings and how they can express and deal with those feelings effectively if they are to mature into adults who have satisfying, lasting relationships. It is the job of parents to teach and expect empathy equally from boys as well as girls, and not to promote the "boy code."

Tips and Scripts for Cultivating Empathy

- **From your child's earliest days, encourage and build your bond with her.** Research has demonstrated time and again that children who are secure in their relationship with a parent have the ability to experience and express empathy.

- **The Golden Rule is alive and well and ripe for teaching to your children.** It may be corny, but it is true. You really should do to others as you would want them to do to you. Say it, do it, live it!

- **Kindness, compassion, and consideration are learned over time.** Cultivating empathy is a process that requires strong models, reminders, and plenty of patience.

- **Respond empathetically to your child's feelings and internal experiences, both positive and negative.** Both boys and girls grow empathy from having been dealt with empathetically.

- **Make sure your expectations are appropriate for your child's age and development.** The child who refuses to share is not necessarily without empathy. She may just be too young. It takes a long time before a child is able to put someone else's feelings first consistently, if not frequently. Some adults still can't. (See the section on being selfish, p. 27.)

- **Never do to the perpetrator the same thing she did to her victim.** After the child has bitten her sister, she will not learn "how it feels to be bitten" if you bite her. She learns that it is okay for a bigger person to bite a smaller one. And she'll concentrate only on her own hurt arm, no one else's.

- **Don't expect empathy all the time, every time.** Encourage consideration of others, but know that there is no such thing as perfection. Empathy is a quality that grows over time and with experience.

- **Welcome and praise the baby steps.** Big acts of kindness are preceded by baby ones. *"You let your brother smell your ice cream. Maybe next time you'll give him a lick!"*

- **Show empathy for your own child.** Interestingly, it is easier for some parents to show empathy for outsiders than for their own children. Treat your child as an individual who has a mind of her own, acknowledging and validating her feelings. Studies suggest that a child is more likely to develop a sense of empathy when her own needs are being met. Children who feel secure and are emotionally connected and healthy are more willing to consider others.

- **Listen to your child.** Taking the time to listen to your child—without necessarily trying to fix the problem—models your empathy. Parents who are responsive to their children, young and old, help them to develop stronger empathy skills. Ask open-ended questions that encourage your child's communication and that demonstrate your concern. Saying *"Help me to understand what happened"* shows that you care what your child experienced, and commenting *"You must have felt so frustrated"* says how much you empathize with her.

- **Set the example.** Young children, especially, are copycats. Parents who show a genuine, deep concern for others, including one another, treating them with respect and sympathy, will raise children who do the same. You create the template for how people should be treated that the child will carry with her for life.

- **Use daily opportunities to point out and generate empathetic feelings for others.** Call your child's attention to situations that require empathy. For example, when watching a television program, say: *"That boy must be feeling so disappointed that he was not chosen in the play."* Or, *"I can imagine how sad that girl feels because her friends talked in such a mean way to her. I feel for her."*

- **Point out other people's empathetic behavior.** *"Did you notice how patient that salesman was? He was so kind to let us try on all those different shoes."* By your example, your child will notice people's positive qualities.

- **Teach your young child about verbal cues.** Children may need to be taught the meaning of voice tones, for example. Explaining to her that her little brother is whining because he is hungry may help her to have empathy for him. Make it a game: Say the same word in different tones and ask your child to guess what you are feeling.

- **Teach your young child about non-verbal cues.** Take time with your young child just to observe other children—on the playground, in the park, even in the grocery store. Guess what someone might be feeling and explain what you observed that led you think that way: *"I'm guessing that girl is really happy because she is clapping her hands and jumping up and down."* Or, *"I think that boy is really angry because he threw his bucket and walked away fast."*

- **Find opportunities to explore other people's points of view.** Asking questions that help your child to get out of herself and imagine how someone else feels is an exercise in empathy. This is known as "perspective taking": *"What would you have felt, had you been the one the girls excluded from the movie date?"* Take pains to ask your question differently each time to avoid your child's eye rolls. Ask the question like you really want to know the answer, and not just as a rhetorical question:

    "I wonder how she must have felt?"
    "Can you describe how she was feeling?"
    "What is your idea about how she feels?"
    "Do you think you would feel that way, too?"
    "Would you have felt differently?"
    "Do you agree with the feeling she expressed?"

- **Point out to your child what she and others may have in common.** Children are more likely to behave empathetically with people with whom they are familiar or with whom they feel some commonality. *"You know Billy, your friend from your soccer team last year? He broke his arm and can't play any sports for three months. How sad is that? He must feel awful. It would be so nice if we made him a get-well card (or baked him some cookies)."*

- **Help your child to become emotionally literate and intelligent.** (See section on emotional literacy, p. 31.) Children need to learn about their feelings and to label them in order to understand the same in others.

- **Catch your child being empathetic.** Let your child know how much it means to you that she is kind and considerate of others, but resist giving rewards for so doing. All children are capable of being spontaneously considerate. The good feeling is its own reward. Don't spoil it by adding a material reward—not ice cream, not a little gift, not a movie date—just your expression of pleasure and pride: *"I am so proud to have a child who cares about other people's feelings. That's you!"* There is little that feels as good to a child as her parents' pride in her, especially if it is not given lightly.

- **Turn the tables.** Encourage your child to put herself in someone else's shoes and recall when she was in a similar situation. *"Remember when you didn't get invited to Jamie's birthday party? You felt so disappointed and sad. Let's remember that as we make out your birthday list."*

- **Model an "internal dialogue."** Pondering out loud teaches children how to think about things. For example, as Mom sits down at the dinner table, Dad might say, *"Boy, Mom really looks tired this evening. Do you guys know how hard she works every day at the office? It's not easy being a lawyer. She has to be on the phone for hours and then deal with tons of paperwork. Then she has to come home and make us dinner. And this is such a great dinner! I especially like the pasta. It's delicious! Let's make sure we all pitch in to help clean up after we're done eating. I really want to give Mom a break."* Expressing such internal talk shows the child how to reason in certain situations, and that might include putting someone else's needs before her own. For the young child, offer simple, clear explanations about how other people feel. *"It makes Elizabeth feel really sad when you don't let her play."* Don't be afraid to let your tone reflect your disappointment. When your child behaves in ways that are thoughtless, let her know what you think. Remember to focus on the behavior and not on the child. Saying *"Refusing to give your cousin a turn was not considerate of his feelings"* is better than *"That was not very nice of you."* It is okay to be frank and honest about the behavior that you don't like, but don't dwell on it. The goal is not to make her feel guilty.

- **Use "I" messages.** Trite as this advice has become, it works, and it is important. No one can dispute how the other guy feels. Saying *"I feel really frustrated when you empty the sand out of your shoes on the floor I just swept"* is an expression of your feelings and not just a put-down of the culprit. The child will get the message and not feel directly attacked, and she is likely to understand how you feel.

- **Beware of your criticisms of others.** Your child is absorbing your offhanded remark about "that old man who is driving so slowly."

She hears it as a negative judgment about old people. The imperfections, shortcomings, and afflictions that people have cannot usually be helped. Compassion is the order of the day, especially if you are trying to teach kindness and cultivate empathy in your child. A client who owns a store told me about a parent shopping with her child who said, "You'll end up just like him, wrapping presents." Can you count the number of bad messages in that comment?

- **Teach your children manners, but be reasonable in your expectations.** Manners are the way cultures keep things pleasant and create polite, respectful interactions. As manners are taught, the foundation for empathy is laid. Using manners means considering another person's position or standing in her shoes. Your child may not really like the underwear Granny Franny has given her, but she needs to say thank you in consideration of Granny's efforts. That is empathy. Tell her: *"I know the gift from Granny Franny wasn't your favorite, but you need to thank her anyway. Saying thanks lets her know you appreciate her effort and it makes her feel good."* Or, *"The dinner was dreadful, you are right. But you need to thank Mrs. Leonard for inviting you. That is the considerate thing to do, and it will make her feel good."* (See chapter 5, p. 98, for a discussion on manners.)

- **Look for ways to counteract the outside influences that do not demonstrate empathy.**

  - Bring into your home books and DVD's that promote compassionate behavior. Nature films stir up feelings of empathy for all living things as well as demonstrate the effect of man's actions on the environment.
  - Steer your child clear of the media that glamorize bad guys, glorify violence, or exhibit succeeding at the expense of others. Research has shown that children who see kindness on the screen tend to imitate it. The converse it true, too.
  - Share real-life stories whose themes are compassion and kindness. Look for heroes in today's society who demonstrate acts of compassion. Point them out in the news, in local lore, and in shared memories from your past. I recently heard about an artist who paints portraits of soldiers who were killed in the war in Iraq and presents

them to the families. This story of compassion and selflessness could be told to a child age eight or older.

○ Surround yourself and your family with people who are compassionate and kind. You do have a choice.

○ Reference people in history whom we remember particularly for their compassion or kindness (Mother Theresa, Gandhi, Martin Luther King Jr., to name just a few).

- **Show how little acts of kindness demonstrate consideration for others.** Opening a door for someone who is holding an armful of groceries, holding an elevator for the person who is rushing to get on, taking in your elderly neighbor's trash are examples of simple acts that exemplify empathy.

- **Sometimes being empathetic means accepting others for who they are at that moment.** Your child needs to learn that she may not know the whole story about a person; the insensitivity or lack of empathy a friend seems to show may just be on the surface. Perhaps the way she is behaving is covering up a deeper sad, hurt, or angry feeling. Empathy means trying to understand a person's feelings, good and bad, as well as accepting people for who they are.

- **Encourage "other-orientation" and acts of philanthropy.** Whether through community service organizations, churches, or spontaneous individual acts, bringing relief to someone in need is the height of empathy. Regularly participate in philanthropic activities as a family. By performing acts of compassion, children can't help but think of how it would feel to be in other people's shoes. Those who live in homes where philanthropy is a habit will grow up to do the same. Look for organized ways for your children to get involved in service. There are many programs for youth (See chapter 9, p. 199, for a discussion of other-orientation.) When children are provided with experiences that demand empathy, they are given opportunities to consider ideas that are bigger than themselves.

- **Consider getting a pet.** If your children are old enough to participate genuinely in its care, not only will they learn responsibility but they will be forced to consider the pet's well being. That's empathy, too.

- **Encourage your older child to be a tutor, mentor, camp counselor, or peer counselor.** Not only will she learn patience and understanding, but she must learn about her charges' needs and feelings in order to be effective in her job.

- **Teach your older child about doing the right thing.** Your child needs to learn to do what *she* knows to be right and not fall victim to social pressure, whether from peers or authority figures. In a famous 1963 study by Stanley Milgram of Yale University, participants were encouraged by an "authority figure" in a white lab coat to administer shocks to a screaming "victim" (both actors); 65 percent of them continued to do as they were told even after the victim feigned fainting. This reminds me of others horrors in history. What an important lesson.

Selfishness

Selfishness is the height of being a brat, isn't it? Having a child who is selfish is a parent's nightmare, but inherent in that label is faulty parenting. In reality, most parents think their child is selfish at some point during her growing years. While it does seem that selfishness is on the rise, it isn't a new phenomenon at all. I feel certain that Odysseus thought his kid was selfish at one time, too.

Being around a child who behaves selfishly is no fun at all. Children who are selfish put their own needs and desires ahead of everyone else's; they want things their way and exhibit little if any flexibility about it; they believe that their needs and feelings are more important than those of anyone else; and they seem to lack the ability to consider what anyone else might be feeling. That is, they appear to lack empathy.

But viewed in the context of cultivating empathy, selfishness is a trait that can be turned around with effort. Know this: Young children are selfish! Selfish is the opposite of being empathetic, and the young child is in the process of learning to consider others. Early on, it's not selfishness per se; it's development, a trait left over from a time when it was necessary for survival. Later on, it's time for a fix.

Tips and Scripts for Dealing with Selfishness

- **Provide a secure home base.** Children who feel tethered to home and family, who feel attached and loved, are more likely to venture out and pay attention to others. Children who are deprived of love, nurturing, and attention focus on themselves and their own needs in order to get those needs met.

- **Consider the situation.** All behavior is motivated, and it is imperative that you stop and think about what might be going on with your child. Her selfishness might be the result of her feeling neglected or jealous (maybe of a new sibling?). It may be the result of "Lousy Local Conditions" (see box, p. 31)—you have been traveling, have houseguests who overstayed their welcome, or a sibling has received a great deal of attention lately. Selfishness can be a cry for help in the form of love and attention.

  Selfishness can also be a reflection of what's going on during certain, predictable times and in certain predictable places, which also falls under the category of Lousy Local Conditions. Does your child behave in selfish ways frequently during the dinner hour? Or perhaps when Mommy comes home from the office? Is she that way whenever you go to a restaurant? When you visit Grandpa? Or on Sunday mornings before she has to go to religious school?

- **Consider your role.** Perhaps you forgot to remove your child from the center of the universe some time ago. Her selfishness is not her fault, but it is the result of you having put her first so regularly that she never had the chance to cultivate the ability to go second, to consider someone else. Perhaps your limits have been squishy and you have backed down whenever she squawked—her wants were made to be more important that your rules. Have you allowed your child to learn not to be so selfish?

- **Think about whether you have been meeting your own needs and in so doing have cultivated your child's selfishness.** Do you spend so little time with your daughter that you would just rather give in and grant her what she wants? Is it just easier to acquiesce to her whining and complaints? Are you giving her so much stuff to make up for not spending as much time with her? It takes effort to put your foot down and to tolerate the explosive outburst when you say, *"I'm just too tired to do that."* But as much as it's not about you, it is about you!

- **Consider with whom she is the most selfish.** Children behave differently with different people. Ask yourself: Is she selfish with her siblings but not with her friends? Is she worse with Daddy than with Mommy? Might there be some people with whom she is not selfish at all? Figuring out "the who" of your child's selfishness will be a clue as to the cause.

- **Teach about selflessness.** Sometimes we get angry with our kids for being selfish, and they don't even know what that means.

  Take the time to explain: *"When you think only about yourself, what you want or need, and you don't think about what someone else might want or need or like, that's called being selfish."*

  For the older child, you can continue: *"Everyone thinks her feelings are the most important right at the moment. That means you think yours are more important than mine, and I think mine are more important than yours. We are both being selfish, thinking only of ourselves. Part of growing up is learning to accept that someone else's feelings are just as important as yours."* And remember to have this discussion when you are not in a heated moment.

- **Make selfishness illegal.** If your child is accustomed to getting her way, especially if she is the firstborn, this might be hard for her. After all, you are changing the rules of the game. You can explain: *"It is time for me to teach you that everyone in this family needs to think about how other people feel. That's called being considerate. I am teaching you not to be selfish and think only of yourself."* Let the child know what is about to happen: *"I am going to let you know when you are behaving in a selfish way and what needs to change, because we are all done with selfishness in this family."*

- **When you see selfish behavior, call it out.** Be very clear that selfish behavior is unacceptable and will not be tolerated. Be specific in describing what has happened and what you expect. For example, you can say, *"Lying on the couch and taking up all the room is selfish; you are not thinking about where your brother can comfortably sit. I expect you to think* *about how he feels and make room for him."* You can say to your older child: *"Choosing to watch that video is selfish and does not take into consideration what would be okay for your brother. You need to find something that is good for both of you."* Then ignore the groans and bad attitude.

- **Impose a logical consequence only if necessary.** Expressing her feelings about being called out for selfishness does not warrant a consequence. Ignore it completely. However, if she is unable to change her selfishness, there can be a logical consequence for the lack of consideration. *"Since you are unable to be considerate of your brother, you have lost the privilege of lying on the couch. Find another place to sit to watch the show."* You can even go so far as to take away all together the privilege of watching the show. But remember, the consequence is only for her selfishness and only for that instance. (See chapter 4, p. 75, for a discussion about consequences.)

- **Most importantly, catch your child being considerate.** It goes without saying that catching the child doing the right thing goes much farther than imposing a consequence for being selfish. Children of all ages want to be well thought of in the eyes of their parents. Be specific in your praise: *"The way you moved over to make room on the couch for your brother was really being considerate. It makes my heart sing to see you be that kind."*

- **Reinforce acts of selflessness.** Point out to your child how her selfless acts affected another person. *"It made me feel so good when you asked me how my day went. I like knowing that you are thinking about me."* Or, *"Your brother's face really lit up when you invited him to play in your room."* This works with children of all ages. Pointing out their acts of selflessness keeps these actions at the forefront of their minds.

- **Rotate meal choices.** Have one night of the week when each person gets to choose either the family meal being prepared or the restaurant. State the ground rules: *"We're all learning to be tolerant of each other's food choices, so every week each of us will get a turn to choose the meal we'll have. Accepting the choice without complaining is part of the plan. You don't have to like it, you don't even have to eat it, but you do need to be pleasant at the dinner table."* When they ask you what will happen if they don't like the food (or the restaurant), you can say, *"I am sure there will be something you will eat."*

- **Rotate who gets to choose the TV show, video, game, etc.** The idea is that each person gets her turn to choose, and each tolerates what the others have chosen. On your regular movie night, take turns selecting the show everyone will watch (with consideration for age-appropriateness, of course). Be sure to recognize the older child's self-lessness in watching *The Little Mermaid* again: *"I know that* The Little Mermaid *certainly wouldn't have been your choice, but it really made your little sister feel good to have us all watch it. Thanks for being considerate of her*

ONDITIONS

...l it, is an expression coined by Laura ...ming the Parent You Want to Be. It ... sabotages the child's ability to be .... Sometimes it results from putting ...nt—letting your two-year-old loose ...our doing. The toddler who misses ...ictim of LLC. The five-year-old who ...s is also a sufferer. The ten-year-old ...r the grumpy teenager who hasn't ...hen it is a case of LLC, it is up to the ...ping on and what needs to be done.

...iteracy

...emotions humans experience and being able to recog... ...d give it a name is being emotionally lit-erate. Emotional literacy is also the language of empathy. Recognizing and naming your own feelings enables you to do so in others. It is a necessary step on the road to empathy.

The extension of emotional literacy, using it in life, is known as being emotionally intelligent. In his book *Emotional Intelligence*, Daniel Goleman describes it as "the capacity for recognizing our own feelings and those of others, for motivating ourselves, and for managing emotions well in ourselves and in our relationships." In short, it is recognizing and doing what needs to be done to achieve a desired outcome in a particular situation involving others. Some people, perhaps due to temperament, may appear to be more emotionally intelligent and better able to do what a particular social situation requires. Perhaps you remember Eddie Haskell from the sixties' show *Leave it to Beaver*? Now, there was an emotionally intelligent teenager. While he was usually up to no good and used his emotional intelligence to manipulate people (note how he charmed June Clever with his daily greeting "Good morning, Mrs. Cleaver. It sure is a nice day out there, isn't it?"), he always knew just what to say. But children who are raised with an eye toward being emotionally intelligent can put this skill to good use, too, becoming adults who have successful and satisfying personal, social, and professional relationships.

Being emotionally literate does not mean just feeling happy. Nor does it necessarily mean wearing your heart on your sleeve, as the old expression goes. It means knowing and understanding your emotions enough so that you can manage them during difficult times, use them in your decision-making processes and better relate to other people.

Because most parents teach their children only the basics—happy, sad, mad, frightened, and maybe surprised—children have limited experience with the full range of feelings. Those might include feeling frustrated, disappointed, irritated, jealous, envious, embarrassed, timid, worried, nervous, disgusted, or impatient, to name just a few. If a child is not familiar with these other emotions, she won't learn to recognize the feelings in herself nor will she know that everyone experiences them sometimes. I am reminded of the preschool age child who is taught to say, *"You hurt my feelings"* to her friends at school. Having limited emotional literacy, she uses that same expression whenever things don't go her way. Whether you tell her it's time for bed, that she must stop throwing her toys, not to hit her brother, or ask her to take a bath she says, *"That hurts my feelings!"*

Tips and Scripts for Building Emotional Literacy and Intelligence

- **Label and discuss your own feelings, positive and negative.** One of the ways children learn about feelings is by hearing about them and seeing them in action. Sharing the feelings you are having, using their real names, expands the child's own vocabulary and understanding of feelings. She learns them in a context. And she learns that adults have feelings, too, and that is a normal part of life.

- **Model your healthy expression of feelings.** How does she learn the appropriate ways to express powerful negative feelings if not by watching you? Let your child see you in the heat of the moment: *"I am feeling really frustrated right now. I have to go for a run to get some of this frustrated energy out."* Or, *"I am really angry right now, so I am going to go in my room and cool off."*

- **Teach "legal" ways for children to express their big feelings.** Parents do a good job of telling their child how she should *not* express her feelings—no hitting, biting, pinching, throwing things, or name-calling. But the child needs to know what she *can* do:

  ○ Hit a punching bag
  ○ Knock down an inflated Bozo doll (the kind that bounces right back up)
  ○ Use a foam bat
  ○ Scream at the top of her lungs outside (or in an acceptable place)
  ○ Stomp on bubble paper taped to the floor (aka "angry paper")
  ○ Write the object of the anger on the bottom of her shoe and stomp on it
  ○ Throw rocks (in an acceptable place)
  ○ Jump up and down ten times or more
  ○ Take a lap, weather and location permitting
  ○ Color hard and fast with a dark color crayon on a big piece of paper

- **Never put down a feeling, even if it's a biggie.** Even if your child is expressing a negative feeling inappropriately, remember that the feeling is legitimate, no matter what it is. It is the behavior that results from the emotion that you may not approve. After the moment has passed, you can discuss what more appropriate ways she could have used to express herself. *"I could see that you were really angry when I told you to turn off the computer. Next time you need to find a more acceptable way* *to express that anger rather than knocking the chair against the wall."* As your child grows older, it is your job to teach her what to do with her feelings, positive and negative.

- **Let your child see how you get over your feelings.** Young children in particular can be frightened by your negative feelings and by their own. They need to learn through experience that people recover; negative feelings don't last forever. You might say: *"I was so angry before. I didn't feel like talking to anyone. Now I am done being angry, and I feel just fine."*

- **Help your child to develop an emotional vocabulary by labeling what she is feeling.** Tell her: *"You are feeling really frustrated because that puzzle is so hard to do."* Or, *"You're feeling impatient with me right now because it's taking me so long to get ready."* Or, *"You are so surprised that Aunt Lorna came to dinner. You weren't expecting that."* Take every opportunity to give the child new language for describing her feelings so she will use that language in the future. You are your child's emotional coach, helping her to understand and label what she is feeling.

- **Take time to listen to your child.** By connecting with your child and absorbing what she is saying, she gets the message that her feelings are important. Honor her feelings—all of them. And then take the time right then, if you possibly can, to talk about them: *"It sounds like you are really frustrated with the way that assignment is going. Is there anything I can do to help you or do you just need to vent? I know how that feels."*

- **Teach about the physical signs of feelings.** Your child can be taught to recognize what bodies do involuntarily as well as what we do with our bodies when we experience certain feelings. *"Sometimes when people get embarrassed their faces get red or flushed."* Or, *"Sometimes when people get irritated they clench their teeth really hard or squeeze their fists tightly."*

- **Help your child learn to decode people's feelings by paying attention to their facial expressions and to their body language.**

  To the young child, say: *"You can tell I am happy now because I am smiling; but a little while ago I was frowning because I was frustrated that our car wouldn't start."*

You can say to an older child: *"I could tell by the look on that clerk's face that he is in a bad mood. It looked like he was angry at something, didn't you think?"* Or, *"I could tell that your baseball coach was irritated by the way he was crossing his arms and kicking the dirt."*

- **Use books, pictures, and illustrations to discuss what people might be feeling.** Create a consciousness about the different feelings people can have by noticing their expressions in pictures and photographs. *"This is the one where Daddy was so angry that the Dodgers had lost. You can just see it in his face."* Or, *"Look at that lion's face in the drawing. He is so sad. Why do you think that is?"* When reading stories, talk about how the characters might be feeling. Ask, *"How do you think that mama owl feels now that her babies have all flown away?"*

- **Compare and contrast feelings.** *"A little while ago you were just furious. You were yelling and stomping your feet. Now you are happy. You are relaxed and your voice is back to normal."* Or, for an older child, *"You were so angry steam was almost coming out of your ears! Now you've settled back down. It took a little time. I know how that feels."* Pointing out the change also gives the child perspective on how feelings have a life span; they come and go. She can recover even though it may not feel that way when she is in the heat of emotion.

- **Provide lots of opportunities for your child to talk about her feelings.** But don't overdo it, and avoid open-ended questions. The child who is asked *"How does that make you feel?"* too often learns to roll her eyes at that question. Instead try, *"I can see that you got really quiet and your face looks kind of sad. Are you feeling sad or angry?"* You will be much more likely to encourage a conversation, and the child will feel understood.

- **Play the game "What would you feel if . . . ?"** Teach your younger child how certain situations might warrant specific feelings. This is a big part of emotional intelligence and it encourages empathy. *"How would you feel if . . . a friend broke your Lego rocket ship? How would your good friend feel if . . . you didn't invite him to your birthday party? What feeling would you have if . . . your dog ran away?"* Playing this game when things are calm is not only fun; it also provides the child with a neutral time during which she can absorb the lesson. The situations and the accompanying feelings will become familiar to her.

- **Imitate faces that express feelings.** With the younger child, stand in front of the mirror and practice making faces that go along with feelings. In so doing, not only will she learn to recognize the feelings of others, but she will become familiar with that feeling: *"Show me what you would look like if you saw a lion walking on the front lawn."* Take turns creating feeling scenarios.

MIRROR NEURONS

Research has shown that humans have in their brains "mirror neurons," which reflect back to the observer the very feeling she is observing. "Mirror neurons make feelings contagious," to quote Daniel Goleman. Seeing an emotion expressed on a face, the observer will sense that same feeling. That's the reason I am moved to tears when I see someone else crying.

In addition, neuroscientists have pointed to the value for children of recognizing and practicing the facial expressions that accompany feelings. In so doing, their mirror neurons actually enable them to experience the feelings they are mimicking.

It is clear that all children have the capacity for empathy, but in order for it to manifest and grow it takes some deliberate work on the part of parents and caregivers. Because it is a trait that provides the foundation on which so many other characteristics develop, it is worth the effort.

❖

CHAPTER THREE

"I Can't Do It Myself; You Do It!"

Building Independence in Your Child

Even though the thought of your grown-up child moving away might leave you gasping for air, having a child who sees himself as an independent, self-sufficient, and capable person is at the top of all parents' wish lists. But it isn't something to which most parents give much thought—that is, until they realize their child isn't heading in that direction.

In recent years there has been a trend for parents to hover over their children, monitoring their every move. This is also known as helicopter parenting. While such parenting is seldom, if ever, good, it is mildly acceptable with very young children who still need their parents' direction. The problem is that helicopter parenting is becoming commonplace among parents of teens, young adults, and even fully grown adult children. Parents insinuate themselves into every aspect of their child's life, from conferencing with their child's college professor to checking (and filling) their adult children's bank accounts. These children have never been given the chance to become independent and continue to get the message that it is not possible—mommy must always be involved. I can tell you that the child who feels independent has been given the message that he has the abilities and is expected to use them.

Not long ago, I was approached about a reality television program that addressed this very issue—adult children who never separated and parents who never let go. If the show does reach the screen, I am sure it will be wildly successful, as there are just too many families in this situation. Ironically, the problem doesn't lie with the adult child. He is looking for ways to fly on his own, but he is worried about the effect it will have on his parents. He embodies the symptom, the disease of which lies with the parent who won't let go. What a sorry state of affairs.

It is well known that children who are independent possess many other qualities that enable them to tackle life head-on and grow up. They usually have a strong, positive sense of themselves. They see the world in which they live as a safe place to be or, even better, they know how to make it safe for themselves. These children are problem solvers and risk takers, and they feel effective in the world. They are often leaders, and they know how to withstand peer pressure. Children who are independent have the sense that who they are and what they do matters. And what more could we want for our children? But how do you get your child there? It certainly isn't by helicopter parenting.

There is a fine line between independence and self-reliance, another trait that is addressed in chapter 7, p. 136. While the two are nurtured with some similar techniques, it is difficult for a child to be self-reliant if he doesn't first see himself as being independent. Independence is the foundation on which self-reliance is built.

The Components of Independence

So many factors and attributes contribute to a child becoming independent. Each is just as important as the next. And, as with so many character traits, there is a direct feeding tube from parent to child in cultivating this one. Independence, in particular, is a trait easily sabotaged by the parent.

Development

As attached as parents are to their infants, the moment that cord is cut, independence begins, whether or not you want it to. So Mother Nature ensures that the parent stays attached to her baby for survival's sake: We are programmed to nurture our young. It is true for all living creatures. I remember a dog in the neighborhood whose puppies were taken away from her right after their birth. This mama dog howled and cried for days. It was painfully sad.

Even though independence is something that is built over time, children are hardwired to begin the process shortly after infancy. There is a developmental component to a child moving away from his parent, becoming autonomous, and practicing his independence. Think about your nine-month-old crawler as he scampers away from you with amazing speed down the hallway. Then he is a walker who darts out the front door as soon as you head for the car. He is independent all right, perhaps more than you'd like at that point. Your two-year-old insists, "No, me do it!" as he pushes your hand away and struggles to put his shoes on, trying so hard to be independent. The eight-year-old who wants to ride his bike alone to his friend's house around the corner is showing you how independent he is. The eleven-year-old who begs to stay home alone or go to the mall with his friends craves independence. Being autonomous, acting independently, is a big part of growing up.

Temperament

There is no question that a child's particular temperament influences his ability and willingness to be independent. The field of temperament was explored by Alexander Thomas, Stella Chess, and their associates in the 1950s, and those studies are still considered the gold standard today. Their New York Longitudinal Study looked at traits of temperament and taught us to identify them in children. One of their findings was that we are all born with certain temperamental traits, which continue to influence our development and behavior in critical ways throughout our childhood as well as in later life.

Temperament is kind of like a filter through which the child views and then navigates his world. When temperament blends with environment, you get personality. It is for this reason that a child can exhibit one personality at home and quite a different one at school. Often a parent will report to me that the child she knows as outgoing, enthusiastic, talkative, and spontaneous is a quiet little mouse at school. Different environment, different personality, the same child.

We learned from the Thomas and Chess research how important it is that parents keep the child's temperament in mind as they craft their expectations for him. Even in the same family, you need to make sure that your expectations are matched to each child and his temperament, as no two children, even multiple-birth siblings, are the same. If a child falls into the temperament category of "slow to warm up" (and that's its real name!), it should not be surprising that being independent is really challenging for him in certain situations. He is independent when he is home and in familiar environments with consistent, well-known players. When in a new environment or even in school, he may be less likely to be so independent.

The opposite of the slow-to-warm child is the one who is "wild" (not a real category name!). This is the child who is totally outgoing, talks to everyone anywhere at any time, and seems to have no brakes. Don't be fooled; this child is not necessarily independent, as he seems unaware of his surroundings, of dangers that lurk, and the cause and effect of his interactions. Despite his outgoing nature, he, too, needs lessons in being independent and using good judgment.

Parents of children who fall in these two, more extreme categories are equally concerned. Both types of children need to learn how to function independently in the world.

Tips and Scripts for Encouraging Independence in the Slow-to-Warm and the Wild Child

- **Accept that your slow-to-warm child is just that.** The message of acceptance gives this child permission to take a risk, as he feels you understand who he is.

- **Do not push the slow-to-warm child.** Pushing this child to do more than he feels he can will backfire and cause him to dig in his heels.

- **Avoid put-downs.** Humiliation is neither a productive nor healthy form of parenting. Therefore, saying *"Aw c'mon, you're not afraid of going into that birthday party, are you?"* is likely to do more damage than encourage independence.

- **Have faith in your child.** You reflect the courage that your child needs to find in himself. Tell him: *"I see that you feel worried about joining the other children, but I know that after a while you will feel comfortable. It always takes you a little time."*

- **Help him to take baby steps.** The reluctant child needs to take small steps and feel successful at each step before moving onto the next. *"I will walk with you to the gate and then you can walk into school yourself. I know you can do it."*

- **Provide alternatives.** *"I will stand at the door of your room with you while you go in and get your shoes."* Or, *"I will stand with you while you speak with Jeremy about taking your bike, and you can do the talking."*

- **Revisit his successes.** Be sure to point out to him, and to his father (or mother) in front of him, what he was able to do: *"I remember when you weren't able to walk into school by yourself at all. You must feel so proud of yourself."*

- **Reiterate your expectations for your wild child in a given situation.** Before he even gets out of the car, say, *"The first thing you are going to do when we get to the park is tell me where you will be playing. If you change places, you are going to come and tell me first. Please tell me what our plan is."* Or, *"Let's go over what you are going to do when you arrive at camp. First, you are going to check in with your counselor. Next, you will ask him what you are supposed to do."*

- **Create rituals and unbreakable rules for situations when independence beckons.** The wild child thrives on ritual and predictability. Knowing what is always expected of him helps him to be safe and independent at the same time.

- **Have clear, logical consequences when the wild child abuses his independence.** All children learn from cause and effect. If the child runs away from you, he must now hold your hand. If he leaves the area he said he would be in, you leave the park. No threats; just follow through. And be sure to give him another chance the next day, reminding him what happened the day before.

The Importance of Feeling Safe

Children who believe that their world is a safe place are likely to try out their independence within it. And why not? They have nothing to fear. The truth is, children are born trusting that the world is a safe place to be. It is adults who give them the ideas about safety and the need for caution. Of course, these are crucial lessons for every child. It is your job to empower your child by teaching him the skills he needs to go out and enjoy his life and to be safe, but you don't want to create debilitating paranoia. In our zeal to keep our children free from harm, we stir up unnecessary fears that can heavily influence their willingness to take steps toward independence. A client mom who came to discuss her child's many fears had an epiphany: "I thought being a good mom meant keeping my child safe, not allowing him to be independent." She thought sheltering her child was what she was supposed to do. Until that moment, she hadn't appreciated how her actions were crippling her child.

Tips and Scripts for Helping a Child to Feel Safe While Encouraging His Independence

- **It is your responsibility to educate yourself and your children about safety.** Be careful not to go overboard. The child who lives in fear will not be independent. It's just too scary. Think of teaching reasonable precautions. The idea is to arm him without alarming him. Teach your children the ways you keep them safe and the ways in which they can keep themselves safe. Whether it involves water, fire, food, biking, or people, your child can be taught the skills and develop the understanding to keep himself safe most of the time. These may include specific safety rules or family rules that from the earliest age are enforced in the same way you expect your child to brush his teeth or wear his seat belt. For example:

  - Only grown-ups answer the front door, unless the child is older than ten or is accompanied by a grown-up.
  - A child never goes anywhere without the supervising adult's permission.
  - A child never goes in anyone's car without the supervising adult's permission.
  - Children must be twelve years old before they may stay home alone.
  - Only children who know how to write down a phone message may answer the telephone unless a grown-up gives permission.

- **Children need to feel confident that there are always adults who will keep them safe.** The idea is to free your child from having to worry. You will not let your child be unsafe; that is your job. Tell him: *"One of the jobs of being a grown-up is taking care of children, and teaching them how to keep themselves safe. There are even grown-ups whose regular job it is to keep us all safe, like firefighters, police officers, crossing guards, and security guards."*

- **Your child gets his cues about safety from you.** Be aware of the messages you are giving your child, including when you don't think he is watching. The child is in a constant state of evaluation. He looks to you and the adults in his world for confirmation about the safety all around him. Feeling safe encourages his independence.

- **Get a grip on your own fears.** Dealing with your own issues will allow you to project the image of a confident, strong parent. If you behave as if you feel safe, your child will feel safe.

- **At the very least, let your child see how you handle your fears rather than being paralyzed by them.** You can say: *"I am not comfortable with dogs, so I am going to walk around that man and his dog."* Being proactive in dealing with a fear is an act of independence.

- **Be careful with your off-handed comments or running commentary.** Avoid phrases like: *"I don't like the looks of that man over there, and I am worried about the way that woman is driving."* Or, *"I thought I heard a noise outside."* Such comments teach the child to be selectively perceptive to danger and encourage fear where it need not have existed for him. How could any child want to be independent under those circumstances? Something bad might happen.

- **Keep your admonitions reasonable and measured.** There are parents who are extreme in the precautions they take and impose upon their children. (*"Don't touch that elevator button; use your elbow."*) Our world is full of dangers of all kinds—criminals and bad guys, germs and filth, bad drivers, and public bathrooms, to name just a few. You need to help your child to feel that the world is safe enough for him to be independent from you. Unreasonable precaution inhibits that lesson. There's just too much to look out for. Set the tone that the world is basically safe, and your child will feel that it is . . . and appropriately move away from you.

- **Teach your child how to be responsible for himself, thereby encouraging his independent moves.** This is not unlike the very young child learning how to look both ways before he crosses the street or learning always to walk around a swimming pool. Take the time to have the discussion about your safety expectations. *"I expect you to follow the safety rules—including no running—when we are at Uncle Jon's pool. If you do, we can stay there. If you don't, you will have to leave."*

- **Give warnings that place the child in charge of himself.** When your child climbs high on the play structure, rather than screaming that it is too high and he has to get down immediately, try saying, *"Climb only as high as you feel safe and comfortable."* And let him know that you cannot climb up to get him down.

- **Avoid giving warnings that thwart your child's risk-taking.** Saying *"Don't go up there; it's too high"* doesn't encourage your child's independent moves. If you are worried about the height, you can say, *"That looks really high. Does it seem okay to you? You be the judge. You can come back down if you aren't comfortable."* Such a comment shows the child that you trust his judgment. One of my favorite ways of reminding my kids to stay alert and be aware of what they were doing was to tell them: *"Keep yourself safe."* It put the responsibility on them.

- **Encourage your child to make decisions for himself.** When your child wants to take a risk that scares you, don't be quick to say no. Instead, you might say: *"I am not comfortable handling snakes, but there is no reason you can't touch them."* Not only will this teach him to pay attention to his own feelings, but he will get a strong message of your trust.

- **The world is a pretty safe place for the vast majority of people.** Children need to be able to trust this reality; their steps toward independence depend upon it. Bad news is delivered into our daily lives at lightning speed, overshadowing the normal, good news. Do not allow that news to thwart your child's sense of safety.

- **Don't squash your child's desire and need for independence.**
For some parents, even the most remote possibility of danger can
interfere with their ability to let go and allow their child more autonomy. It is important to consider each individual child and circumstance before laying down the law. Try to compromise when you can
and allow your child to take baby steps toward independence. For
example, while you cannot allow your child and his friend to go to the
movie alone, you will allow them to sit by themselves as you sit a few
rows behind them in the theater.

WALKING TO SCHOOL ALONE

Even though you walked to school alone when you were only six years
old, times have changed. Today we know more about the world and about
kids. But there are no laws or predetermined ages to guide us in such decisions.

Many realities and variables must be considered in deciding when and
if your child is ready to walk to school alone, including not only the environment and the inherent dangers but also the child's development and maturity. It is a fact that children are slower to recognize and react to danger.
Unlike adults, children have difficulty judging how fast cars are going and the
velocity of small versus large vehicles. Their peripheral vision is just two-
thirds that of an adult, and they often have difficulty knowing where sound
is coming from. And, of course, children can be restless and easily distracted.
In thinking about your child's readiness to walk to school—or anywhere—
consider the following:

- Is your child responsible? Does he complete his basic household responsibilities?
- Does your child follow through with requests you have made?
- Does he follow basic rules without reminders, such as buckling his seat
  belt, washing his hands after using the toilet, etc?
- Does your child argue with you about your family safety rules or break
  them? For example, does he forget to call you when he arrives at a friend's
  house?

○ Does your child consistently follow basic street safety rules without your reminders, i.e., does he pay attention to traffic signs, stop at the curb before crossing, look both ways before and while crossing, pay attention to driveways, etc?

Readiness is a gradual process. When your child begins asking to walk on his own, you will need to consider the possibility. With that in mind, look at the following considerations and steps you might take as your child progresses toward walking to school alone.

○ Model following street safety rules, always. This includes jaywalking and crossing (while driving or walking) when a light is red or just about to turn green. When you bend the rules your child learns to do the same, providing him with a false sense of safety.

○ Even with the most competent and mature child, it is generally accepted that no child under ten years old is ready to walk to school all by himself.

○ Consider your neighborhood and know the history of events involving children's safety that have occurred. In some areas, it will never be okay for children to walk unaccompanied by an adult.

○ Explain to your child the reason you have your rules, excluding the graphic details that may create unnecessary fears. Remembering that children think they are invulnerable, you might say, *"Not all people follow the traffic rules, and I worry about that."* Or, *"I wish I could say that all people are kind and treat children well. Just because a person looks friendly, doesn't mean he is friendly."*

○ Walking to school independently doesn't have to mean going alone. Walking with a group of children is always a good idea at any age.

○ When walking with your child anywhere, give him bits of responsibility as you go: Let him cross the street alone. Have him tell you when it is safe to cross. Practice. Practice. Practice.

○ Explain that there is only one direct route to school. No exceptions.

○ Arrange "safe houses" along the route. This may necessitate meeting neighbors you have not previously known, introducing your child, and making an arrangement that your child may go to that house if there is a problem. (A few years ago two ten-year-olds on their way to school ran to a house on their route when they were frightened by a van that was driving very slowly next to them on the street. The neighbor called their parents and the police. The van was a painter looking for an address. The girls reacted exactly according to previous instruction.)

○ Take baby steps. Say goodbye to your child a block before his school, while you are still watching.

○ Walk behind your child as he walks with a friend, letting him go farther ahead and explain that is it for your peace of mind.

○ When and if your child does begin to walk to school alone, let him know that you will do a "spot check" and follow him once in a while. It makes you feel comfortable to know that your child is following your rules.

A parent never stops worrying about her child's safety, whether he's walking to elementary school or around a college campus. The best any parent can do is to teach safety precautions and hope that their use becomes a habit.

The Role of Conflict

While conflict is inevitable in raising children—you have your ideas and they have theirs!—sometimes it interferes with the goal of helping your child become independent. In such cases, the focus moves from the task at hand to the conflict, undermining the child's independence.

Tips and Scripts for Removing Conflict that Undermines Independence

- **Conflict arises when a child has a plan, and it's not your plan.** Just the fact that your child has his own idea is an act of independence. He can think for himself. This is often the case with the two- to five-year-old child. (It is different from when the child is just being defiant. Then he knows what you want, and he's not going there. The defiance is the motivation, not the different idea he may have.) When he has a plan, he is showing you that he has a mind of his own. While that's a good thing, often his idea doesn't work for you. The trick is to honor his plan without squashing his independence.

You can say: *"I know you want to climb onto the counter and help me bake. Let me bring the bowl down to your table so you can reach it."* With this script you are staying on track and not letting a conflict arise over climbing on the counter. The focus is on the child's goal of helping you to bake. Or, *"Oh, I see you are getting out your paints. That's a great idea, and you can paint after lunch. Let's put them on the counter so we don't forget. Right now it is lunch time."*

For the older child: *"You came up with a great plan to meet Terry and work on your skateboard ramp. Let's think of a day when that can happen, as today we have to visit Grandpa. Can you call him right now to set that up?"* By saying yes before you say no, by honoring the idea and the planning, you validate the independence, and you are not focusing on your disagreement and the potential conflict of interest. Stay away from the fight, and keep your eye on fulfilling the plan.

- **Adult impatience leads to conflict that thwarts independence.** There are times when you need something done quickly. *Quick* is hard for children who want to do things themselves. But you hurry the child along, even taking out of his hands whatever it is he is trying to accomplish because you can do it faster. And what message does the child get? *"I might as well not do it; Mommy does it faster."* Bye-bye independence. When you are really in a hurry and are not just being impatient, you can say, *"You are working so hard on that zipper. Next time you will show me how you can do it all by yourself. Today is not a day when I have time to wait for you. I'm going to help you finish. I love that you are learning to zip."*

- **Adult standards for perfection may conflict with the child's execution of a task.** He's a child, what do you expect? Children learn by doing, by making mistakes and doing lousy jobs. But your child won't try again if he feels that he just can't meet your expectations. (And the same holds true for your spouse, by the way. If you want him to take the initiative and do the laundry, don't criticize his folding!) Accept the job he has done, praise his great effort, and do not redo or correct his job. *"Wow! You made your own bed. You must be so* *proud of yourself!"* Let it be imperfect or just lousy. It is the independent initiative that counts in this case, not the outcome.

- **Beware of the conflict that arises when the child's independent act raises fears in you.** When your child gets himself on the public toilet all by himself, and you go nuts because he has forgotten to use the paper seat cover, let it go. As discussed, the conflict inspired by your own fear will infect his independent moves. Later, way later, you can say, *"Remember when you went to the toilet all by yourself? I loved the way you took care of yourself. Next time remember to use a seat cover."*

- **Conflict arises when a child won't do what you want him to do.** In some cases the child won't follow through with a request that requires his independence. It may be because of fear; it may be because of laziness; it may because it's hard to break old habits, especially if he is accustomed to your doing his work for him. Instead of focusing on the conflict that will arise when you attempt to force him, craft your request so that the child is able to fulfill some of it.

For the younger child: *"Which part of getting dressed do you want to do? Put on your shoes or your pants? I will do the other part."* (The answer *"No part"* is not an option. Not making an effort leads to not getting dressed and not doing whatever comes next.) Avoid the conflict, but have the expectation. If you believe he can do it, he will believe it, too.

For the older child: *"I will wait for you right here while you carry the notice into the front office. I know you can do it."* Or, *"I will stand with you while you tell your teacher why you were unable to complete your homework. It is your homework, and she needs to hear from you."*

When to Compromise

Inevitably, there is going to be much more conflict as your child (elementary school age and older) struggles to be independent. It is his developmental task to separate from you. But you know the dangers that lurk on the streets and at the mall; he isn't thinking about the latest child-snatching. He wants to be grown-up and independent. Your caution, stemming from your fear, works against his natural inclination to move away. It often leads to a conflict between you.

Here are ways to lessen those conflicts and honor your child's efforts to be independent, without throwing the family safety rules out the window.

Tips and Scripts for Ways to Compromise without Compromising Your Safety Rules

- **Let the ages for various permissions be known early on.** Your family safety rules, which you have previously discussed, should also include the specific ages at which your child will be allowed to do certain activities—stay home alone, walk to the store, ride his bike to his friends house, go to a movie alone, etc. Surprise rules leave room for the protest, *But I didn't know!*

- **Recognize that as your child matures the family safety rules will need to be modified accordingly.**

  For the eight-year-old: *"Tell you what, I am going to stand on the porch and watch you walk down the street all the way to Joshua's house by yourself."*

  For the ten-year-old: *"Here's what makes me feel comfortable. You can ride your bike to Joshua's house, two blocks away, and the minute you arrive, you call me to say 'All Clear.'"* Or, *"Yes, you and Jonah can sit in the movie theater all by yourselves. Daddy and I will sit in a row far away from you."*

  For the thirteen-year-old: *"I will drop you off in front of the theater five minutes before the movie begins, and I will pick you up in the same place five minutes after it ends."*

  The compromise avoids a full-blown conflict and gives the child the message that you trust him and that you are giving him independence incrementally. He is earning it every time he follows through.

- **You get to determine the exceptions.** There may be an activity that you would never allow in the city that you might well allow when you're in the country. Your child needs to understand that different circumstances in different environments yield different opportunities for independence. When you are visiting relatives out on the farm, you are more likely to let your seven-year-old wander a bit farther than when you are in New York City.

A friend of mine who is cautious with her children shared with me the story of allowing her nine-year-old son to take a last run down a ski slope all by himself, including going up on the lift. She knew that he was well aware of the safety rules for skiing, and there were plenty of adults to help if needed. The payoff in his sense of pride and independence was immeasurable.

- **Different rules for different children.** Some children in the same family will be able to handle more freedom and independence earlier than others, based on age, development, and temperament. That is just the way it is despite the protests of *"That's not fair!"* It's not a bad thing to have to be old enough to be granted some independence. (Family safety rules, however, apply to everyone in the family.)

Necessary Conflict

Before the child takes an independent plunge, he is often frustrated. He wants to be able to do something, but he can't. The big "I can't do it" feeling is the opposite of independence.

There's a conflict between what he wants to be able to do and what he thinks he is able to do. Or he may be simply frustrated by the fact that he can't do it just the way he wants to. That very frustration is the feeling to be overcome—it is a necessary conflict. Learning frustration tolerance is one of the peaks all children must climb in order to grow up and become independent.

Tips and Scripts for Dealing with Necessary Conflict

- **Teach your child to stretch his tolerance for frustration.** Some children need help learning to tolerate frustration. Working with the child so that he can learn to grin and bear it, bit by bit, will stretch his ability to tolerate frustration. *"You are working so hard on that puzzle.*

You've almost got it. Keep it up, because you're just about there." Such encouragement not only plays on the child's willingness to keep at it but also gives him the message that he can do it independently, without your help. Next time, he'll be willing to work harder because he's familiar with the feelings and the process: Frustration leads to increased effort, which leads to his success.

- **Conflict from frustration can lead to the development of independent coping skills.** When a child is young, it's Mommy or Daddy who makes him feel all better. But as he grows and they are not always there to soothe him, he has to learn what he himself can do to feel better. You have heard stories of the college student who put a fist through a dorm wall out of frustration or conflict. Clearly, he didn't learn coping skills. Take the time to share with your child some of the things you do to soothe yourself when you feel frustrated: *"Sometimes when I am so frustrated that I want to scream, I go somewhere where I can scream! I have to get all those feelings of frustration out."* Or, *"When I am really frustrated, I go for a run. I run really hard and run all those feelings right out of my system. That helps me to feel better."*

- **Suggest what your child might do to discharge some of that frustration.** There will be different suggestions for children of different ages.

  For the younger child: *"There are lots of ways to get that frustration out. You can jump up and down twenty times. You can stomp your foot really hard. You can go outside and scream loudly, at the top of your lungs. You can run as fast as you can across the yard five times."*

  For the older child: *"It looks like kicking your soccer ball really hard across the yard might help you feel better."*

  In the face of frustration, none of the above may be possible, so your child needs to learn skills for tolerating the feelings in the moment: *"When you think you are going to burst, try taking three really deep breaths. Breathe in through your nose and out through your mouth, like this"*— and then demonstrate the technique. It works for people of all ages. You are putting him in charge of taking care of himself. That's independence.

- **Children can be taught to be resourceful in the face of conflict.**
  Instead of being quick to jump in and solve the problem, as most parents do, stay close, do nothing, and wait. After awhile, you can empathize with your child: *"That is just so frustrating. I know exactly how you
  feel."* And be exasperated right along with him. Avoid sounding con-
  descending. Likely this will bring on more complaints and whining,
  which are for your benefit and which you must not absorb. Be patient
  and when you see an opening, try saying: *"What do you think you might
  do?"* You're putting the ball squarely in his court. You can follow with,
  "I know you will feel so much better when you come up with a plan." When
  he does offer an idea, be sure to praise the resourcefulness and not the
  plan. *"You always figure things out."*

Independent Play

"How do I get my kid to play by himself?" is a question I am frequently
asked by parents of children of all ages—and almost always in reference to
their firstborn child—you remember, your "practice child?" By necessity,
the second and third children learn to play independently. You just don't
have the time to sit and play with them; there's too much else to do. But that
firstborn, boy, did you ever blow it. In the parent's zeal to be the best parent,
she hovers. She is the helicopter parent. And the child never actually learns
what it feels like to play by himself because you or someone else is always
there.

Tips and Scripts for Teaching the Child to Play Independently

- **If your child is still a baby or a toddler, leave him alone to play
  for short periods of time.** Of course, you are always closely supervising your child, but being in the same room with your child and
  playing with your child are two different acts. Your child needs both.
  Leave him alone to explore his hazard-free world. When you see your
  young child amusing himself, absorbed in his play, don't interrupt.
  Busy yourself with something else, and when he is done and begins
  to make noises, don't be quick to come to his rescue. Something else

may catch his attention. If not, give him a minute and then join him. He is learning how to entertain himself.

- **Narrate the plan for your toddler.** *I am going to work in the kitchen while you play by yourself.* He will get the message that being together, doing your own things, is the way it is supposed to be.

- **Expect that your preschool age child will play by himself.** While the three- to five-year-old certainly grows and learns with your help and guidance, he needs plenty of time to be by himself. When he complains that he wants you to play with him you can say, *I am going to play with you after I finish my work. Now we are having time by ourselves for a while. Later I want to see what you have done.*

- **Always being with your child when he is very young leads to the expectation that you will be with him 24/7 even when he's older.** Expecting your child to play independently is the step that precedes expecting him to do his homework and to partake of other activities by himself. Your child will act in the ways that are familiar to him.

- **Gradually build a tolerance for playing alone if yours is the child, regardless of age, who has not been able to do so thus far.** It is not reasonable to expect a child who has always had your undivided attention suddenly to play by himself now. He is accustomed to having you right there in the thick of things and must get used to the rules being changed midstream.

  Try saying, *"I am going to sit right here and read my mail for a few minutes, and you can play with your toys."*

  Don't emphasize the "alone" aspect to the child who is unaccustomed to playing by himself. Keep the amount of time very short at first if your child has no tolerance for playing independently. And be sure to heap on the praise in the end. *"You played with your toys by yourself while I read my mail. You must be proud of yourself. That was terrific."* Then slowly lengthen the time when you regularly do things separately each day.

- **Keep your irritation or anger out of the request.** After all, it isn't your child's fault that he doesn't know how to play independently.

Your child will pick up on your negative tone, and that will draw him closer to you. That's not what you want.

- **Some children try to stay connected by talking to you.** Playing independently means without having any connection to you. If your child continues to talk to you, asking you questions, or showing you his work, you can say, *"I will listen to all you have to say after I am done with my reading. Right now we are just being by ourselves quietly."*

- **Resist the temptation to tell your child what to do.** At some point every child I have even known has said, *"I don't know what to do, I don't have anything to do,"* or my personal favorite, *"I'm bored."* Beware. These are hooks! You are going to get caught. Your child has plenty to do. Have you looked on his toy shelf lately? You can reply with a simple, *"Oh, I know you will find something to do."* And leave it at that. The first time it may not work. But the second or third time, he will figure out that he needs to find something to do independently of you. And, to the claim of being bored, try saying, *"That is great! I know you are going to figure out something really interesting to do."* By the way, there is no such thing as being bored at home. Children who are bored are trying to engage you. (For an extended discussion on being bored, see chapter 7 on self-reliance.)

The Parent's Role

Learning to be independent is a process that unfolds over all the years that it takes a child to grow up. It doesn't happen quickly. It is cumulative, like putting scaffolding on a building. Each step supports the next, and independence gradually blossoms. The more steps your child takes on his own, the more confident he feels—and independence grows out of confidence.

As discussed, some children are temperamentally predisposed to being outgoing risk-takers and may be more independent than you asked for. If this is your child, then you know what I mean. They are challenging in a different way; their independence needs to be applauded but harnessed and channeled at the same time. Building independence in any child, regardless of his temperament, requires you, the parent, to be deliberate, consistent, and patient.

Tips and Scripts for Encouraging a Child to Become Independent

- **In the business of everyday life, expect your child to be independent.** Throughout your daily life look for opportunities for your child to do things and be by himself. Whether it is brushing his teeth or playing by himself, expect that he will do it. Even an infant can learn to fall asleep independently . . . if you allow him to. The parent's consistency in her expectations sends the message of her faith in the child's independent ability. Just thinking *You can do it* is contagious, if you believe it.

- **Have routines in your child's daily life.** Routines shape a child's life and offer predictability. Not only does the child know what is expected of him, but he knows how you expect it to be done. He needs you neither to tell him what to do nor how to do it. Independent action will be the order of the day.

- **Create limits and boundaries.** While it seems strange, it is within such limits that children feel safe enough to take risks. Boundaries breed confidence as they provide a limit beyond which the child cannot go. They provide the security and stability that allow him to take a risk. Being able to take a risk is a tributary to being independent.

- **Be clear about what is and isn't negotiable.** While negotiation may be a marketable skill later in life, it undermines the young child's push toward independence. If he can negotiate with you, it will cause him to question who is really in charge. If it's the child, that means he may not be safe—in which case he'd better stick close to home. So much for his independence.

- **When a task is begun, expect it to be completed.** Children grow accustomed to the parent finishing their tasks. Do not accept less than what you have asked for.

- **Expectations for independence must be appropriate to the child's age, development, and temperament.** For the child who is terrified of the dark, sending him upstairs alone may be too much to ask. But telling him you will stand on the landing and talk to him as he walks up the stairs is a first step.

- **Help your child to be successful.** Give him small tasks at first that he can complete. In so doing you will allow the thrill inherent in doing something by himself to grow in your child. Buy him shoes with Velcro instead of laces until he is old enough to learn to tie (five years old). Give your three-year-old elastic waist jeans so he can take them on and off himself. The idea is for your child to feel successful in his independence.

- **Give your child choices.** Usually two choices are plenty. More can be overwhelming. Making a choice for himself helps the child to feel involved in the decision-making process and encourages his independent action. It was your choice, after all. If you say *"Do you want to run up the stairs or walk up backwards?"* he will still get up the stairs, but it may remove the conflict in getting him there.

- **Life is filled with decisions that need to be made.** It is usually easier (and certainly quicker) for a parent to make decisions for the child, but you'll regret it later on. The child must learn to make decisions for himself and to stick by his choices. The sooner the better.

- **Allow your child to suffer the consequences of his actions and choices.** While it may be hard for you to bear, children need to learn the consequences of their choices, both good and bad. Next time he will make a better choice or take a different action. For the younger child, most logical consequences are imposed by the parent. You can craft them to be appropriate to the child's age and development. For the older child, the consequence, usually part of the action or choice, may seem harsh to you. No one likes to see her child suffer or be in emotional pain. But it is a crucial life lesson, one that helps a child to learn how to make better independent choices the next time around. *"You chose to wear your favorite basketball jersey to school and now it is stained with paint. I know how sad that makes you. Next time you will make a better choice about what you wear to school, I know."* No buying a new jersey. (See chapter 4, p. 75, for a discussion on consequences.)

- **Encourage problem solving.** It is tempting, especially when you are in a hurry (and who isn't?), to jump in and solve your child's problems. In so doing you are creating dependence. Help him to solve his problem by saying, *Describe the problem to me.* Sometimes just in restating the problem the child is able to see a solution. But if not, continue with, *"What are your choices for how you might solve that?"* Or, *"What have you tried so far?"* and then, *"Why didn't that work?"* Sometimes just offering to be there while your child works on the problem is all the support he needs. *"I know this is really a tough problem. I am going to sit with you while you try to figure it out."* Be prepared to respond to a loud *"But I can't do it!"* with *"Okay. Then you don't have to do it."* And move on. Your child simply may not be ready for that level of challenge, and you don't want to make a big deal about that.

- **Avoid "directing" your child.** While it may be more expedient and easier to tell your child what to do and how to do it, doing so undermines his independence and his sense of being able to do things himself. Instead, invite his participation and accept his way of completing the task. *"I sure could use your help to clean up the playroom before Grandpa arrives"* is likely to elicit the help you need from your child. Make sure it is followed by: *"You really helped me out in the playroom and figured out where everything went. Absolutely great!"*

- **Give hints, not answers.** Some children need a few suggestions as to how they might approach a problem. Be careful not to give the solution, as you will be the problem solver. Remember, your goal is to encourage the response *"I can do it!"* and hear the word "I." Problem solving is empowering.

- **Help your child to learn conflict resolution.** Teaching a child the skills to negotiate his conflicts is a big step toward feeling powerful and independent. Whether it is helping your preschooler to use the words you have taught him rather than his fists, or giving your elementary schooler specific scripts to use in playground disagreements or disengaging from bullies, he will feel strong and capable.

  For the young child: *"I don't like it when you take my shovel. Don't do it."*

  For the older child who is being teased: *"Does it make you feel good to make me feel bad?"* Having a script at hand gives the child the courage to respond.

- **Be careful with your praise.** Keep your eye on the goal—independence—and praise the act rather than the outcome.

To the younger child: *"Wow! The playroom was a total mess and you put every single car away."* Or, *"You used so many different colors in that painting."*

For the older child: *"You raked the whole hillside and carried all the bags to the curb. That was incredibly helpful."*

Take pains not to over-praise your child, as it will become an attention getting device. (For more information on how to avoid raising a praise-junkie, see the discussion on praise in chapter 4.)

- **Support your child's interests; they may become his passions.** You may have dreamed of having a baseball star, but you seem to be getting a song-and-dance man. Your child needs to live his life, not yours. He is autonomous, and that's a good thing. Your support and encouragement of his interests underscore that reality. Praise the person he is becoming. *"I just never dreamed I would have a child who is such a talented dancer."*

- **Help your child to learn to tolerate disappointment.** Tolerating disappointment, like tolerating frustration, is a task that children must master in order to grow up and function independently in the world. When a parent rushes in to "make it all better," to minimize the disappointment, the child is deprived of the opportunity to learn to recover. For example, you can say: *"It feels really bad to lose an election. You tried so hard to win and did everything you could. Right now it hurts so much. I really do know how that feels, so disappointing."* An understanding hug is good medicine and is better than running to buy an ice cream to soothe the pain.

- **Children must learn that disappointment happens in all realms of life, and it isn't their parents who save them.** Always cushioning the blow or avoiding it altogether won't help with this lesson.

- **Teach your child to use his "bootstraps."** Your child needs time to feel bad, even to mope a bit after a disappointment. But he will always begin to feel better when he has a plan and picks himself up by the bootstraps, as my mother used to say. Being proactive is a step in learning how to recover. It is always good medicine. Change and growth will not come out of being inert.

- **Encourage your child to advocate for himself.** Elementary schoolers (and older ones) can be expected to interface with their teachers and coaches. Whether it is talking with the teacher about a late assignment or discussing a bad call with a coach, it is the child's job to speak up for himself. It is tempting for all mother lions to roar on behalf of their cubs, but the lesson of independence will not be learned. The tales of high school and even college students whose parents are calling the professors to complain about assignments make my skin crawl. The child needs to learn to take action on his own behalf. If he doesn't want to do it, so be it. He will have to live with the consequences.

As the saying goes, it is a parent's job to give her child roots and wings. The roots part seems easy; it's the wings that can be a challenge. Encouraging and allowing your child's independence is a step in the right direction.

❖

CHAPTER FOUR

"Where's My Jacket?!"

Teaching Responsibility

How many times has your daughter "lost" her sweater at school? (This is different from the socks that get eaten by the dryer.) The sweater goes with her on the bus in the morning, but it just never comes home. It's so maddening! Taking care of possessions is just one of the many ways we define being responsible. And while your child is not born a responsible human being, she is born with the capacity to learn to be responsible and to do things like keeping track of her sweater.

It is easy to see which of the parents who come to my seminars and groups have a sense of personal responsibility. At the end of a session, these are the people who, having enjoyed the proffered refreshments, throw their trash away in the prominently placed wastebasket. Then there are those who leave their trash sitting on the table, which I find amazing. Just who do they think is going to clean it up? I guess clearing their dinner plates wasn't a part of their upbringing.

Children in whom responsibility is cultivated at the earliest ages, who are allowed plenty of time and opportunities to become responsible, are not brats. They see the connection between their actions and the consequences of their behavior, both positive and negative, and they learn to be accountable for the same. Children who are taught about responsibility know how to think about the particular situations with which they are confronted. They develop into the people who know how to organize and complete tasks, to set goals and work toward them. Responsible people are trustworthy people. They are on their way to being self-reliant and independent adults.

By first learning to take responsibility just for herself, then for herself as part of a family machine, and then in the context of a larger community (the school, the baseball team, the church or temple, the city, the national organization . . . the world!), a child will gain great satisfaction from her accomplishments and contributions.

Cultivating responsibility in your child is not only about your child's learning to accept or take responsibility, it is about *you* inviting, giving, and expecting it. And it starts at a very young age, younger than you think. Hundreds of years ago, children as young as four or five were responsible for tasks that we can't imagine giving to a twelve-year-old today. A five-year-old was responsible for watching over her three younger siblings, fixing their meals, bathing them, and keeping them safe while their parents were out foraging or working in the cornfield all day. Now parents wonder if they should leave a twelve-year-old home alone for an hour while they run an errand. Many adults have memories of being responsible for the family laundry or dishes, cleaning bathrooms (yes, toilets!) when they were only seven or eight. Perish the thought today. In the underestimation of your child's ability, there lurks a self-fulfilling prophecy: *Mom doesn't think I can do it, so I can't do it . . . and I won't do it.*

Children today are not raised to feel that they play an important role in the family. Yes, they believe that Mom and Dad love them unconditionally, and many actually have an inflated notion of their own place in the family. But they do not have the sense that the family unit needs their assistance in order to function. In fact, with so many families, it is the help—the nanny, the housekeeper, the gardener—without whom a family cannot operate. The nanny calls in sick, and the family machine grinds to a halt. Perhaps the only responsibility the child has is to care for herself and do her homework. Responsibility grows out of being genuinely needed and valued for your contribution to the smooth running of the whole.

Research has shown just how important feeling needed is to human beings, as well as the impact of the lack thereof. A depressed adult often expresses the feeling that her life has no purpose. She doesn't feel necessary to anyone; she is absorbed in herself. When a person is feeling down in the dumps, one sure way to recover is to do something for someone else. That is just how powerful the need to feel significant is. Making a meaningful contribution in a family, being given responsibility, certainly sends the message of personal value.

Teaching your child to become responsible is not an easy task. It takes a whole lot of effort, but it absolutely can be done.

The Parent as Saboteur

It is actually easier to sabotage the child's development of responsibility than it is to encourage it. Often, a parent's own needs get in the way of her child's as the child stretches to meet her responsibilities. As is the case with cultivating independence and self-reliance, there are times when it is just plain easier to do the job yourself. Perhaps you are in a hurry. ("Oh here, just let me do it," you say as your three-year-old struggles to put on her leggings because she feels cold.) Maybe you know that you can do a better job of it. ("Here, I'll fix that for you," you say as your seven-year-old only half wraps the peanut butter sandwich that she is responsible for making.) You might be frustrated. ("Oh, never mind. I'll just do it myself. The dog can't starve," you sigh, when your eleven-year-old has to be reminded repeatedly to feed the dog.) And sometimes you just run out of steam. ("Forget about it. It's not worth fighting about," you grumble when your twelve-year-old doesn't bring the trash bins in right after school, which is when you want the job done.) But doing the job for your child simply robs her of the opportunity to take responsibility for herself.

Learning responsibility requires the teacher to be patient and flexible. Often that can be really hard, especially at the end of a long day when your fuse is pretty short. But it's the big picture that must be kept in mind. In the end, when your child feels good about what she can accomplish and has a strong sense of her own importance to the family, you will have a responsible child.

These days, parents have really full plates; there are so many things to take care of in the course of each day. So they create all kinds of systems for getting the job done. Too often, that means outsourcing. While that might make your life easier, it doesn't model taking responsibility yourself. How can you expect your child to make her own bed when the housekeeper makes yours? Too many of us hire people to do the jobs that you, dear parent, or your child could and should be doing. Isn't it a parent's responsibility to teach the child to ride a bike? That's what I asked myself when I saw the advertisement in a local paper for "The Bike Coach." Responsibility starts with you.

Being responsible means many things: keeping your promises; following through on your commitments; obeying rules; making good choices; and looking out for your own well-being and for the well-being of family, extended family, neighbors, friends, and others, just to name a few. That's a whole lot for a child to learn.

Tips and Scripts for Teaching a Child to Be Responsible

- **Always keep your promises.** Following through is a big part of being responsible. Saying *"I know I promised I would be at your performance, but I just couldn't make it"* says that sometimes it's okay to be irresponsible. It isn't. If you might not follow through, don't promise. Instead, tell your child: *"I am going to do my best to make it home before you go to bed tonight. I hope it can work out. If not tonight, another night for sure."*

- **Stick to your own commitments and insist that your child do the same.** Your child needs to see that even if you don't really feel like going to your book group, you have made a commitment to be there, and so you go. *"I am so tired tonight, I really don't want to go to my book group. But the others are expecting me to be there, and so I am going. I have a commitment to the group."*

  Your child has begged you for ballet lessons, and after one or two, she doesn't want to go anymore. After you give her the chance to explain what she doesn't like about it, you can say: *"When we signed you up for ballet class, we made a commitment that you would be there. So, you do need to go. Whether you participate is up to you and the teacher. But I am honoring the commitment by making sure you go."* Or, *"I know that playing soccer is not what you expected it to be, but you have made a commitment to the team, and they are counting on you to be there. If you don't want to play, you can talk to your coach about it"*. You can add, *"When this series of lessons is over [or next season] you don't have to sign up again. That will be your choice."*

  Of course, another issue is the money you have paid for the art class your daughter was begging to take and is now no longer interested in; however, the emphasis should be on her keeping a commitment.

- **Teach your child about obligations.** Your child needs to learn that both promises and commitments are also obligations, things that we have to do. *"When you say that you will do something, when you make a promise or agree to do it, you are giving your word. That means you have to do it, you are obligated."*

For the child older than five years, you can add, *"When you meet your obligations, doing what you said you would or promised to do, you are a person who can be trusted. That is part of being responsible."* Directing a child to fulfill her commitments, sometimes insisting that she do so, is a parent's obligation.

At some point in the process of growing up, most children change their minds about things they said they would do (continuing lessons, keeping a play date, being on a sports team). A parent needs to help her child to think carefully about a commitment she is going to make before it becomes an obligation. *"You need to be clear about what signing up for Club Soccer will do to your schedule and other activities. It means that you will have to go to two practices and two games a week. That also means that you will not have time for playdates or for other extra activities."* However, if the child makes a commitment to someone else that was a bad judgment call, you might have to make an exception, stressing the importance of thinking through commitments before they are made. Teaching your child to say, *"I have to ask my Dad,"* to buy the time the child needs before taking action, will work for many years.

It is not uncommon for a child to accept the offer for a playdate, which is like making a promise, and then to change her mind. Perhaps a better offer comes up; perhaps she has gotten cold feet. In teaching the child the lesson of keeping one's promise, the child needs to consider the other child's feelings. *"When you change your mind about your date with Samantha, you are disappointing her and hurting her feelings, and you are not keeping your promise of a playdate."* As discussed in chapter 2 on empathy, there is a developmental component involved. Being able to get into another person's shoes is a perspective that grows little by little. If a child changes her mind about a playdate because of separation anxiety or fear, it will be up to you to help make that date easier for your child, but canceling the date does not send a good message to your child about being responsible.

- **Discuss with your child how you make good choices for your-self.** Think out loud. Most children don't get to witness their parents making decisions; they are usually only privy to the plans after the decisions are made. Children need to be taught how to weigh options and to consider the possible effects of their choices. *"I am trying to decide when I will do the grocery shopping. I can go this morning or after I pick you up from school. If I go after I pick you up, you might not have enough time to do your homework. If I go now, I will have to hurry, but I think it is a better choice."*

- **Teach your child how to think about a choice.** The lesson starts with an awareness of the possible outcome of their choices. Ask your child, *"What would happen if . . . you don't do your math tonight . . . you don't invite Stacie to your party? . . . you don't go to soccer practice?"* and wait for her thoughtful answer. Yours is not meant to be a rhetorical question. The child needs to learn to think ahead to the consequences of her choice. Then allow her to experience them. *"So you are saying that if you don't do your math homework, you will have to skip recess and do it. Is that okay with you? It is your choice."* And, of course, you can throw in the kicker, *"You remember, in our family, there is no computer time until all homework is done, right? I am just reminding you."* It's a reminder, not a threat.

- **Follow the rules.** Sounds obvious, doesn't it? Following rules is being responsible. But you would be surprised at how many adults don't—and they even break the rules in front of their children. *"Oh, it won't matter, just this one time."* But, of course, it does matter. As a school director, I frequently admonished the parents who would jay-walk across a terribly busy street, pulling a child along behind them. Last time I checked, jaywalking was illegal and really unsafe. If you want your child always to use the crosswalk, especially when you're not there to keep her safe, don't jaywalk!

- **Never do for your child what she can do for herself . . . or at least make a genuine attempt.** This includes picking up after herself, making lunch, doing homework, and other developmentally and age-appropriate tasks. If you are the saboteur, as discussed earlier, she will not learn that she should be doing the task for herself—or that she can do it.

- **Let your child know what meeting her responsibilities does for you or for the family.** Tell her directly: *"Because you sorted the laundry, I had time to bake cookies for the family. Your help is really important to me."* Or, *"Everyone got to school on time today because you were so responsible about being ready."*

- **Allow your child to have responsibilities.** There are plenty of opportunities every day. Here are a few.

A two-and-a-half- and three-year-old can:
- Carry her own jacket, lunch box, backpack into/out of school
- Put away some of her toys
- Put her wet bath towel over the tub edge, on the counter, or anywhere that isn't the floor
- Put stuffed animal friends back on the bed in the morning
- Lay out her own clothes for school the night before (three years old)

A four- and five-year-old can:
- Clean up her play area
- Make her own bed by putting animals and pillows in their correct places on the bed
- Hang up her wet towel over the rack
- Put dirty clothes in the hamper
- Clear her own meal plate
- Choose her own snack at home (have prepackaged choices ready in the pantry or refrigerator)
- Lay out her own school clothes the night before

A six-year-old can:
- Make her own lunch (you make the sandwich; she puts in the extras)
- Pack her own snack for school (from the precut/prepackaged choices)
- Make her own bed, including pulling up the covers
- Pack her own back pack and ready her things to take to school the night before

An eight-year-old can:
- Decide when to begin her homework and then follow through on completing it
- Decide when she will practice for the lessons she takes and follow through on regularly keeping those practice times
- Pack her own bag to take to lessons, practice, and overnights . . . and remember to take that bag with her!

- **Allocate regular family or "community" chores.** Not only does having family chores strengthen the child's sense of belonging, but it also helps her to see the importance of everyone's contributions. No one wants to be taken for granted. (See the section in chapter 9 on personal and community chores for a detailed discussion.)

- **Along with your child, prioritize the day's activities, including responsibilities.** Make sure that your child knows what can happen after her responsibilities have been completed. Tell her: *"You can practice roller skating after your homework is done."* Or, *"You can use the computer after you have cleaned the pet's cage, because it's Tuesday [cage-cleaning day]."*

- **Post visual reminders of the child's responsibilities.** Make a list of the things you expect your child to do and put it someplace where it can be readily seen. For the nonreader, use a pictorial list. For the reader, list one-word tasks, such as:

  - Vitamins
  - Teeth
  - Lights
  - Homework
  - Lunch

  Too many tasks will short-circuit the process. For household chores, post a chart that includes the child's name, the days of the week, and the chores to be done. (For an example of a job chart, see chapter 9, p. 191.)

- **Don't be a nag! Part of learning to be responsible is remembering to meet your obligations.** The visual chart will be a memory aid. But if you, the parent, have to remind the child, she won't learn to do it for herself. That "remembering muscle" needs to be exercised.

If the family sits down to dinner at an unset table, the child will certainly get the message about not having done her job. The disappointment of others can be a powerful teacher, and it's much more effective than nagging.

- **Allow the child to experience the consequence of not making responsible choices.** Most children only forget their jackets on a cold, snowy day once. Decide upon the consequence for inaction, let the consequence be known, and allow it to happen. Lesson learned. No saving your child if you want the lesson to be absorbed. (For a longer discussion on consequences, see p. 75.)

- **Keep your eyes open for different ways that your child can be responsible.**

At the grocery store: If your four-year-old loves to have her own mini basket like those found now at many stores, let her spot the items needed (which is a good visual exercise) and fill her basket. Send your seven-year-old to the next aisle to get her own cereal (always with her safety in mind) and ask her to bring it right back to you. Encourage your nine-year-old to write a list of items she would like in her lunch and let her fill her own basket with those items when you shop together. Try your best not to correct her choices (except if it is an unacceptable choice). Rather, praise her responsible choices.

At the restaurant: Allow your child to order for herself, using her good manners. It may take a little time for the more introverted child to find the courage to speak up. Ask this child to request just one item from the waiter rather than ordering the whole meal.

- **Invite responsibility.** Demanding that your child be responsible can be a recipe for defiance. But when you respectfully express your need for her help in an effort to make her responsible for certain things, she will glow in having a purpose. Try saying, *"It would really help me out if you would be responsible for turning off the lights in the house before we leave. I know I won't remember, but I can count on you to do it."*

- **Take advantage of activities that inherently teach children the importance of being responsible.** It may be a bother for you to engage in these activities at first, but the lessons in responsibility that are learned while doing them are priceless and will last a lifetime. The following are a few suggestions:

- **Care for a garden:** A vegetable (or flower) garden takes consistent care and attention. The thrill of growing your own salad is contagious, even for adults. But for the child who has had to plan, cultivate, water, fertilize, and weed his plants, the lesson in responsibility is immeasurable and the result is tremendously satisfying. On a scorching hot day when no one wants to be outside, she has learned that she will have to water her tomatoes or they will die.
- **Care for a pet:** The benefits of having a pet, in my mind, far outweigh the drawbacks. You don't have to start with a golden retriever. Start small. A goldfish is easy: Feed it daily and change the water in its bowl weekly. A box turtle needs food and water and a place to live, which gets cleaned every now and then. A hamster or mouse ups the ante a bit with its need for attention, food, water, and weekly cage cleaning. And the responsibility increases with a cat or a dog. In choosing the appropriate pet, be sure you are putting your child in a position to be successful in its care. I don't know many six-year-olds who are good at cleaning up dog poop, but that is one of the responsibilities that comes with having your own dog.
- **Remember others with a gift or card:** Regardless of the occasion, helping a child to think about someone else is a step toward cultivating empathy and being responsible for the well-being of others. When a friend has to cancel a date because of illness, instead of taking your child out for ice cream to assuage her sadness, help her to make a get-well card for her friend. When a classmate loses a pet, encourage your child to make her a picture to let her know she is in someone's thoughts.

- **Let your child speak for herself.** Children as young as four and certainly older ones should be encouraged, if not expected, to speak up for themselves. *"Will you tell Amy's mommy that I don't like carrots?"* should elicit: *"If you don't like carrots, you can tell Amy's mommy."* If she doesn't want to say it, then she'll have to deal with the inevitable carrots on her plate. Children can be taught to take responsibility for their needs, complaints, and excuses when another adult is in charge.

Stepping in to do the talking only retards the child's learning to speak for herself and take responsibility for her actions, choices, and feelings. *"It is your job to tell Mrs. Elson why you didn't do your homework last night."* Or, *"You will need to tell Coach Allen why you will not be at practice next week."* Sometimes the first step in encouraging your child to speak up is to offer to accompany the child. *"I will go with you to talk with Mrs. Elson, but it is your responsibility to tell her how you are feeling."* Do not give in to such demands as *"No, you tell her,"* or you will be undermining your goal.

- **Model being responsible in your world.** Children who live with responsible parents are much more likely to be responsible themselves. Take the opportunity to be responsible whether or not your child is with you. It will become your habit, and in time it will become hers. So many clients say to me, *"My father always used to . . ."* as the reason for doing any number of things. Your responsible acts will be etched in your child's memory forever.

- **Set the stage for learning social responsibility.** Reaching out to help others—neighbors, friends, and people in the community— teaches children another form of responsibility. Bringing in your neighbor's mail when she is out of town or taking the newspaper to the porch of an elderly neighbor shows your child how you take responsibility for others.

- **Look for opportunities to make your child feel needed.** Having responsibilities outside of the nuclear family (either for older or younger people) can generate feelings of self-worth. Tutoring a younger child in math, for example, or working as a "mother's helper" for a neighbor's toddler are jobs from which the child gets the sense that she is needed. Programs that use peer counselors, camps that have counselors-in-training, even multi-age group settings all contribute to making the helper child feel effective in her world. Having her work make a difference to someone builds the foundation for being socially responsible.

- **Social responsibility begins at home and with extended family.** In many large families, the older children are expected to take care of the younger ones. It's the only way the family can actually make it. These children learn very early on about social responsibility. In families who are not dependent upon siblings' taking care of each other, it will have to be encouraged, but should not be demanded. An older child might read to her little brother when he is feeling sick, sad, or just needs to be occupied, for example. The adoration of the younger child for her sibling, coupled with your appreciation for the help, should fuel more social responsibility in the future. However, if such requests lead to struggles laced with resentment, a different approach may have to be considered.

"Sometimes we visit Grandma because she needs help in the house, needs errands to be done, or just because she gets so much pleasure out of seeing you children." Being socially responsible includes giving help and companionship and making other people feel good.

- **Include your child in your acts of social responsibility.**

  ○ Allow your child to accompany you when you vote. Voting is the responsibility of every citizen.

  ○ Take your daughter with you when you pack food for distribution to the needy. Have her help you bag and bring your donations to the local charity.

  ○ Pick up and throw away the litter on your path in the park, and say, *"Taking care of our parks is everyone's responsibility. That's why I am throwing this litter in the trash bin, even though I didn't drop it."* Our planet needs each of us to be responsible for its keeping.

  ○ When your community has a clean-up or beautification day, participate with your child.

  ○ Let your child know what causes you support and why you have chosen them. Talk about the ways in which you give your support—the checks you write, the time you volunteer, the auction for which you solicit items.

Becoming socially responsible is a habit that will grow if it is a part of a child's life.

The Role of Praise

The ultimate reward for being responsible is the sense of satisfaction that it brings. But it takes some time to get there. In the meantime, external reward in the form of praise gets internalized to become intrinsic reward.

Praise, when used deliberately and thoughtfully, can go a long way toward encouraging your child to make responsible choices. Yet most parents do precisely the opposite: They draw attention to the child's lack of responsibility. This is negative reinforcement, to be sure. Critical, direct, and offhanded comments just make the child feel bad: *"I can't believe you walked on the new rug with your muddy shoes. When will you remember to take them off at the door?"* Real learning doesn't grow from feeling bad about oneself. Such comments may give you the chance to shed some of your anger, but they don't encourage the child to be responsible. Because all children really do want to be well thought of by their parents, catching them making responsible choices will go a long way toward encouraging more of the same.

Tips and Scripts for Praising Effectively

- **Be specific in your praise.** Describe the child's responsible action, rather than using platitudes. Be sure to use the word "responsible" in your praise: *"You carried your jacket and lunchbox in from the car today, and I didn't even have to ask you. That was so responsible of you."*

- **Describe the effect of the child's responsible choice.** In so doing you reinforce her ability to look beyond herself: *"I appreciate your making a few trips to carry in the grocery bags. I am so pooped out today and my back was really bothering me."*

- **Don't even bother with "good job."** What the heck does that mean, anyway? Children hear those two words so much that the comment means nothing except that Mom's happy. Alfie Cohn, author of eight books on education and human behavior, calls comments like these "verbal doggie biscuits." This loosely tossed and hollow praise will not motivate the child to be responsible again. It just signals that everything is okay—for now. The words, not absorbed, are usually gone as quickly as they were said. (See appendix, p. 227, for *100 Ways to Say "Good Job!"*)

- **Use your tone rather than a judgment word to express the praise.** Saying *"You cleaned up the whole playroom!"* with surprise and pleasure actually communicates more genuine praise than does *"I am happy that you cleaned up the whole playroom."* Remember, the goal is for the child to be intrinsically motivated to be responsible. When praise is all about your happiness, the child will grow to need you and your reactions. This is extrinsic motivation in the making—exactly the opposite of what you're trying to cultivate.

- **Use the word "I" sparingly.** If your praise starts with the word "I," then it is about you and not about the child. Make every effort to start your praise with the word "you."

- **Show appreciation for a chore completed, but do not necessarily thank your child.** For responsibility taken, children can be recognized and even shown appreciation. But thanking the child for something she is expected to do may make it seem like she didn't have to do it in the first place: *"I so appreciate the way you set the table without my having to ask you, and you did such a careful job of placing the silverware."* No thank-you stated; appreciation expressed. Message received!

- **"Gossip" about your child's shows of responsibility.** This is a form of praise. As if she is not listening, talk about the things your child has done to reinforce the action and get more of the same. *"Oh, Janie, I just don't know what I would do without Kate. She is so helpful to the family in doing her chores. Today I was just exhausted, and her dust-bustering the kitchen floor was a lifesaver."* Fake the phone call if necessary. Your young child won't know if anyone is on the other end, but she will hear your side of the conversation.

- **In front of your child, show appreciation to others in the family for doing their parts.** Take every opportunity to reinforce that every member of the family contributes to its smooth running and makes a difference. *"I really appreciate how Daddy makes spaghetti for this family. We all just love it."*

- **Recognize different children at different times.** Often praising one child and then her brother because he has whined, *"What about me?"* dilutes the recognition you have given the first. In response to the above plea you can say, *"Right now I am just talking about what Heather did for the family,"* and leave it at that.

The Role of Consequences

In order for your child to be responsible, she needs to be given responsibilities and allowed to feel the consequences of her choices and actions, good or bad. Developing responsibility is a process of gradual, incremental learning. When a child accomplishes a task and experiences success, the responsible choice she has made is reinforced. That is a positive consequence of being responsible and, hopefully, it leads to more of the same.

For the two-year-old child who is fully ensconced in the learning mode, it's all about exploring and trying things out for herself: *"Me do it!"* she exclaims. For her, the consequence of her actions is not as potent as the glee and power she feels in doing it herself.

At four years old the child is fully capable of experiencing the consequences of her choices. She can generalize the lesson of cause and effect, applying it to similar situations in the future. Older preschool and elementary-school children have the cognitive and conscience development to understand making responsible choices.

Teaching a child that her actions bring results is one of the lessons on the pathway towards becoming responsible. Inherent in the lesson—in choosing your actions you are also choosing the consequence of those actions—is the lesson of accountability.

It's tricky business to allow your child to experience the consequences of her actions. It can take you right to the "you're the meanest mommy in the whole wide world" place. While no one likes to be in that position, it is necessary to bring the lesson home. You are going to have to be quite unpopular as you allow your child to suffer the consequences she has brought on herself.

There are three different kinds of consequences: natural consequences, logical consequences, and illogical consequences.

Natural Consequences

These are the results of actions that happen without any intervention from anyone. When the child doesn't put the cover on her favorite green marker and finds that it's all dried up, the lesson is obvious. The child who forgets to wear her shin guards isn't allowed to play in the soccer game. Chances are she won't forget them again; she will remember to bring them to each and every game because sitting out an entire game was just no fun at all. I cannot stress enough the power of the lesson of the natural consequence. It fuels responsibility, and, best of all, it isn't even your fault.

Logical Consequences

These differ from natural consequences in that you or the adult in charge structures them. The critical point is that logical consequences are directly related to the action or behavior. They make sense to the child and therefore seem reasonable; she doesn't view the consequence as an arbitrary decision the parent has made. The child who has left her homework at school might have to fess up to the teacher in the morning and do her homework during recess. The child, who threw her tennis racket and broke it when she lost the game, now owns a broken, unusable racket. Maybe she'll have to work to earn the money to help pay for the repair. With logical consequences, it's clear who is responsible.

Illogical Consequences

These are the ones that don't really make sense, but you think it will teach the child a lesson and make her more responsible. It is not related to the child's choice of action at all, but in your view it will have the most impact on the child—she'll really feel it. The four-year-old didn't clean up her toys, so she can't have a playdate. The third-grader didn't do her homework, so she can't have dessert. You know about illogical consequences because that's what parents impose when they can't think of what else to do. Illogical consequences don't teach lessons that last.

The lessons of natural and logical consequences are clear and easily understood by the child. In choosing her actions she also chooses the consequence. Next time, she will do her homework because it wasn't fun at all, and it was embarrassing, to have to spend recess in the classroom finishing her work. It makes sense, so the child actually feels accountable for her choice of action and usually makes an effort not to make that choice again.

The lesson of the illogical consequence is that Mom is mad at her for doing something. The emphasis is on what the parent imposed and not on what the child brought on herself by not making a responsible choice.

As children reach the middle elementary-school age (usually around eight years old), the logical consequence may not be directly related to the infraction. The child is now old enough to comprehend that the causes and effects of her actions are directly related. Rather, the consequences of not doing what was expected of her at this age may be the removal of her privileges, as previously discussed with her. In her book, *The Blessing of a Skinned Knee*, Wendy Mogel outlined what we owe our children. Explain to your child that while you are responsible for her, she will always get from you shelter, food and clothing, an education, and medical attention, and that everything, and I mean everything else, is an extra or a privilege. You and your child will be astounded by the length of the list of her privileges that you make together (TV, computer, iPod, telephone, playdates, overnights, movies, extracurricular activities, practices of all kinds, etc.). The consequence for her behavior or choice of action is the removal of one of these privileges for a meaningful, but not ridiculous, amount of time. It works!

Whether using the logical consequences appropriate to the younger child or the removal of a privilege, below are suggestions for effectively structuring the consequence.

Tips and Scripts for Imposing the Consequences of Irresponsible Choices or Actions

Remember, the goal in implementing consequences is to ignite some constructive learning. It is not for your child to feel horrible! Consequences are not punishments.

- **The consequence must be related to the action.** It might take you a little time to think about what it should be, but allow yourself that time to figure out an appropriate consequence. Don't shoot from the hip or allow your own parent's methods to dictate what you do. Tell your child: *"When you choose not to put your toys away, there is a* *consequence. I need to think about what it will be, and I'll let you know in a minute."* Wait only a very short time before returning with the consequence. *"Part of owning toys is taking care of them and putting them away. You chose not to put your toys away so you cannot have them for a few days."* Learning to structure logical consequences takes time. You'll get better with practice.

- **You can involve the older child in deciding her consequence.** With an elementary-school child the consequence might be obvious, so you can say, *"What do you think is the consequence for not putting your bike in the garage, as is our rule?"*

    How funny it is that children often come up with illogical consequences or ones that are harsher than yours would have been? Those who come up with an appropriate consequence are the ones who, at last, get it!

- **Consequences should be reasonable, both to your child and to you.** Consequences that are reasonable, that are structured with the child's age, development, and severity of the offense in mind, are also respectful of the child. Though it may not at first seem that way to the child because she is angry at herself for blowing it, she gets it and will be more accepting of receiving her due when the consequence is reasonable. Not watching television for a month is not a reasonable consequence for not turning it off when she was supposed to. But losing the privilege for a day or two certainly is. *"When you choose to watch more TV than you are permitted and are not responsible, you are also choosing the consequence of not watching TV tomorrow and Thursday at all."*

    Make sure that as you structure the consequence you don't choose something that will punish yourself or the rest of the family. If you have been looking forward to going to the beach on Saturday, staying home with your child is probably not the best consequence.

- **Mind your anger!** Though you might be frustrated, fed up, disgusted, and just plain angry with your child, your emotion will get in the way of the lesson. I polled a group of parents regarding their own parents' responses when they blew it growing up. Several parents replied that a father calmly saying *"I am disappointed in you,"* without demonstrating anger, was the most powerful statement of all.

- **Don't editorialize; let the consequence speak for itself.** While it is tempting to add your two cents' worth, don't do it. Your child knows she has made a mistake; she doesn't need you to rub her face in it. Not only will the additional lesson be lost, but so will the power of the consequence. It will all be buried in the landslide of your words: *"Blah blah blah."*

- **The consequence should be decided and known to your child in advance.** Although it is difficult to anticipate everything that could happen, you are usually in a position to let your child know what her responsible behavior will bring, positively and negatively. Have a discussion with your child about the possible appropriate consequences for a misstep. For the child who is not getting her homework done, over the weekend you might bring up the topic and say, *"You are responsible for getting your homework done every night. Let's decide what the consequence will be for your not following through."* And when it inevitably happens, you are not the villain when you say, *"So, since you decided not to do your homework tonight, that means you also chose not to have your outside play time tomorrow."*

- **Beware of manipulation.** The more "gifted" the child, the more manipulative she is. I swear it! Much as you might appreciate the skill, you must not let it work for her: *"You choose the action, you choose the consequence"* is the rule. Most teachers and bosses can't be manipulated. That's life. Your child will be crippled if you don't allow her to learn to deal with those responses.

- **Tolerate the reaction.** Even though your child claims to hate you, that you have ruined her life, and she wants to live in a different family, she knows full well that you are right, and you will have gained her respect. By giving in you are abdicating your responsibility. Put on your Teflon suit. An eye roll never hurt anyone.

- **Consistency counts.** Consequences that are sometimes implemented and sometimes not lose their efficacy—and so does the parent. The child needs to internalize the lesson that her choice of action is the reason for the consequence. Irresponsible choices will always yield the same result. If you are wishy-washy in your implementation, if you allow your clever child to talk you out of it, the lesson will be lost. Enough said.

- **Follow through until the very end.** I know this may sound harsh, but the consequence is the consequence. If there is no television for three days, don't reduce it to two days. Not only are you being irresponsible, but also the consequence will lose its punch. Remember, it is not you who is punishing the child. The consequence is of her making.

I am reminded of this classic example: A parent tells the child whose shoes are not on that the family will be leaving without her. No shoes, no go. As Mommy picks up her keys and shepherds the other family members out of the house, the child rushes frantically to the door, saying: *"I'm coming! I'm coming! I'm putting my shoes on."* Mom acquiesces and waits as Abby quickly (and finally) puts her shoes on. And no lesson is learned.

Chores

Everyone knows that chores teach responsibility. In fact, many parents use the words chores and responsibilities synonymously. That's how basic chores are to the process of raising children. It is 100 percent true that having chores builds a child's sense of responsibility as well as her sense of value to the family unit. While there are many widely differing opinions regarding at what age a child should be given chores and what they should be, most people agree that children should have chores.

Children as young as a year old can and should be introduced to chores. Of course, to these children it's a kind of game—putting the Cheerios back in the bowl, for instance—but it forms the foundation for cultivating responsibility. Two-year-olds actually love putting the zoo animals back in their basket and putting the basket on the shelf. Three-year-olds can easily put their soiled school clothes in the hamper. So the answer to the question of when you should start giving your child chores is: earlier than you think.

I have clients with a thirteen-year-old son who is an endless source of frustration to them. He is certainly a typical teen, but on top of that he is an unusually difficult child who simply won't do his chores. The son is wearing them down. (And they are pretty weak at following through with the consequences for chore-shirking.) At our last meeting, Dad said, "Frankly, I just got sick of hounding him to do his chores. I don't want to have that relationship with my son, so I have just stopped expecting him to do them. Now he does nothing, and we don't fight about it." Talk about letting your child down! Yes, doing chores can be an uphill battle with some children, but giving up is worse. In that case, the message is: "I have no faith in you; you are not a vital member of this family; I don't care."

Tips and Scripts for Getting Your Children to Do Chores

- **Do your own chores.** Make sure that your child sees that everyone in the family has specific chores that he does religiously. Talk about it: *"It's time for me to cook dinner. It's one of my chores. Daddy does the dishes. That's his chore."* I know it sounds ridiculously obvious, but children don't see the things that you do as chores; they see those things as what defines you. You can let them know that it isn't something that you love doing but that you do it because it is your responsibility. Once in a while you can throw in *"You know, I don't feel like cooking dinner tonight. I'm not going to do my chore,"* and see what happens.

- **To begin, choose chores at which the child will easily succeed.** Children as young as three take pleasure in doing jobs. Their thrust toward autonomy *("Me do it!")* fuels their desire to do chores. Take advantage. Offer small, easy tasks. They can:

  - Put one napkin on every placemat
  - Carry a (small) pile of towels to the laundry room
  - Line up all the shoes by the door
  - Put all the cars in the basket

- **Be sure that chore assignments are appropriate to the child's age and development.** You want your child to be successful and not overwhelmed by her chores. It is reasonable for a four-year-old child's chores to include making her bed by putting the pillow where it belongs and placing the stuffed animals back on the bed. It is not reasonable to expect that child to neatly replace the comforter. A twelve-year-old can do the family dishes, but maybe not the pots and pans.

Chores that are manageable—that have a beginning and an end—are more likely to be done again and without complaints.

- **Take the time to teach the chore.** Even though your child has watched you make her bed hundreds of time, she may still need a lesson. Show her how to do the tasks you expect her to do. She may not know that the napkin goes on the left under the fork. However, this is not about quality control; it is literally about teaching. Accept her learning curve. Then be a great cheerleader as she improves: *"When you first started setting the table, you didn't remember which side the fork went on. Now you do it so well every time. Way to go!"*

- **Communicate your reasonable standards for a chore.** Being responsible means doing the whole job. Along with teaching how to do a chore, your child needs to learn your reasonable expectations. If it is her job to clean the cat's litter box, she also needs to know that you expect her to put in fresh litter. Emptying the small wastebaskets might also include taking the harvest out to the big trash bins.

- **Be willing to lend a hand when the chore is overwhelming.** Straightening up the playroom may be a regular chore for your four-year-old after a typical day, but after a four-person playdate the chore will be less overwhelming and more likely to be successfully completed when you step in to lend a hand. *"This room is so messy today. I am going to help you with your straightening chore. I will pick up everything with wheels. You can put away everything with four legs."* Be sure you step in to help before your child starts complaining about the size of the job. Otherwise she will quickly learn that complaining works!

- **Create an incentive to finish the chore.** The incentive might be how happy the child's siblings will be to find their clothes neatly piled on their beds, or what she will be able to do when the chore is completed.

- **Involve your child in choosing her chores.** You can give her some choices, make some suggestions, or you can make a list of all the chores that get done by someone in your family. It's going to be a long list, and the longer the better. Start the chore assignments with: *"There are so many things that need to get done in this family. I'm willing to do* *the laundry."* And then see what each of your children is willing to do. Put names next to the chores as they are chosen; everyone in the family will be listed. Children who are involved in the choice of chores will be more willing to cooperate. They will see themselves as part of a family unit, every one of whom contributes to the smooth running of the whole.

- **For people who have household help, ask them to leave the chores for the child to do.** If it is your child's chore to put her toys away before bed, neither you nor the household help should do it. It is the child's responsibility, remember? (See the section on consequences, p. 75, for a discussion of what to do when a child doesn't meet her responsibility.)

- **Have consequences when chores aren't done.** Decide upon and make it clear what the consequences will be. Children learn the lesson of taking responsibility when they experience the consequences, both positive and negative, of their work or lack thereof. It may pain you to have to follow through with the logical consequence, but the power of the lesson trumps your pain avoidance. *"I know you were hoping to wear those jeans today, but when you don't put them in the hamper, they don't get washed."*

- **Never redo a chore a child has done.** Be prepared to accept the job the child has done, even though it may not be up to your standards. If it is a genuinely poor attempt, you can request that it be done properly, but if it is simply not up to your adult standard, leave it alone. (I can't tell you how many times I have overlooked a counter not perfectly well sponged.) At a later time, you can address how you expect a chore to be done. It is about giving information only: *"I want to show you how to feed the dog so that most of the food gets in the dish."*

- **Mind your critical self.** The surest way to turn off your child (or your spouse) from doing a job and feeling good about having done it (and wanting to do it again) is to be critical. Often "good enough" is in fact good enough. If the job is not up to snuff, you can say in a neutral voice: *"I think you need to go back and finish your chore. It's not quite done."* Then drop it.

Personal Chores vs. Community Chores

Each family will have a different idea about what they expect from their children on behalf of themselves and for the family unit. Not only must children learn to do things for themselves, but they need to learn to "do their share" in the context of the entire family. Personal chores are those that relate directly to the child's belongings and well-being. These might include her personal hygienic care (bathing, tooth brushing, hair maintenance, etc.), room care, and cleaning up after herself (putting toys away in the family room, clearing her place at the dinner table, hanging up a wet bath towel, etc.). Personal chores are expectations; we all need to learn how to take care of ourselves.

Community chores are those that contribute to the smooth running of the family on a regular basis. They are chores that absolutely need to be done by someone. These might include table setting, dish washing, dishwasher unloading, pet feeding, etc. The family is dependent upon each member, including the child, to contribute her efforts. If she doesn't do it, it doesn't get done. In addition to the not-so-fun community chores, children should be allowed to do some of the bigger chores, like meal choices/planning and preparation.

The following is a list of community chore suggestions:

- Set the table
- Clear the rest of the table, after each person clears her plate; push in the chairs, put placemats away, sponge off the table, dust-bust under the table
- Empty the dishwasher (starting at age six; breakables may require help)
- Empty the silverware container of the dishwasher (at age four or five)
- Empty the small room wastebaskets into the kitchen trash
- Sort the laundry by color or by owner
- Put clean socks together by pairs
- Carry laundry to owners' rooms
- Bring in the newspaper
- Bring in the mail
- Take out the big trash bins; bring in the empty trash bins

- Feed the pet; fill the water dish
- Clean up the pet poop
- Water outdoor plants
- Weed small garden areas
- Remove dead leaves from plants
- Pick up/rake leaves from specific areas
- Sweep patio/porch/walkway/garage
- Dust-bust the car
- Dust-bust anywhere!
- Wash (spritz) the car windows
- Sweep/dust-bust kitchen or common areas
- Sponge off family room table; straighten the magazines

I could go on and on. Be creative. Anything that you might need done, a child can do all or part of it, depending upon her age.

There are different schools of thought about whether to compensate monetarily for doing personal or community chores. I believe that children need to learn the connection between work and reward (stickers for young children, money for children at least seven years old). They need to have ways to earn money and also need to learn to manage their money as part of their responsibility lessons. It is up to each family to decide what works best for them, have a plan, and consistently follow through. (For a discussion on allowances, see chapter 9.)

The good news is that you'll have no shortage of opportunities to teach your child to be responsible; there are always jobs that have to get done. The more challenging part is dealing with the child's learning process—the complaints, the whining, and the avoidance. Without question, however, it's worth the effort, as you are teaching your child how to *be* in the world.

❖

CHAPTER FIVE

"No, *You* Go to Your Room!"

Creating a Respectful Child

"If I spoke to my father the way my child speaks to me . . . " That's the reaction of so many parents who can't believe what their children say to them. It's curious that each generation of parents says the same thing about their offspring: "Kids today just don't show their parents any respect. It wasn't like that when I was growing up." Disrespect just smacks of being a brat.

It's really hard to grasp all the nuances and expressions of respect. Yet with your young child's first explosion of back talk, in your horror, you stumble for a response and let loose with: "That is so disrespectful! You may not talk to me that way!" While he has no idea what that means, he sure knows that you are not happy. But he'll learn fast. From that day forward, he hears that word "respect" all the time, and in many different situations: when he defies you, when he talks back, when he doesn't follow rules, when he doesn't use his manners, when he doesn't look someone in the eye, when he is expressing his real feelings at the moment ("I hate you!"), and even when you talk about one of his wonderful teachers whom you admire.

What Is Respect?

Both a noun and a verb, "respect" can also be made into an adverb and an adjective. Respect is a biggie! For most of the world, respect means thinking of someone else, considering his needs, desires, and position. It is an acknowledgment. When you are expecting your spouse at a particular time and he calls to say he'll be a little late, it is a show of respect for you. When he asks if you mind if he changes the TV channel, it is an act of consideration, and that is respect, too. There is a language of respect, the acts we do and the words we use that are a kind of universal communication. Shaking hands, saying "pleased to meet you" are mannerly acts of respect. Respect is one of the ways we show that we acknowledge a person's status. When people meet the queen of England, they bow or curtsy as a sign of respect, which acknowledges that she is the queen.

An even more abstract meaning of respect is as an expression of the esteem in which you hold someone. You need not even have met him, but you admire or respect him. I respect Warren Buffet because he is a man who stands by his economic principles and literally puts his money where his mouth is. I respected Ina, my own children's preschool director, for her devotion to her school and to my children.

From the perspective of the child, regardless of his age, the first definition of respect is having to behave and act in specific, acceptable ways in certain places and at certain times. Sometimes it is the way you talk to someone, and sometimes it is following the rules. Respect isn't only with regard to people. The child also needs to learn about respecting things. For example, he must respect his books by taking care of them, not tearing pages, not walking on them, cleaning them up, etc. Gradually, the child comes to understand that being respectful is one of the ways that he acknowledges another person, and he demonstrates his growing understanding of life's operating instructions. Implicit in demonstrating respect is the understanding, *I know what I need to do in this situation.*

Respect is such a complicated concept. If it's hard for an adult to wrap his arms around it, can you imagine what it's like for your child?

From the Developmental Perspective

The child comes into this world factory-equipped with only the basics, things like instincts, temperament, a thrust toward becoming autonomous, and the need to explore the world. The child model doesn't come with behavior options like kindness, thoughtfulness, and respectfulness. Part of his journey on the pathway of growing up is learning what it means to be respectful and why he needs to be respectful.

The toddler, from eighteen months to two-and-a-half years, is blossoming. His language skills are just developing. And he is figuring out that through his language he gets his needs met. Often that is done with little finesse, as he says to Daddy at bedtime, *"No, go away. I want Mommy!"* You might think, *How disrespectful,* when in reality it's just his newly mastered and still raw way of expressing what he wants. The toddler is totally in the figuring-out stage. He is the explorer scout! Everything is new, waiting to be discovered and experienced, and he is all about information input. *When I say this, Mommy does that; When I don't say this, here's what happens,* and so on. The toddler is fully capable of generalizing the skills he learns, behavioral and interpersonal, to new situations, but it takes repeated experiences and lots of time on his part. Truth be told, children spend their growing years doing a whole lot of road tests. And you have been anointed the policeman. It takes tremendous patience on your part. In order to learn what he is supposed to do in any number of situations, the child must do the opposite, and sometimes to you that looks like disrespect.

Respect is a foreign concept to the toddler. But this is the time when the foundation for understanding respect is laid. This little guy is all about himself: *I see it, it's mine; I want it right now.* While he is interested in and even fascinated by other children, in particular, considering another person's feelings doesn't come naturally. His empathy is just starting to unfold. (See chapter 2 for an in-depth discussion of empathy.) He knows how he feels; he has yet to learn that how you feel is important, too. He does learn that there are powerful people in his world: his parents, his grandparents, and his caregivers. His awareness of the hierarchy of the people in his life, who has power and who makes things happen, begins to grow. But the toddler can't practice respect and consider another's needs, because he doesn't quite get it yet.

The preschool-age child, the three- to five-year-old, is still in the mode of understanding the rules of the road, too. But his is a super highway. A big part of his learning is the acquisition of social skills. He is beginning to understand his effect on others, both at home where he feels secure and loved, and in the bigger world of school. Emotionally, this child, especially the four-year-old, can be intoxicated by his own power and the effect he has on others; he is working hard to figure out the extent of his reach. And you can see this play out in three-year-old girls, whose language skills suddenly seem so advanced. They use their tongues as swords, roll their eyes and *tsk* just like teenagers! These preschoolers are practicing their autonomy, defying you, discovering their own tastes and desires as well as expressing their individual wills. What's respect, anyway? You think your child is being disrespectful; he thinks he is Tarzan, king of his world (or she thinks she's Miley Cyrus, queen of hers). Practicing disrespect is the first step in developing an understanding of respect, both the need for it and its usefulness. Learning respectful behavior is an interpersonal skill, and it requires a whole lot of trial and error.

The preschool-age child's empathy is growing. It was not so long ago that he was all about me me me. Considering others and learning the power and importance of respect—learning how he gets his needs met in the context of other people—is an ongoing lesson. Sometimes being respectful and considering other people gets trumped by the preschool-age child's lack of impulse control, as well as his powerful needs, desires, and emotions.

The ability to tolerate frustration and disappointment and being able to delay gratification—the three peaks that must be conquered in order to grow up—are really challenging to the preschool-age child. Developing these abilities is among the prerequisites for being able to demonstrate respect. In reality, what parents may view as disrespect is often the actions of a child trying to scale one of these peaks.

The elementary-schooler, the six- to ten-year-old, gets it. He has the foundation for understanding what respect means, even though he may not be able to articulate it. He knows what being respectful means and how it is demonstrated. This child has cultivated empathy, and he has practiced his social skills. He knows the rules of the game. Whether he follows them all the time is a whole different story. The challenge with the "Satanic six-year-old" as he can be fondly referred to, is that he often finds it especially difficult always to be respectful toward the people with whom he is the most comfortable. He spends a lot of time strutting his stuff, demonstrating his power and his will, and experimenting with new ways of making his mark. Words, expressions, and "attitude," the likes of which you have never seen before (unless you have an older child who has survived this stage of development) come home with him and are given a trial run with you. Believe me, you will have lots of opportunities to teach this child about being respectful. Don't worry, though, you will never hear from his teacher that he has talked back to her. He probably never will, because he gets it.

The preadolescent, age eleven and up, is well versed in the meaning and practice of respect in all its forms. This child is becoming emotionally and socially intelligent, and knows the role that respect plays in both. But like all people, sometimes this child just loses it. The middle schooler is often his own victim, caught between raging hormones and the incomplete wiring of his neural development. He is a *Stranger in a Strange Land.* Working on the developmental task of individuating, becoming his own person, separate from you, can mean defying you, questioning you, and yes, even being disrespectful to you. At least he expresses much of the disrespect under his breath, muttering as he rolls his eyes and skulks off to his cave.

Tips and Scripts for Teaching Respect

- **Treat your child with respect.** Respect begets respect. Children who are spoken to with respect are shown the model of respectful interactions. The parent who screams at his child, *You may not scream at me!* makes no sense to the child. Your child will parrot the words and tone you use with him, and you're liable to get it right back. It was James Baldwin who said, "Children have never been very good at listening to their elders, but they have never failed to imitate them." Children who live with disrespect—including overhearing when you talk that way with your spouse—practice disrespect.

- **When speaking to your child, be as respectful as you would be with a friend.** Would you say to a friend: *"What in the world are you wearing? Did you pull that out of the trash?"* Or, *"Put your napkin on your lap. What do you think this is, a pig sty?"* Flip remarks, sarcasm, and humiliation do not demonstrate respect.

- **Listen to your child.** Listening is a way we show respect. Positioning yourself to receive his communication, whatever it might be, sends a strong message about your respect for your child's thoughts, opinions, and ideas. If you cannot stop at that moment, honor your child by saying, *"I really want to hear what you have to say, and I want to give you the attention you deserve. I am going to finish this and get right back to you."* (If necessary, review chapter 1, "Did You Hear Me?: How to Talk to Your Kids.")

- **Don't talk over your child.** Doing so drowns out his words and gives the clear message that what he is saying doesn't matter. No respect there. Let him finish.

- **Catch your child being respectful.** Especially with young children, use the word "respect" when you offer praise. *"When you shook Mr. Schulman's hand, that was really respectful,"* and *"You showed how much you respect Buddy Dog when you cleaned out his dog house."* Take every opportunity to praise examples of respect in order to expand his grasp of what being respectful means. With an older child, you might say: *"I know you don't particularly like Mrs. Smith, but that was really respectful of you to help her carry her packages."*

- **Monitor the media/television programs your child watches.** While you can't control all of the outside influences on your child, you can be selective about the ones that he is fed through the media. *The Simpsons, Sponge Bob Square Pants,* and *iCarly,* for example, provide models of disrespectful behavior that become acceptable through familiarity. If you are able to watch such programs with your child and editorialize, all the better. *"Wow, that Bart is being so rude and disrespectful to his mother. That sure wouldn't be okay in real life, would it?"*

- **Use the examples of disrespect that real life will give you.** There have been plenty of examples of sports figures who mouth off to referees, politicians who speak disrespectfully to colleagues, entertainers who behave or speak in shocking ways in public. Use these examples as powerful fodder for family discussions. Starting with *"So, did you hear the way Serena Williams spoke to the linesman at her tennis match? What did you think about that?"* makes for meaningful and meaty dinner table conversation and brings the lesson home without pointing a finger at the child.

- **Help your child to learn more effective and respectful ways of expressing his feelings and opinions.** Just telling your child that his way of speaking was disrespectful doesn't give him the tools he needs in order to show respect. He needs to hear many different examples of what he or others should say. *"If the congressman had said, 'Mr. President, I really don't agree with you,' that would have been respectful.*

But calling the president a liar sure wasn't. That was really awful." Children need to learn that name calling and hurling insults at anyone are disrespectful.

- **Substitute the word "respectful" for the word "appropriate."** Too often a child's misstep is met with the parental response: *"That's not appropriate."* That doesn't offer much of a lesson, as the word "appropriate" becomes a one-size-fits-all word. If you mean to say "respectful," then say it. Be direct.

- **Honor your child's differing opinion.** It is not necessary that your child thinks the way you do. In fact, you want to encourage his independent thinking. Honoring the expression of his own opinions is one way that you demonstrate your respect for him. *"I like knowing that you have your own opinion. And I respect you for having it. That's one of the things that makes us each different people."* No put-downs!

- **Allow your child to disagree with you.** Disagreement is not necessarily a sign of disrespect. Your child may be furious because of a consequence you have imposed, a privilege you have taken away, or a decision you have made. Let him tell you, respectfully. Then say: *"I hear that you disagree with my decision, and I understand why. I respect you for telling me, but I am not changing my mind."* At least he feels heard and therefore respected, which saying *"I don't give a hoot what you think"* would not communicate.

- **Have clear limits and enforce them.** In addition to making a child feel safe, having limits shows your concern and respect for him. When you impose the limit firmly and calmly, your child feels respected and sees that you respect the rules that are in place, too. Respect your child by letting him know in advance the limits and boundaries for him or for your family.

  In so doing you are giving the message that you know he will follow through, and that expectation oozes respect. *"You may use the hose outside as long as you keep the water off the patio. I know you will follow the rule."*

  The older child may respond with *"I know, I know. Do you think I don't know to call you when I get to Josh's house?"* He means that you don't trust and respect him. And you can reply, *"I know you will respect the rules."*

- **Respond to rule- and limit- breaking calmly but with authority.**
  Describe what happened specifically and the result of such behavior.
  Respect is not born from screaming, belittling, embarrassment, humiliation, or intentional pain—and it won't lead to genuine learning
  that will inform future behavior. Try: *"I asked you to turn off the television,
  and you did not. Now you have lost the privilege of watching any more today."*

- **Modulate your reactions to your child's misbehavior or bad
  choices.** Don't overreact when your four-year-old calls you a "poop
  head." Remember that sometimes a lack of impulse control trumps
  using respectful words. It's likely that your child is trying to get a rise
  out of you. Instead, try: *"If you are angry at me, you can certainly tell me,
  but calling me a 'poop head' doesn't tell me anything."* You can add, *"In our
  family we don't call each other names."* Then leave it at that.

    There is no need to rub it in when you are responding to some-
  thing your child may have said or done. Overreacting and carrying
  on says you do not respect him and his ability to absorb what you
  have said. In addition to teaching him not to listen, your overreaction actually detracts from the lesson you are trying to teach. *That's
  just Dad exploding again,* he thinks. The child's behavior, which led to
  your reaction, is lost in the shuffle as it's all about you now, and he is
  off the hook.

- **Don't shoot from the hip.** In your most clumsy moments, when
  you don't know what to say or what consequence to impose, you reach
  into the ever-present luggage in which you carry everything your parents ever said to you and pull out the very comment you swore you
  would never say to your own child: *"Children should be seen and not
  heard!"* Not only is that comment and others like it the height of your
  disrespect, but also you will lose your child's respect. He knows you
  fumbled! It's all over your face.

- **Sharing your feelings is not disrespectful.** *"It makes me really angry
  when you do not do what I asked"* is neither disrespectful nor illegal.
  When delivered without vitriol, it is honest and will be heard.

    While there are people who believe that saying *"I love you but I
  don't like what you did"* is a good thing and shows respect, I do not. It
  merely confuses the child and gets you nowhere. Perhaps it assuages

your guilt over being angry. In my opinion, it's okay to be respectfully angry. It's honest.

- **Speak to the behavior, not the child.** Say what you mean. *"When you call me names, I do not want to be with you,"* Or, *"I do not like being with you when you stick your tongue out at me."* Then walk away.

- **Saying nothing can be a powerful response.** Especially with older children, merely walking away, not commenting, but letting your child know you are not happy by your facial expression and your leaving, sends a strong message.

- **Do a revisit . . . later.** In the heat of the moment, the child goes deaf. His head is filled with his anger or yours. When there is distance from the incident, when you've both cooled off, he will have the perspective to review what happened and why.

With a child four or younger, a simple review will do: *"You wanted more ice cream and Daddy said no. You felt so angry that you started throwing your toys, and I had to stop you. Next time you can say, 'Daddy, I am really angry at you.' And I will know how you feel."*

With your five-year-old, at a calm moment, in a comfortable place, ask him, *"What is your idea about what happened today in the grocery store?"* and then pay attention to his entire response. If he got it all, you need not add anything except *"I am glad you understood what happened. I think you will respect the rules next time."* And be done with it. If you get the old *"I don't know,"* (and by the way, he does know!), you will need to go on, always starting by validating his feelings: *"You were really mad at me when I said you couldn't buy candy at the grocery store. You were so mad that you had a huge meltdown, screaming at me and showing disrespect to me and all the people in the market who had to hear you. So I had to take you out of the store. I think you learned three things. One is that No means no, and I will not change my mind even if you have a meltdown. The second is that you must respect the rules for behavior in the grocery store. And the third is that when you disrespect the rules, you will have to leave wherever you are."*

For the ten-year-old: *"You were really angry with me when I wouldn't let you stay up and watch another program, and you let loose with language we don't use in this family. It's okay for you to be ticked off with me. Next time you need to find a more respectful way of telling me."*

- **You are not your child's friend.** Your child has enough friends. You are his parent. Being a parent sometimes means being disliked (even hated by your four-year-old). Your child may not like you, but he will respect you because you made the hard call and you followed through.

- **Make the tough call.** Even though yours will be the unpopular decision, you will gain your child's respect. Parents who have a backbone in the face of *"You are the meanest Mom in the whole world"* are the ones on whom children know they can rely. In addition, the respect you show for your job as parent sets an example you hope your child will remember when he must be responsible or when he is a boss, a coach, or a parent.

- **Fearing you doesn't mean respecting you.** Sometimes what might look like respect is really fear. Genuine learning, figuring out what is expected and necessary, is not an outgrowth of fear. It comes from a healthy understanding of what is going on. Through repeated experiences and his trusting, mutually respectful relationship with you, the child learns to comply and behave because he sees that it works. Fear is a closed-down place where this does not happen. Thinking *I'm going to teach him to have a healthy respect,* as you raise your open hand over your child's behind, just doesn't work.

- **Apologize only if you have made a mistake.** If you have been disrespectful to your child, apologize for that and that alone. Do not apologize for a consequence or response if it was respectfully delivered. *"I am sorry that I yelled at you this morning, Brooke. That was not respectful of me. I should have told you more calmly that I was angry."*

- **Don't confuse being a spineless parent with respecting your child.** The parent who looks away from the obvious limit-testing or disrespect, who tries to sweet talk her child out of misbehavior, or who chooses not to impose the threatened consequence is not "respecting her child." She is a wimp.

Teaching Respect in Daily Life

In the way you set up your home, establish rules, and run your family life, you will find opportunities to teach your child about respect.

Tips and Scripts for Manifesting Respect in Everyday Life

- **Allow each person his own private space.** Every member of your family needs a nest, a place to call his own. By having his space respected, he will learn to respect that of others.

- **Never violate private space.** Always ask permission to touch or enter private spaces. If you expect your child to stay out of your office, you'd best stay out of his private space, too.

- **Children need to have personal possessions.** Give your children their own things and don't require them to share. Forced sharing causes children to hang on tightly, to say nothing of feeling resentment. Granting ownership encourages their letting go.

- **Beware of having too many community toys or things that just "belong to the kids."** Children who have their own stuff will learn to take responsibility and care for it. That is a form of respect. And they will learn to respect other people's stuff at the same time. Of course, this is a hard lesson for the toddler who wants and believes that everything belongs to him!

- **Make knocking a rule for everyone.** Even if a door is ajar and not closed, get in the habit of knocking. It shows that you respect other people's privacy.

- **Give yourself some privacy.** I am sure that many a parent hasn't used the toilet alone in years! Once a child is three years old, has toilet skills, and can understand your need for privacy, ask for it: *"I am going to use the bathroom now, and I would like some privacy. I will be out in a few minutes."* Then tolerate the screaming and door-banging. It's a lesson. And it gives him permission to ask for the same, if it is safe.

- **Insist that siblings (and you) ask before borrowing.** Asking permission shows that you respect ownership. If a child says no, respect his answer. A fight or a tantrum may ensue, but the lesson of respecting one another's choices and decisions will be learned. What goes around comes around; just wait until the previously maligned child is asked to share and gives his sister a big fat no!

- **Do not take your child's possessions away as a form of punishment.** How would you like it if your husband took away your favorite necklace because you were late for dinner? It's not his to take. The same holds true for your child. Only possessions that are not treated with respect or are used improperly can be temporarily removed. *"Throwing your fire truck across the room is not treating it with respect. You may not use it for the rest of the day."* That works. So does *"You left your bike outside all night, and the rule is that it goes in the garage when you are done. You have lost the privilege of using it for two days."* That makes sense. *"You were not kind to your sister so I am taking your Light Saber away,"* makes no sense. Neither does: *"I am taking away your iPod because you spoke to me so disrespectfully."* Both of these teach the child that you don't respect his ownership. With the child older than seven, if you have previously discussed his privileges and he knows that the temporary removal of the iPod privilege is the consequence that will result from his show of disrespect, then such a response is fine. (See the discussion of consequences, p. 75.)

- **For the five-year-old child, clean out and throw away items only with him or with his permission.** Children younger than five see their possessions as extensions of themselves and often find it difficult to part with anything. For this child, create a rotation. *Let's keep out only as many toys as fit on the shelf. The rest will live in the closet until you want to trade them for the ones on the shelf (in the garage, in the storage room). Let's see what works.* Involving the older child in the clean-out or getting his permission to do it, says you respect his possessions, his wishes, and his needs. *It's time to clean out your toys (your books, your Legos, your art supplies, your American Girl doll outfits). Would you like to do it by yourself or do you want my help?* It may be a painful process, but it teaches your child how to make decisions about what stays and what goes and how to organize.

Manners

Manners walk hand in hand with respect. As a child learns to navigate his social world, manners become important as a common language, one that makes life easier for people and demonstrates respect. It is both respectful of a system of "rules" for interaction, for playing the game, and it is respectful because it considers other people. Using your manners recognizes another person's existence and needs; they make that person feel comfortable. As such, there is a developmental component to the child's ability and willingness to use mannerly behavior. Certainly, beyond the rote parroting of manners, the child needs to be on the road to developing empathy. (See chapter 2.) The toddler learns that in order to get his juice he needs to say "Please." That's a road rule. The four-year-old knows what is expected of him when it comes to manners, but it may not be his priority at the moment. He is a powerful and busy guy. Using a napkin to wipe his mouth just doesn't matter to him. The seven-year-old may be in a sour mood and remembering to say "please" or conform to your expectations is low on his list. The eleven-year-old begrudgingly uses his manners with you when it's in his best interest. There is a certain acquiescence that is implied in using manners.

The child's temperament also plays a role (see chapter 3, p. 39). The more introverted child, the one who takes time to warm up to people, will be challenged by looking your business partner in the eye, shaking hands and saying, "Pleased to meet you."

The good news is that, as with being respectful, most children do use their manners when they are out in the world. They just don't always use their manners with you, the person whose love they know is unconditional.

Tips and Scripts for Teaching Manners

- **Demonstrate manners.** Children who live with adults (and that means all of them in the home) who practice good manners daily will absorb those manners. But don't expect the payback right away, necessarily; just know that the message is being transmitted. It will surface when he sees how it serves him.

- **Lectures about manners don't work.** Demonstrating manners works much better than lectures, which usually fall on deaf ears. (*"Blah blah blah."*)

- **Don't turn it into a power struggle.** Your young child just might sacrifice whatever he wants in the service of winning. It should be as simple as: *"When you use your manners by speaking respectfully, you are more likely to get what you want. If you don't, you certainly will not."* Remember, you can't force anyone to talk!

- **Recognize the use of manners.** When your child isn't expecting it, catch him using his manners: *"It really makes me feel good about helping you when you say thank you."* Or, *"You were so polite in the way you greeted Mrs. Leonard. I know it made her feel good, and it made me feel proud of you."* Genuine, specific praise is a great motivator.

- **"Gossip" about your child's mannerly behavior.** Let you child eavesdrop on the phone conversations where you tell someone about the good manners he used. *"I wish you could have heard Anthony today when he thanked Mrs. Orenstein for the playdate. He used such good manners and made me so proud of him."* Remember, once in a while you can fake the phone call. Your young child doesn't know if anyone is on the other end. This technique is manipulative, but it does the job. You can also talk about the good behavior to your spouse during dinner—a great technique for any age child. I know I've suggested similar actions before for other challenges, but this is one of the most versatile tools in your toolbox, so don't be afraid to use it!

- **There is no "magic word."** My skin crawls when I hear a parent say, *"What's the magic word?"* It's not magic; it's necessary. Just remind your child that you would appreciate his using his manners when he makes a request. *"I know you know how to ask for more crackers using your manners. Want to try again?"* And when he doesn't, no crackers . . . and no comment from you. And for the older child, a simple *"Excuse me, what did you need?"* might do the trick as a reminder. If he is missing the boat, you might have to be straightforward and say, *"When you ask me politely, I will be willing to help you."* Remember, no lectures or judgments. And sometimes, simply not responding as the child rudely demands what he wants over and over, gives you the opportunity to say, *"I am happy to give you what you want when you ask me using your manners."*

- **The behavior yields the consequence.** That's the message. If your child isn't willing to thank his host for the playdate or thank his grandma for the gift, there is a consequence for that lack of respect. Of course, finding the logical consequence is difficult at first, but you will get better with practice.

Children under the age of four will be challenged by using their manners when it comes to some situations, especially those that involve non-family members. But expectations for older children should be highter.

- Before a playdate tell your older child: *"When the playdate is over, I know you will remember to say thank you and goodbye to Justin's mother."* The consequence for not doing so? *"Not saying thank you and using your manners means that you will not have another playdate."* And when Justin's mother calls to arrange a date, you get to say, *"I'm sorry, Mrs. Schulman, Todd can't have a playdate until he learns to say thank you to his host."* Now follow through . . . and even fake some phone requests that same day for dates that you will turn down.
- Before the birthday celebration or Christmas, provide reminders: *"When you receive a gift, it is using good manners to thank the person, even if it isn't your favorite gift."* Moreover, *"Saying thank you shows that you appreciate Aunt Lorna. She remembered your birthday. It is respectful."* And the consequence, *"Saying thanks is part of getting presents, and you may have the gifts when you do."* The converse is implicit. Even with children aged seven and older, who should be writing thank you notes, you can say, *"You may have each gift after you have written the thank you note."* Then tolerate the grumbling, you mean mommy! (For an in-depth discussion on consequences, see p. 75 in chapter 4.)

Manners That Are Rules

Following rules of all kinds is a way that we demonstrate respect. It shows an acceptance of the need for order in the world, and it acknowledges the operating systems that have been established to do so.

Table Manners

There are rules about how to behave at a meal table, whether at home or in a restaurant. Using table manners shows that you respect the other people who are eating, whether it is your family or other diners in a restaurant.

- **Children need to eat with adults in order to learn table manners.** Feeding your children alone, early, while you and your spouse eat later, or eating with your children only once a week, will not model the manners they must learn. Children need regularly to see manners in action, the table behavior that shows respect for everyone.

- **Both Mom and Dad need to practice the same manners you expect of the children.** It can't be okay for Daddy to reach across the table, if eleven-year-old Jared can't. Daddy's belch isn't excusable, even with a laugh and *"Oops, don't know where that came from!"*

- **Have reasonable table rules and expect them to be practiced.** Base your expectations on the age and development of each person at the table. They may vary for different aged children. (And that's right; it isn't fair. Oh well.) It is reasonable to expect a four-year-old to use his utensils. Your three-year-old will likely hold the fork in one hand and put the food in his mouth with the other. It's a skill he is just mastering. Your six-year-old can keep his napkin on his lap, not using his sleeve to wipe his mouth. Your ten-year-old can contain his newly found skill of burping really loudly. Everyone can politely ask for food to be passed and to be excused when he is finished.

- **State in advance what your expectations are for your family's mannerly mealtime behavior.** *"Everyone at our table is expected to ask politely for food to be passed, I expect you to use your utensils and not your hands to eat your food;"* and *"The dinner table is not a place for screaming."* Remember not to lay on too many rules at once. Practice one or two at a time.

- **Follow through on the consequences for not using manners.** Your children are clear on your expectations, so don't waste your breath on repeated warnings. *"You know that people who use* *their sleeves to wipe their mouths have no place at this table. You are excused."* Believe me, it won't happen again. Yes, his dinner is over.

- **Young children don't belong in restaurants.** I know this isn't a popular idea, but I believe it. It isn't reasonable to expect a two- or three-year-old to follow the rules in a restaurant. First of all, restaurant food is slow food. Meals at home are fast food; you call your child in for dinner, and there it is. Waiting for dinner to be served in the restaurant is an invitation for mischief. Second, there are no exceptions in restaurants. Even one scream when the food is too hot gets raised eyebrows from the diners next to you. And third, restaurant eating just takes too long. Young children can't sit that long. Get take-out instead!

  The trend of the child-friendly restaurant where it is acceptable for kids to run around, be a bit noisier than normal, and not have to think about keeping the food on the table, to say nothing of the plate, is my idea of a bad idea. It sabotages the child's learning what is expected at the meal table.

- **Anticipate trouble.** If you think that one of your children is liable not to follow your table rules, bring two cars. Be prepared to leave with the culprit, and let the others finish. Your night may be ruined, and you may not get your favorite burrito, but the lesson will be learned. Be sure to go back to that restaurant very soon, if not the next night, and give your child a chance to be successful. Tell him, *"The last time we were here, we had to leave because you weren't able to use your inside voice. I know you will be able to use it tonight."*

- **State your expectations before you enter the restaurant and get ready to follow through.** *"There are other diners at this restaurant whom we need to respect. They want to have a pleasant meal and don't want to hear children yelling or see them running around. You need to stay in your seat and use your inside voice. If you don't, we will leave."*

Telephone Manners

Children love the phone. They love it because they see you on it so often, especially with the omnipresence of BlackBerries in our culture. Many young children see the phone as a toy, especially if the parent has given it to him to occupy or soothe him. Hear this: The telephone is not a toy.

There are safety issues at stake in allowing young children to answer the phone. You never know who is going to be on the other end and what information that person will be able to extract from the child who answers. My rule of thumb is that until a child is old enough to say, "My mommy isn't available" as opposed to "Oh, my mommy isn't home," and understand why, or until he is old enough to say the above and write a message or remember to tell you (usually when he is older than five), young children should not answer the phone. In this era of caller ID, parents have gotten very lax about letting a child answer. The problem is that the young child is unable to differentiate between answering when you know it is Grandma and just picking up the phone when he hears it ringing.

Using the phone is an opportunity to practice manners and respect. Doesn't it bug you when you call someone, and a young child picks up the phone and says, "Who is it?" I suppose I am old fashioned about this one, but it makes me nuts!

- **Have rules for phone use when your child is old enough to use it.** Children can be taught to answer the phone by saying, *"Hello, this is Jessie."* Though it may not be imperative, it is one way that a child shows respect for the caller. They can also be given a whole litany of acceptable, mannerly phone responses from which they can choose, including:

    "Who may I say is calling?"
    "Who is calling, please?"
    "Just a moment, please."
    "Can you hold on a moment, please?"

    Explain to your child that in order to be allowed to answer the phone, he must use his manners. Otherwise, no answering.
- **Encourage your callers to let your child know how much they appreciate the manners he used.** Friends and family will do you that favor. All kids love to be praised, and it encourages more of the same behavior when it comes from someone besides you.
- **It's another story with tweens.** Older children, especially those who already have their own cell phones, are accustomed to a

different phone language. But the way they talk to their friends is not acceptable when speaking to adults. Tell them: *"'Hey dude' doesn't work when you answer the house phone."* They will need reminders.

- **Do not allow interruptions or intrusions when you are on the phone.** Given that the phone takes your attention away from your child, she perceives it as the enemy and will attempt to interrupt you as often as she possibly can when you are using it. When you allow your children to break into your conversation, it is disrespectful to the caller. Of course, you need to make every effort to limit your lengthy calls to when you are childfree. Teaching your child (and your spouse!) not to interrupt takes time, but it can be done.

When you go to make a call or answer one, say to your child, *"I am going to be on the phone for a very short time. I do not want to be interrupted, even if you say excuse me."*

When your child inevitably interrupts, excuse yourself to the caller and say, *"I asked you not to interrupt me. If you do it again, I will take this call in my room where you cannot bother me."*

When he interrupts again, go into you room, close the door, tolerate his screaming and door-banging, and finish your call.

When you come out and after he has calmed down, explain, *"When you interrupt me while I am on the phone, you may not be in the same room with me."*

It is a good idea to practice by making fake phone calls until your child understands what will happen when he interrupts you. It's cause and effect. Try making ten such calls in a row. Your young child doesn't have to know if they are real or not. Keep the calls short and allow your child the chance to be successful at not interrupting. Then praise him to the hills. Respecting your telephone needs and not interrupting is really hard for the child who hasn't learned to delay gratification. Funny how when the phone rings, he has something he really needs to tell you.

- **Not even once can you allow the child's interruption.** If it works one time, he'll keep trying again and again. The lesson is lost. The older child who interrupts usually does so because his interruptions have been tolerated. That was up until now. Time to stop.
- **Try your best not to allow anyone to interrupt.** I have a friend whose husband always interrupts our calls, and she allows him to do it; she answers him. It really feels disrespectful of me.

Back Talk

Whether you call it talking back, being sassy, or being fresh, it's all the same, and it feels like the height of disrespect. Just ask any parent who has a child. When your child talks back it makes your blood boil. *How dare he?* you wonder. It feels like he is questioning your position and authority, and it's just so defiant.

All children talk back at some time or other, as they try out their wings, cultivate their individuality, and in the process learn about respect. With young children, their behavior is not a reflection of a lack of respect. The three-year-old may be expressing her will or flexing her newly acquired, expert tongue muscles. The four-year-old Tarzan may be pounding his chest, testing his power. The five-year-old may be looking for your attention, negatively. The six-year-old may be experimenting with boundaries of language, trying out what his buddy's older brother taught him. And your preadolescent, well, just look out as he expresses his separateness from you, letting you know just what he thinks in so many words! The good news is that seldom will you hear that your child speaks with disrespect to his teachers or coaches. He saves it for you, because you love him best.

Tips and Scripts for Handling Back Talk

- **Don't take it personally.** Your child's back talk is an expression of whatever the heck he is feeling—defiant, rebellious, mad at you, mad at his friend, hungry, tired—but it's not about you. He is shedding his feelings by trying to lay them on you. Don't take the bait.

- **Back talk is fueled by your response.** As your child tries his darnedest to get your attention, the surest way to perpetuate his back talk is to respond. Just because your father used to say, *"You had better watch your mouth, young man,"* doesn't mean you should repeat his words. It won't work.

- **Save your anger.** Of course back talk makes you angry; it feels so disrespectful. But don't go there. Children, especially over the age of four, feed on a good fight. It can actually feel good. He loves the sparks or he wouldn't have gone there. Don't give him any reason to continue the exchange. Your explosive reaction will only invigorate his.

- **Do not respond; do not engage.** The single best response to back talk is the nonresponse. If it has no effect, it's not likely to be repeated. Simply ignore him.

- **Put some distance between you two.** Even just walking some feet away and picking up a book can be enough distance. I suggest removing yourself immediately, going into your room, and closing the door, as long as no younger child is put in jeopardy by your doing so. Sending the child to his room will only signal that talking back to you gets your attention. Moreover, your child will be angry with you for having to go to his room, removing the subject of back talk from center stage and making his punishment the new focus.

- **If you must say something to your child, four and older, try:** *"I don't speak to you that way, and I won't listen when you speak that way to me."* Make sure you have a very serious, firm, "I mean business" look on your face and then walk away. Not one more word. Not even a side-glance or a finger wag. Leave.

- **Not responding doesn't mean back talk is okay.** There are those who feel they must respond in a big way otherwise the child will think back talk is okay. Not so! Your child knows full well what is acceptable, and your nonresponse underscores that reality.

- **Discuss the behavior after the storm has passed with a revisit.** When both of you have cooled off, address the back talk.

With the four-year-old: *"You were really angry when I asked you to go to your room, and you talked back to me. That is not showing me respect. I hope I will not hear that from you again."*

With the six-year-old: *"If you are angry at me, you can tell me, and we can talk about it. Speaking to me with disrespect will not solve any problem you may be having, and I will not listen."*

With your eleven-year-old: *"When I asked you to take in the trash, you gave me a really disrespectful response. Do you think I was wrong in asking you to do that? Is there a way I could have asked you differently?"* That message says that you do care about what your child feels. Now take the time to listen to his response. When you are genuine in your revisit you are likely to strike up a productive conversation that will lead to changed behavior, as your child will feel respected.

- **"I hate you" is okay.** I can just hear you exclaiming, *"It is? No way!"* Children need to be able to express their feelings, including being really angry with you. *"I hate you"* is not back talk; it is an expression of how your child is feeling at that moment. First of all, you are a grown-up, and your child shouldn't be able to hurt your feelings. Okay, it stings a little, but you know very well that your child doesn't really hate you. When his fury has subsided, you can let him know that you didn't absorb his words and that it is safe to express his feelings, even the big ones like anger, to you: *"I know that you were really angry at me when you said 'I hate you.' Next time when you feel that way, let's talk about it, and I will try to help you with your feelings."*

  A child needs to feel that his relationship with his parents is so strong that it will not be damaged by his expressions of anger. He needs to know that you know he was angry but that you are strong enough to take it, even though you may not have liked this disrespectful talk.

- **Resist the urge to say "Well, then let me show you the door."** When your child says he wants a different mother or wants to run away, ignore it. It isn't about you. He is just expressing his feelings at the moment.

- **Refrain from saying "I am sorry you feel that way."** Remember, it's not about you. You need not apologize for anything, including whatever you did to make him so angry. And it dilutes the meaning of an apology, by the way.

While it may seem that teaching your child to be respectful shouldn't be so difficult, you can see that it encompasses many different areas of child-rearing and is filled with many pitfalls. If you are in the throes of dealing with a particularly mouthy or disrespectful child, it is likely to feel downright daunting at times. Remember, children who are feeling pretty good about themselves have an easier time being respectful of others. How interesting it is that the very child who crosses the line with you at home knows just how to behave when out in the real world. With deliberate, consistent attitudes and expectations, respect will grow over time. There is promise, so have at it!

❖

CHAPTER SIX

"I Didn't Do It."

Instilling Honesty in Your Child

"I'm pretty sure your child's not going to grow up to be a criminal," I told the parent who was despondent over her son's denial regarding a broken lamp.

There's no question about it. Every parent wants her child to have integrity—to tell the truth, to take responsibility for her behavior, to respect people's ownership of their property, to follow the rules, to be an upstanding citizen. We all know that honesty is the best policy, right?

But if you take a close look at the world in which kids are being raised, examples of dishonesty are everywhere, almost in epidemic proportions: People lie to authorities, to the media, and to those whose money is being invested; they steal from the government and from businesses; they "work the system," cheat on tests, and break rules. Unfortunately, I could go on and on. Because bad news speaks more loudly than good news, each day brings another story whose theme is dishonesty. We just shake our heads in disgust. These daily doses of dishonesty are making us immune to the importance of being honest. What's the big deal, anyway? Everyone is doing it.

The plain truth is that honesty is critical to the moral fiber of every individual. Experts agree that people who are honest feel better about themselves. They are able to enjoy stronger friendships, are more successful in school and in other pursuits and, in the long run, have deeper, happier marriages. It is from honesty that so many other desirable traits spring forth. Honesty is also an antidote to bratty behavior.

There is no shortcut to instilling honesty in children. Not only is it a journey on the pathway to growing up, but learning to be honest has developmental components, too.

The Development of Honesty

Toddlers spend lots of time in the world of fantasy. In fact, much of their learning emanates from pretend play. It is the way they process their world and gain mastery over much of what they are experiencing. "I am driving to Disneyland. Fasten your seat belt!" Honesty doesn't even enter the picture.

This same toddler is just beginning to learn about right and wrong. There are lots of boundaries to be crossed and limits to be tested. It's hard to comprehend those limits when she is just figuring out cause and effect, *I did this, and that happens.* In fact, this is how she begins to develop that sense of right and wrong. The look on Mommy's face tells the tale. When you are two-years-old, on a kind of animalistic level, you know that some things are not okay, but you need other people to tell you so. If you are stopped, you feel some shame. But if you're not caught, you feel just fine. It will be a while before this child internalizes that voice of the conscience.

The three-year-old, even a few fours, subscribe to "magical thinking." If she says it, she believes it happened or that maybe it will. The little one, who can be intoxicated by her power and effect, loves to make things happen . . . even if it isn't real. It's a kind of wishful thinking, not to be confused with lying. Distinguishing fantasy from reality is a challenge to a child of this age. Telling her "It's just make-believe" doesn't do the trick, especially when she awakens at midnight, screaming about monsters in the closet. To her mind, there *are* monsters in her closet!

The four-year-old begins to develop a conscience. Built on her loving, trusting relationship with her parents, she identifies with and internalizes them as her conscience. At first her behavior was controlled by them (and other trusted adults in her life), but as this four-year-old grows, she develops self-discipline that is based on her knowing right from wrong. When you are four, even if no one knows you have done something wrong, you feel guilty. This is great developmental progress. Doing the right thing is part of who she is, of her self-concept: *I am a good kid, and I do the right thing.* This child is a work in process, figuring out who she needs to be. Learning to be honest is part of this.

In order for the child to understand how her honesty affects others, she has to have empathy. (See chapter 2.) You won't get too far asking a two-year-old, "How do you think it made Emily feel when you took her flash-light?" The very young child is still egocentric. She is just beginning to work on empathy; her world is mainly all about her, at least for the moment. But with your five-year-old, it's a whole different story. You can say to her: "I'll bet it made you feel really bad when Elizabeth said she was inviting you to her birthday, and then she didn't invite you."

The elementary-schooler is a lot more social. Now her models for honesty and doing the right thing come from others, aside from her parents and care givers. While the family unit remains important, there is a shift to the peer group. She is part of a community, and she wants to belong and be liked. Sometimes that means doing the right thing and sometimes that means doing the wrong thing (which her peer group might be doing), including being dishonest. These children spend more waking hours in school than they do at home, so teachers, in addition to peers, wield a powerful influence. Being the kind of person her teacher expects her to be can nourish the development of integrity and honesty.

The adolescent is working hard on her developmental task of individuating. She needs to separate from you in order to figure out who she is. It is natural for middle- and high-school-age children to distance themselves from their parents for this reason. This age child experiments with ways of being in the world, especially when she decides that some of your values and ideals just aren't cool enough. Sometimes dabbling in dishonesty goes along with being part of a particular peer group. (That doesn't make it okay; it just explains it.)

Most children are developmentally predisposed to enjoying the benefits that come from being honest. Not only are they are highly aware of other people's reactions to their honesty, but it just plain feels good to know that you have done the right thing. However, there are some people whose dishonest behavior is pathological. Genetic evidence exists that "antisocial personality disorder," as such behavior is called, is hardwired. It isn't necessarily the result of growing up in a particular environment. This person's perceptual apparatus did not allow her to internalize her models of integrity and honesty. Her dishonesty has become habitual and part of her personality. Likely, this is not your child. However, if you feel that your child's dishonesty is chronic and beyond what seems to be typical experimentation, you need to consult a mental health professional.

Here is the good news: The most widely accepted theory about how children grow into honest human beings is that they learn it from their parents. Just a little pressure, right?

- **Honest parents raise honest children.** You are constantly under your child's surveillance as she learns by living with you how to be honest. Children spot hypocrisy faster than you can imagine. Everyone blows it once in a while. So when you do, admit your mistake and share with your child how you will handle the same situation in the future. *"It was wrong of me to keep the cookies that the bagger accidentally put in my bag. I didn't pay for those, and my keeping them was not honest. If that ever happens again, I will take them right back."* While you and I know that you would do that, it is doing it deliberately—so your child sees it—that packs the learning punch.

  If you receive more change than you should, let your child see you doing the right thing. *"The cashier gave me too much change. I need to go back into the grocery store and give her two dollars back. It is not my money."* When you find something in a public place, try to take it to the lost and found. I am reminded of the time my son Lucas found a batting glove at the Palisades Little League Field. He wanted it so badly and pouted all the way to the Lost and Found in the park office. When he checked later in the week, much to his disappointment, it had been claimed. Then when he lost his glove later that season, he expectantly checked with the office for days. No glove was turned in. Unfortunately, not everyone does the right thing. But Lucas learned that in our family it was important to do so, and I bet he will teach his children to do the same thing.

- **Love your child unconditionally, warts and all, and build her positive sense of herself.** The child who feels loved and has a strong sense of self is less likely to feel judged and then crumble when she makes a mistake. Since the child knows that all people do good and bad stuff, she will have less of a need to be dishonest, and when she takes a misstep, she won't have to lie about it. Remember, high self-esteem is not an outgrowth of hollow, nonspecific praise. It comes from your valuing your child for what she is and what she can do. The child who is given the opportunity to work and succeed, to accomplish the smallest of tasks all by herself, for example, is the one who grows healthy self-esteem. She feels powerful and big.

- **Expect everyone in your family to be honest.** Mince no words in sharing your expectations for your children. *"We are a family who believes that being honest is very important. I always try to be honest, and Daddy and I expect you to do the same."*

  To the younger child: *"When I ask you a question about what happened, I expect you to tell me the whole, real story. That is being honest."*

  To the older child: *"Everyone in this family is expected to be honest and truthful, and that includes following the rules and telling the truth. That is one of the ways I know I can trust you."*

- **Teach about trust.** From a young age, children need to hear about the role that trust plays in your relationship. Teach that "trust" is a word we use to say that we can count on people to do or not to do certain things. *"Trusting someone means that you know she is going to do the right thing. It means you believe what she says and that you can rely on her."* Continue: *"When I tell you I will pick you up after school, you know that I will be there because you trust me. I do what I say."* You can give examples, such as: *"When I remind you to do something, like brush your teeth, and you do it, that helps me to trust you. When I ask you to tell me the story of what happened when your brother got hurt and you tell me the whole, real story, I believe you because I trust you."* It is in a context that children really learn the meaning of trust, so use the word often and in a positive way.

  The older child can more easily see the role that trust plays in your relationship, that when you trust her she will be able to do more things. *"When you follow through and do what we have agreed on, I trust you. When I trust you then I can give you more privileges."* As children get older, parents hold the magic key card, which is the very reason preteens and young adolescents want to be trustworthy: They want to get more privileges, like a drivers' license! Your days are limited, so use them well to stress how important your trust is. *"Earning my trust goes a long way in getting to do the things you really want to do."*

- **Don't give your child a reason to mistrust you.** If you make a promise, follow through. If you aren't sure you can fulfill a promise tell your child, *"I will try my best to be there. I cannot promise, but I will try. I only promise when I am absolutely sure."*

- **Catch your child being honest.** No matter how small the act, specifically praise honesty. *"You were really honest when you let Caroline have her turn, even though she didn't remember she was next. I admire that about you."*

- **You are your child's teacher, not a policeman.** Your job is to help your child to learn to be honest. You don't want your child to live in fear of being caught for doing something wrong. Instilling fear does not help a child to develop courage to tell the truth. Learning to be honest is an outgrowth of a loving, trusting relationship and does not come from living under a magnifying glass. Stop looking for misbehavior or dishonesty, but don't ignore it, either.

- **Children make mistakes.** It is part of their learning process. Do not be overly harsh in the consequence for their misdeeds, missteps, and misbehavior. This may discourage them from taking responsibility or telling the truth about it. Talk with your child about doing it better the next time, emphasizing the behavior and not the dishonesty.

- **Develop an honest relationship with your child.** In order to do so, a parent needs always to take into account the motives for the child's dishonest behavior. All behavior is motivated; nothing happens for no reason. When a parent speaks to and emphasizes the motive, she will be likely to get more honest behavior the next time. Saying *"I wonder why you didn't want to tell me that you had homework tonight?"* allows the child space to share with you what is really going on with her. When she cheats on a test, rather than lecture her, try to get to the core: *"It sounds like you were really worried about not doing well on your spelling test. What can we do to help you to learn your words so you will do well all by yourself?"* Such a conversation allows you to teach appropriate (and not dishonest) means for getting her needs met or meeting her goals for herself.

- **Emphasize owning your own stuff.** When a person admits responsibility for what she has done, she is being honest with herself and with others. It is an acknowledgment of wrongdoing and implies a recognition of the need to do better. It also feels really good, in much the same way as does confession, I think. A child can be taught the positive effect of owning her stuff; it usually leads to a less severe consequence and often leads to forgiveness. Everyone deserves a chance to do it better next time. *"When you take responsibility for your mistakes, it lets me know that you will try to do a better job next time."*

Parents who model owning their own stuff are the most likely to get the same from their child: *"I didn't speak kindly to Grandma on the phone just now. I feel bad about that. I am going to call her and apologize."* Parents who are quick to blame and punish, who do not go to the cause and the solution, breed children who don't own their own stuff.

- **Help your child to understand the power of honesty.** Elementary-school children can learn how being dishonest affects relationships by identifying the feelings accompanying dishonesty. *"It must have made you feel so disappointed and sad when Leanna said she was taking you ice skating and then she invited Felicia. Leanna wasn't honest with you the way friends should be."* This age child can empathize and therefore see how important integrity in friendship is.

- **Teach that being honest doesn't always feel good in the moment.** You will need to teach your older child (preadolescent and older) that sometimes doing what you know to be honest and right may not feel like the best choice because sometimes you lose out. Knowing that you did the right thing will feel good in the long run because nothing feels as good as a clear conscience. *"Sometimes being honest means not going along with what everyone else is doing. Sometimes it feels like you are losing out. But in the long run, you will feel so good because being honest is always the right thing to do."*

- **When's it's done, let it go.** No one is honest all of the time. When an incidence of dishonesty is over, consequence imposed, be done. Refrain from bringing it up, over and over, months later. Your child must not feel defined by her transgressions. She needs to regroup and do a better job next time.

- **Listen to your child.** Instead of ineffective lectures about the importance of honesty, let your child talk. Do your best to figure out what prompted the dishonesty or misbehavior. *"I am trying to understand why you needed to tell me that your sister spilled the paint on the carpet. I think you were worried that I would be so angry at you if I knew that you spilled it."* Now listen to what she says and acknowledge her feelings. *"I understand that you thought you would get in trouble for taking the paint into your bedroom. It is our rule that paint stays in the playroom."* Wait and listen some more. Then help her to think about how she can handle her paint plans differently next time. *"What do you think you can do next time you have the urge to paint your walls?"* and suggest, *"I can help you to find a place outside to paint if you come to me with your ideas."*

- **Beware of "I'm sorry."** Everyone agrees that children need to learn to say they are sorry. It is the socially acceptable thing to do. It certainly helps a parent to feel better when faced with the scorn of the victim's parent. *"I'm sorry"* can turn into an a battle of wills, the parent insisting on it and the child stubbornly refusing to say it. Saying *"I'm sorry"* is an admission of guilt; it says that the child has culpability. For the child often that means relinquishing her control, and now the battle is about getting the child to speak the words. But what you really want is for your child to *be* sorry, to feel remorse. When you insist that a child says *"I'm sorry,"* often you are just teaching her to lie. She may be apologizing for her misstep or for being dishonest by being dishonest! Further, the child soon learns that *"I'm sorry"* is a magic word, just like saying *"please."* Mom leaves her alone and it's over. No lesson learned. But *I'm sorry* is not a get-out-of-jail-free card. Rather than force your child, chin in chest, to mumble, *"I'm sorry,"* help her to find a way to make amends for her misbehavior or dishonesty, to show contrition. It is often in the demonstration of remorse that the child learns to feel genuinely sorry. *"Eating Clare's candy when you didn't have permission was not okay. We need to find a way for you to make Clare feel better. Perhaps you could buy her some more candy with your own money. Or we could bake her some cookies, or make her a picture to show her you feel sorry."* For the child who doesn't have any money yet, she can do a job for you for which she will be paid, and with it buy the candy for Clare.

- **Let her make things right.** Helping a child to make amends also helps to assuage her guilt and make it "all better." *"Let's get the carpet* *cleaner and see if we can get that paint out of the rug."* Cleaning up your messes, literally and figuratively, goes a long way in cleaning your conscience.

The Conscience

The conscience is a moral compass that points us in the direction of being honest, among other things. A child's conscience develops over all of her growing years. While its power can be seen in the four-year-old, the foundation for conscience is getting laid down before this age, though it is a long time before it is solidly in place, often not until the teen years.

As the child grows and is able to think in the abstract, she also becomes capable of self-reflection, usually not until she is coming into her teens. Self-reflection is a requirement for a fully developed conscience. The child can watch herself and evaluate her own behavior. While this ability began long ago with her not wanting to disappoint her parents who love her so much, she has internalized that parent, and it has morphed into wanting to do the right thing.

Tips and Scripts for Developing Conscience

- **Cultivate a loving, accepting relationship with your child.** Seems pretty obvious, I know. I repeat it here because it is just that important. It is through her loving attachment to you that the child internalizes your acceptance of her, both the good and the bad, and is able to stay on track, move on after her misstep, and do better the next time.

- **Teach your child about her "little voice."** Your child can be taught that she has a little voice that lives inside of her that tells her what is right and what is wrong. Pointing to your solar plexus say, *"Deep inside of every one of us, we have a little voice that tells us what we should and shouldn't do. You need to stop and listen to that voice. It will tell you if what you are about to do is okay."* Then take the time to model out loud how you listen to your little voice. *"There is extra change at the checkout stand.*

I would like to have it, but my little voice is reminding me that it doesn't belong to me. I need to give it to the checker."

- **Guilt is not all bad.** While it is not advisable (nor is it healthy parenting) to try to make a child feel guilty, guilt is an important feeling that emanates from the growth of the conscience. Guilt happens because there has been or is about to be a violation, and the violation is often in a relationship. Guilt works as sort of a warning light. Feeling guilty can be a positive thing because it forces you to think about what you shouldn't do or what you have done without anyone telling you to do so. It gives you the chance to decide what to do to fix the situation.

- **Neither eliminate nor overuse expressions such as "I am proud of you."** While the child needs to derive satisfaction intrinsically, she also needs to know that her behavior affects you. She will stay on track by not wanting to disappoint you, and she will feel good, basking in your happiness with her. It's a balance.

Lying

Let's be honest: Everyone lies. Some lies are big and destructive; others barely count. Society even accepts some lying and forgives the offender by turning a blind eye. Does that mean lying is okay? No. But lying happens, along with all kinds of behaviors that are not so great. Regardless, it is a parent's job to inculcate her child with the importance of telling the truth.

Most children lie about something at some point during their growing years. And most parents are horrified by it, fearing that their little angel is on her way to becoming a pathological liar. Not so! In fact, turning the child's dalliance with lying into a catastrophe is not a good idea. Learning to tell the truth, just one of the ways in which people are honest, is a process that takes time. Children do not learn to be honest and tell the truth from one or two of your lectures or from your finger wagging. Like all learning, it will take trial and error on the part of the child. It will also take patience, understanding, and a whole lot of calm on the part of the parent.

I cringed a bit when I heard the parent of a four-year-old say that her child lied to her. "Lying" sounds horrible, dark, and unforgivable. Lying in this sense of the word is a deliberate, manipulative deception that is used to get away with something while making someone believe something else. Young children don't have the experience or the developmental ability to "lie" in this way. Rather, they are manipulating or bending reality to meet their needs at the time. They are certainly not trying to hurt anyone or to be disrespectful, nor are they aware that they may be doing either. It's about them, not anyone else, anyway.

Children bend reality for a reason. As discussed, the three- or four-year-old child is learning to distinguish fantasy from reality. As far as she knows, it could be real—the truth. *My daddy does play basketball with the Lakers, really he does . . . I think.* This age child engages in the aforementioned "magical thinking." She wanted something to happen so much that maybe if she says it, it did happen. From a different perspective, if she tells the story the way she wants it to have been, maybe it really did occur that way. Many a preschool teacher has reveled in the child's excitement about a new puppy only to discover that the latest addition to that household is actually a baby sister.

Then there are the tall tales young children tell that are hard to classify as lies: mommies who fight off bears that came in the kitchen window, daddies who fly real rocket ships. These kinds of stories are a normal part of early childhood.

As the child grows, she is well tuned into how her behavior and choices affect her parents. Displeasing you doesn't feel good. Knowing you will be happier if she has put her toys away, she just might reply *"Yes"* to your inquiry, when the truth is *No,* the toys are still all over the playroom floor. In the moment, she doesn't stop to think that you will see them still scattered on the rug; she just wants to please you. She bends reality so you will be happy with her. She's not lying.

Intentionality also falls under the category of owning your own stuff. If you didn't mean to do it, then it isn't your fault, and in the child's mind, she isn't responsible. So she sees reality differently. *"I was going to give my sister a sip and the juice spilled on the new suede couch where she was sitting. I didn't spill it."*

Sometimes children just make mistakes. They say it wrong. The child who claims that you yelled at her when you sternly reminded her to stop playing and come to the table might say, *"You screamed at me."* You know you didn't scream; that's not the truth. But she felt screamed at.

As she gets older, the child bends reality to protect herself from getting into trouble. She doesn't tell the truth as a way of trying to dodge an anticipated consequence—whether it's your wrath or a privilege being removed.

Children also change reality and revise history in order to avoid blame. Lying is not the issue here; rather, the problem is that your child, anticipating some negative consequence, will avoid accepting responsibility at all costs, including denial, throwing blame on someone or something else, hiding the evidence, or another form of not owning her own stuff. Hence the expression, *"I didn't do it."* I am reminded of the parent who enters the kitchen to find milk spilled all over the counter and yells, *"Who spilled the milk?"* Does she really expect a child to run in and say, *"I did it. Punish me!"* Instead, she will get a chorus of *"Not me! Not me! Not me!"* echoing from each bedroom down the hall. The child who operates out of a fear of consequences leaps to avoid ownership. She becomes artful at hiding the truth, blaming others and pointing a finger—all to save her own hide. You will see suggestions for encouraging ownership of your own stuff in the following Tips and Scripts section.

Tips and Scripts for Encouraging Truth Telling

The foundation for raising children who tell the truth begins with creating an environment where it is expected, modeled, and safe to do so.

- **Create an environment where it is safe to make mistakes and to tell the truth about them.** Parental overreaction yields a child who doesn't feel safe to tell the truth. Who wants to suffer your wrath? Make sure that the consequences for your child's misbehavior are appropriate to the child's age, development, and the nature of the falsehood. Proportion is important. You don't kill a fly with a bulldozer.

  Being quick to make accusations of dishonesty and imposing severe consequences for bending reality can lead to less truth-telling, not more. When your child is young, tread lightly on the reality bending, and instead praise the truth telling. *"I am so glad that you told me the real story. When you tell me the truth, I believe you and I trust you."*

- **Stay calm.** When a parent gets visibly angry, the child's energy will go into defending against that anger. None of us learn when we are in an emotional state. Use a calm demeanor and keep your goal in focus: The child's misbehavior wasn't okay, first and foremost, and neither was her dishonesty about it. It is not true that a child needs to feel bad, to bear the brunt of your anger, in order to behave well.

- **Don't go to the "lying" place.** Calling your child a liar is overkill, and it is labeling her. If you use the label enough, she might as well just be one anyway, and the lying might become chronic—a self-fulfilling prophesy. Remember, your child will believe about herself what you tell her she is; you are your child's mirror.

- **Call it like it is.** Your child is just trying to get her needs met, including steering clear of punishment or your disappointment in her. When you know the story your young child is telling is not the truth, let her know that you're aware of what's going on instead of admonishing her. To the child who has announced to her class that she went to Disneyland, you can say: *"You really wish that we would go to Disneyland. I can tell by the story that you are telling. One day we will go there."* For now you can say, *"I am making up a pretend story about going to Disneyland."* When you know the older child's story is an excuse and not the truth, you can say, *"Now I would like you to tell me the whole, real story. What were you doing instead of completing your homework?"* And leave it at that.

- **Mind your own fibbing.** When you ask your child who has answered the phone to say, *"Tell him I am not home,"* you are asking your child to lie, and you are giving her the message that such dishonesty is okay. You are doing the same thing when you tell the ticket lady at the theater that your child is younger than she is so that you can pay less. Parents need to model telling the truth if they expect their children to do the same.

- **Communication is key.** From an early age, point out to your child the difference between make-believe and real, keeping in mind the child's capacity for understanding based on her development. *"This stuffed lion is pretend. There are no real lions here or anywhere near our house."* Or, *"This make-believe pizza we are eating is delicious."* Or, *"We are pretending to drive to Grandma's house. Beep, beep! Get out of my way!"*

  If your child is going to get a shot at the doctor's office, let her know. *"We are going to see Dr. Bob for your five-year-old checkup. He is going to give you a shot. It will hurt for just a minute, and then it will be done. Then we're going to the park to have some fun."* Not only are you modeling telling the truth, but you are also helping your child learn to trust you. Tolerating her meltdown can be tough, but the lessons the child learns will be worth it.

If you are going out after your child is asleep, let her know the truth. *"After you are sound asleep, we are going to a movie. Brenda is staying here with you. When we come home, I will tiptoe into your room and give you a kiss."* While it may be hard the first or second time you do this, she will soon learn that Mommy always comes back and gives her a kiss goodnight. She will also learn to trust that you tell her the real story, and she will learn to do the same.

- **Catch your child being honest when she doesn't expect it.** Look for opportunities to point out your child's truth-telling. *"You told me the whole real story about how Jack got hurt because you hit him. I like knowing the truth. Or, I appreciate that you told me the truth about how the mud got tracked into the house. Now I see that it was an accident. Will you please help me clean it up?"* Notice that the focus is on the fix. As discussed, children need to learn that there are ways to make amends for their missteps.

- **Praise your child's truth-telling.** Sometimes it takes courage to tell the truth because the child knows she will have to deal with the consequence. The child who feels good about herself, who accepts that she is lovable despite her mistakes, is more likely to tell the truth and suffer the consequence of her misstep. In order to encourage more of the same, and especially if this isn't your child's first foray into dishonesty, lighten up on the consequence for the misbehavior, or give her a one-time get-out-of-jail-free card and praise the honesty. *"I am proud of you and appreciate your telling the truth. This time only there will be no consequence for watching more than your hour of TV."* Many parents have the misguided notion that they need to give a whopper of a punishment, something she'll never forget, in order to prevent a repeat of the unwanted behavior. As mentioned, such disproportionate consequences eat away at the child's self-esteem and attachment, and may even have the opposite effect. (See chapter 4, p. 75, about consequences.)

- **Notice and praise others' truth-telling.** It is a parent's job to help the child process the world in which she lives. Look for opportunities to point out real examples of truth-telling and share your approval. Tell your child about the time a friend of yours told the truth when she said she was late because she had totally forgotten about her date with you. Pass on to your child the story about her neighborhood friend who admitted to her dad that she had made a mistake and scraped the side of the family car with her bike.

- **Position yourself from the positive, instead of wagging your finger.** Begin your conversation about a consequence with, *"Because you told me the truth about who wrote on the closet door, I am taking away your markers only for this afternoon."* In so doing, you are getting mileage out of emphasizing the truth telling.

- **Don't set your child up to lie.** If you know she hasn't brushed her teeth, don't ask her if he did. Just ask her to brush her teeth. If you sent her to wash up for dinner, and you know she didn't use soap, say: *"Please go back and wash your hands with soap this time."* This very scenario occurred with my son, Ben. I knew he hadn't done a thorough enough job when, after protesting that he had washed his hands well, he proceeded to sniff them! The best response is to ignore the protest and say, *"Please do a better job, using soap this time."*

  When you know your older child has homework, and she is playing a computer game, simply state the rule: *"You know our rule is no computer games until after your homework is done."* And expect her to comply. Don't give her the chance to lie about not having homework by asking her if she does. This is also known as not asking your child a question to which you already know the answer.

  Stating your expectation gives the child no chance to lie. *"Let me know when you have finished your job"* (cleaning your room, setting the table, taking in the trash). It will get done, and she won't need to lie.

- **Avoid the phrase, "Are you telling me the truth?" There aren't many kids five and older who would answer no to this question.** Additionally, this question offers on a silver plate the chance to lie. Such suspicion also delivers the message that you think your child doesn't tell the truth, which leads once more to the self-fulfilling prophecy: *If you don't think I tell the truth, then I won't tell the truth.* It doesn't encourage truth-telling.

- **Try a do-over.** Sometimes it is effective to give your child a chance for a do-over. You can say, *"Would you like to start over and tell that story* *again? This time, tell me the whole real story."* Don't comment about her not telling the truth; just ask her to tell the story as it really happened.

- **Beware of demanding the truth.** Sometimes we inadvertently sabotage truth telling by demanding it. As discussed, a lie can be protection against a feared consequence. When you start out by saying, *"Tell me the truth,"* the child already knows she's in for trouble. So why tell the truth? When you say *"If you don't tell me the truth, you will be grounded for a month,"* the child is likely to stand by her story. She doesn't feel safe telling you what really happened. In the end, she's going to lose anyway.

- **Keep your eye on the real issue: the behavior about which she is being dishonest.** Your goal is to modify the misbehavior that motivated her dishonesty. Put your emphasis where it belongs, on the misstep. The consequence is for that act. The lack of truth telling just increases the consequence. It's a double whammy.

- **Give your child a chance to be honest.** Try: *"You know that there will be a consequence for your behavior. When you tell me the truth about what happened, the consequence will not be so big."* Or when you discover that your nine-year-old was dishonest: *"Because you went ahead and watched TV after I told you that you could not, you may not watch TV for two days. Because you did not tell me the truth when I asked you about it, I am adding two more days to the consequence. Next time, I hope you remember that I expect you to tell the truth. That is how I learn to trust you."* And you can add, *"You are responsible for your behavior and the choices you make; you are also expected to be honest and own those choices, even the bad ones. You will get in trouble, but not telling the truth makes it big trouble."*

- **Allow your child to make restitution for her misstep.** When the child denies a wrongdoing, instead of quizzing her, simply tell her what she needs to do to make amends (according to her age and development, of course) and expect that it gets done. She will appreciate the chance to make restitution and absolve herself of her guilt. *"Here is the spray and a rag. Please clean the pen off the wall in your room and let me know when it is done."*

- **Your child is not responsible for your feelings.** If a child mis-
  behaves or takes a misstep there is a consequence, period. But many
  children are raised to believe that they must hide the truth or change
  it to protect their parents' feelings. It is for this reason that saying a
  child's behavior makes you sad or mad will not lead to her truth-
  telling. No child wants to be responsible for a parent feeling bad, so
  she'll just have to lie.

  However, there will be times when saying *"I'm proud of you"* or
  "That made me so happy" is in order. While the idea is to encourage the
  child's intrinsic satisfaction in having done the right thing, knowing
  that you feel good about her behavior will help to create her own
  good feelings. The key is to find the right balance between the expression of your feelings and making hers important.

- **Let bygones be bygones.** Don't revisit past transgressions. You are
  not only rubbing salt in the wound when you emphasize past undesir-
  able behavior, but you are also shaming her. Genuine learning does
  not spring forth from shame. Lying and dishonest behavior does.

- **"The Boy Who Cried Wolf."** I think every parent remembers to
  use this tale. The lesson is a good one, but don't use it too soon. Even
  five-year-olds do not understand this tale. You will know what I mean
  after your child's third week of nightmares that the wolf is going to
  eat her up! Instead, tell stories from your youth and your own forays
  into the world of lying. Not only do children love hearing them, but
  they make effective learning tools. Your child will be relieved to know
  that even Daddy makes mistakes and learned a lesson.

White Lies

Honesty is multilayered and has many social implications. Children need to
be taught the importance of telling the truth, but sometimes telling the truth
isn't really speaking the truth, it is sharing an opinion. And that opinion
might hurt someone's feelings or even be disrespectful. When you receive a
gift that isn't to your taste you wouldn't say, *"This scarf is hideous. Why in the
world did you think I would like this?"* You protect your friend's feelings and

appreciate her intentions by not giving her your "honest opinion." Instead, you tell a white lie: *"Thank you for this scarf. I love the colors."*

Children are brutally honest; they call it like they see it. So the art of white lying does not come naturally to them. In order to understand the reason for using a white lie, the child needs to have developed empathy. She needs to know how it feels to be in someone's shoes and hear the cold, raw truth: *"That scarf is really ugly!"*

White lies certainly are lies. But sometimes they are necessary, as a form of kindness, respect, or as a show of manners. Children older than six need to be taught that telling the truth should not be confused with saying what you think whenever you want. One of the ways that we show respect to other people is by not saying what we really think and by remembering that different people have different opinions. The truth might actually be harmful or hurtful to someone else. Here is a possible explanation:

"Sometimes telling someone the truth about what you think or feel isn't such a good idea. It's not a good idea if it's going to hurt her feelings or be disrespectful. That is when you might need to tell what is called a 'white lie.' If a friend asks you if you like her jacket, and you think it's really babyish, you wouldn't say, 'No way! I think it's babyish.' You would tell a white lie and say, 'I like the colors. You are lucky you got it.' And that wouldn't hurt her feelings. If Grandma gives you socks for your birthday when you were hoping for a special DVD, you wouldn't say, 'More socks? Who wants these?' You would say, 'Thanks, Gran. You know I can always use more socks.' Even though you wanted to scream, 'Socks are the worst present in the whole world, ever!' White lies are what you say when you don't want to hurt someone's feelings or be disrespectful, even though you might not really mean it."

There will be times when you may need to manipulate reality as part of your parenting. For example, when your child asks if the plane you are about to board is going to crash you don't say, *"Gee I hope not."* Instead you say, *"No, this plane is not going to crash. I am going to New York and coming right back home in three days."* In order not to sabotage your five-year-old's rapidly approaching bedtime, you might need to tell her that you are going out to dinner with your friends and not the whole truth that you are going to grown-ups' night at Disneyland. In a few places in this book I have recommended something I call the "fake call." In reality, this is dishonest, as you are pretending that you are talking to someone on the phone. But both of these examples fall into the category of white lies, as they serve the distinct parenting purpose of protecting someone. I do not advocate lying to children. But sometimes with young ones, you might change the story because it is in their best interest.

Stealing

While many a parent is mortified when her child steals, it is not out of the range of what some young children do. And it doesn't mean that you have a kleptomaniac on your hands. At around eighteen months, the child's awareness of ownership kicks in. In fact, here is when Toddler Property Laws take effect:

> What's mine is mine.
> What's yours is mine.
> What's his is mine.
> What's hers is mine.
> I played with it a while ago. It's mine.
> I might play with it later. It's mine.
> I am thinking about it. It's mine.
> I like it. It's mine.

These children are beginning to differentiate between what is and isn't theirs. The egocentric little creatures think that all of it is theirs. And why not? It's pretty much been that way until then.

The four-year-old has a firm handle on the concept of ownership, but her grasp on her impulse control can be shaky. Sometimes she sees something, and her desire trumps her ability to listen to the little voice inside that tells her that she can't have it just because she wants it. The parent who checks her child's pockets after nursery school and discovers a favorite school car tucked away knows this tune.

But when an elementary-schooler appropriates something that isn't hers, you have to take a closer look at what might be going on. The seven-year-old who steals may be giving the parent a wake-up call. Before this dishonest behavior becomes a pattern, the stealing should be seen as a message that she needs something. She might not even know what she needs. But whatever it is, she doesn't know how to ask for help. Does this child have the means to get the objects of her desire? Does she have enough spending money? Does she feel the need to keep up with her friends who have things she doesn't have? Sometimes a child this age will steal as a metaphor for getting the attention she lacks; she might as well steal it if it isn't readily given to her. On top of that, she will certainly get the attention she wants if she steals. Negative attention, positive attention, it's all attention.

A client of mine shared that her seven-year-old son had stolen lots of things, most of which belonged to his older brother's friends. She was horrified. We uncovered that this little boy had been treated like an appendage of his brother, the star of the family, for his whole life. Not only was he desperate for some of his parents' attention, for some of the spotlight, but he also needed some friends and a life of his own. When his parents began consistently giving the boy their attention ("special time") and cultivating a life for him separate from his brother (playdates and extracurricular activities of his own), the stealing stopped.

The preadolescent who steals is scarier business. While she may know the difference between right and wrong, stealing may be the accepted modus operandi of her peer group. The initiation into the "in crowd" means doing what her pals do. Perhaps it's a thrill. Perhaps it's defiance. These kids justify their actions with thinking along the lines of, *Hey, no one is getting hurt. The store has lots of money; they won't even feel it. I don't have a lot; I deserve it.* The child is torn between her loyalty to the values of her posse and to her family values. But stealing of this sort is antisocial behavior, which can have some serious and longer lasting repercussions.

Tips and Scripts for Dealing with Stealing

- **Recognize that stealing is a sign that your child needs something.** Try to figure out what is motivating the act. Have the discussion with your child about how to meet her needs. *"It seems like you would like to have more money, so much so that you took money that doesn't belong to you. Let's see what we can do to make that happen. Do you have any ideas?"* Of course you can make suggestions, like doing some chores at home or even helping the neighbors with small jobs.

- **Stay calm.** If you get very angry or lose your temper when you address your child's stealing, she may get just what she is looking for:

your attention. A jumbo-size reaction may compound the offense as it may drive your child to lie about the details just to escape your wrath.

- **Make it clear that you are criticizing your child's behavior, not her.** At the same time, let her know that the world will not end because she stole, that she can make amends for what she has done. It is important that your child knows that you have faith in her ability to make a course correction. You can also explain, *"One of my jobs as your mommy is to teach you right from wrong. Taking things that don't belong to you is wrong. Now you know that lesson."* And for the older child, *"Stealing is wrong for two reasons. It's never okay to take something that doesn't belong to you or that you didn't pay for. It is also against the law. Grown-ups get in a lot of trouble for stealing. Kids are taught by their parents about what is right and what is wrong."*

- **Never tell a child that she will go to jail.** First of all, it isn't true. Second, fear is not the best teacher. Learning happens when the child experiences the consequence for her behavior.

- **Teach that stealing is hurtful.** Somewhere down the line, someone is hurt by stealing—the shopkeeper who loses money, the manufacturer, or even the person who trusted you to be honest. Stealing also demonstrates disrespect. *"When you take something that doesn't belong to you, you are showing that you don't care about the person's feelings or respect him. Stealing hurts the person you are stealing from."*

- **Take every opportunity to point out the wrongness in stealing.** When stealing happens in your child's world through kids' books, TV shows, or videos, talk about it with your child, creating the proper spin. *"Well, that little bunny certainly did not make the right choice. Stealing vegetables from Mr. McGregor's garden was the wrong thing to do. It is never okay to steal."* Your older child may benefit from hearing the "neighborhood news." *"I heard that Jeremy Johnston was caught stealing from the hardware store. That sure was a bad choice he made. I'll bet he is in a lot of trouble."* Even sampling fruit from the produce section or taking just one small piece of candy out of the bins are both acts of stealing from the grocery store.

- **The older child needs to understand the reality of your economics.** Take the time to explain to the child who is six years and older, *"Sometimes we have to make choices about what we want to spend our money on and what we can afford. Just because you want something, doesn't mean you can have it or that we want to spend money on it right now. If there is something that you really want, we can talk about how and when you might have it. That's called planning and budgeting."*

- **Point out that stealing erodes trust.** *"When you take things that do not belong to you, it causes me not to trust you. When I trust you, I can allow you to do things by yourself because I won't have to watch over you."* Then the child needs the opportunity to win back your trust by doing what you specifically describe: *"You may go on a playdate to Heather's house, but I need to trust that you will not take any of Heather's things that do not belong to you. Let's give it a try. I want to be able to trust you."*

- **Children should not be insulated from the consequences of stealing.** Although you are embarrassed, do not make excuses for the child's misstep. She is let off the hook when you say things like, *"Oh, all kids steal."* Or, *"She was really tired and just didn't know what she was doing when she put Kate's coin in her pocket."*

- **The consequence should be proportional to the stealing.** The child needs to experience the consequence of a bad choice so that it will not be reinforced. But the consequence that is imposed should be in proportion. Stealing a pack of gum is bad, but not as serious as stealing an iPod, for example. A consequence should make the child uncomfortable, even unhappy, so that she will listen to her little voice the next time she is tempted to steal. For example, the child who steals gum should pay back the store for what she took, delivering the money and making the apology in person. After the child who steals the iPod returns it to the store, she should make restitution by doing some work for the store owner. She may also lose the privilege of going to the village or the mall for a few weeks.

- **Regardless of from whom the child has stolen, the child herself must make her amends.** Whether it means bringing the toy car back to the teacher in her classroom or returning the coin to her friend, it is the child who needs to do the job in person—regardless of her age. The act needs to be accompanied by an admission of what she has done and hopefully a gesture of remorse. *"I am returning the car that doesn't belong to me."* Discourage the victim from excusing the child by saying, *"Oh, that's okay. It's no big deal."* If that happens, you can add, *"Actually, it is a big deal. In our family, it is not okay to take something that doesn't belong to you (without paying for it)."*

For the older child, an act of contrition is critical. Help your child to think of something to do to make amends. If it is a friend from whom she has stolen, perhaps he needs to give that child something of her own, as an act of apology. If a teen has stolen from a store, the teen can be of some service to the store, sweeping the floor or washing the store windows, even making a donation of her own money (that she may have to earn) to the store manager's favorite charity.

If you do not know the owner of the stolen item, it should be confiscated and donated. A suitable consequence or loss of privilege, proportional to the age of the child and the offense should be imposed.

- **Do not allow your child to appropriate loose change that is lying around.** Doing so undermines the young child's ability to learn when it is and isn't okay to take something that she knows is not hers.

- **Stealing within the family is still stealing.** Stealing within the family is tricky because, while it is stealing, families take the act less seriously. It is just as important for the child to be held accountable for taking from family members as from anyone else. All the children in the family will absorb the lesson. We call this "ambient learning." When the victim is a sibling, it is especially important that she feel protected from the child who took her possession, and a consequence must be imposed. *"You took those Lego pieces without your brother's permission. They do not belong to you. You have lost the privilege of going into your brother's room and of using your own Legos for the next two days."* Children need to learn to respect the property of siblings and parents; it should be required and enforced.

- **When it's over, let it be over.** Your trust may have been violated, but your child needs you to move on and to learn to trust her again.

- **Spanking? No way, no how.** Today, no one believes that spanking is an acceptable consequence for missteps, and most will agree that it mainly teaches the child that someone who is bigger than you can physically hurt you. Before you give in to the urge to spank (as some parents do when it involves a major misstep) remember that those who are spanked often become the children who hurt others outside of the home and, later, the parents who in turn are liable to spank their children. Spanking only takes the emphasis off the original misdeed and begs the question (spoken or unspoken), *"If you can't control your urges, how can I be expected to control mine?"*

When the stealing is chronic, it is time to seek the help of a mental health professional. Now there are two equally big problems: the stealing and the motivation. Both need attention.

The Tooth Fairy, Santa Claus, and Other Childhood Myths

Every year as the winter holidays approach, parents raise the Santa Claus question. "Is it a problem if I let my child believe in Santa Claus?" Some worry that exposing children to Santa, the Easter Bunny, or the Tooth Fairy is teaching them that untruthfulness is okay—and that later on, when the truth is discovered, children will consider their parents liars. But does passing on such folklore really erode children's trust in their parents?

From the very beginning, young children are read fairy tales and told fanciful stories. They look at picture books that have talking dogs, cows that can type, pigs with wings. They don't even question if they are real; they are just there to be enjoyed. Fantasy plays a big part in young children's lives. In fact, one of their most powerful learning modes is playing "make believe." As children grow, their awareness changes right along with their intellectual development. They wonder, question, and try to make sense of the world as it comes into focus with their more highly developed thought processes. It takes time for young children to learn to distinguish fantasy from reality.

Remember the classic movie, *Miracle on 34th Street*? What a metaphor it was for the role of fantasy in everyone's life. Is there really a Santa Claus? A fat man in a red suit who carries all the toys for all the children in the world on a flying sleigh, delivering them all in one night (down chimneys even!)?

Santa Claus is the spirit of Christmas for those who celebrate the holiday; he embodies the joyous feelings and the attitude of the season. The Easter Bunny serves a similar purpose and the Tooth Fairy celebrates the rite of passage of losing a tooth.

There is nothing wrong with passing on the cultural myths of these fanciful beings with the young child when they are appropriate to your family. It brings pleasure to parent and to child. But what happens when the jig is up? It is not uncommon for little Isabella to announce to her friends at school, "Your mom is the Tooth Fairy, you know." What a crushing blow. And it might happen long before you are ready for the fun to be over. What do you do?

Tips and Scripts for Dealing with Childhood Myths

- **Recognize that every culture has its myths.** From the beginning of time, different cultures have woven fanciful stories to answer their questions and help people understand the great wonders and enigmas in the world. They have created traditions to mark and celebrate various parts of their lives. The creation of their folklore and traditions keeps the culture alive, as these tales are passed down, adult to child, over generations.

- **Adults take great pleasure in passing down their myths.** It is one of the joys that come with being a parent. We are reminded of how it felt to be young and naïve, as we relive our childhood through our children.

- **Think of Santa Claus, the Easter Bunny, and the Tooth Fairy as traditions of your culture.** In so doing you can relieve yourself of the sense of guilt you may feel imagining that you are teaching your child that lying is okay.

- **Let your child be your guide.** You will know it is time to explore the truth when your child asks you, *"Is Santa Claus real?"* These kinds of truth-seeking questions usually come when the child is somewhere between the ages of six and eight. Sometimes a neighborhood saboteur causes the question to be asked before its time. Be prepared to follow your child's lead, telling neither too much nor too little. In answer to that question, you can say, *"Well, what do you think? Do you think he is real?"* Based on your child's age and development, she will begin to question it herself. But if she presses further, you can say, *"Some people do believe that Santa is real. When I was your age, I did."* And if you are pushed against a wall, *"As a grown-up I don't believe that Santa Claus is a person who brings presents down a chimney. But I do believe that the story of Santa Claus is part of the way we celebrate Christmas. Thinking about him makes me feel happy and warm and excited about the holiday. He is part of the spirit of Christmas."*

- **Allow your child to come to her own conclusion.** If your child has learned the difference between fantasy and reality, she will be able to think it through for herself. Ask her, *"What is your idea about what the Easter Bunny does?"* As your child tells you that a rabbit puts all these baskets together with chocolate and candies and toys, and he hops around from house to house and leaves them for all the kids in the world, the truth will dawn on her, if she is ready.

- **Validate her feeling of loss or disappointment, if you detect any.** Learning that your mom is the Tooth Fairy can be devastating news for a child. Be sensitive to her feelings, as there is a real loss of childhood in the revelation. *"It must make you feel sad to think that the Tooth Fairy isn't real. I remember how I felt when I found out. I really wanted her to be real, and I was disappointed that she wasn't."* You can add, *"Part of growing up is learning the truth about some of the stories you believed when you were little."*

- **Enlist the help of your older child.** If after the older child gets it, you are worried that she will spill the beans and ruin it for her little sister, bring her on board. *"Telling kids that there is a Santa Claus is one of the things that grown-ups do for little kids. The story is passed on from grown-up to child, over and over, just like Grandpa passed on the story to me, and I told it to you. Now you can help me pass on the story to your little sister. She will love to believe in Santa just like you have for all these years. We'll let her enjoy that story until she is old enough to know about Santa."*

You can also explain to your older child how grown-ups like to participate in all the magic of the holiday. That doesn't mean they aren't telling the truth. *"Daddy and I love to decorate the house and talk about Santa Claus because that's one of the ways we pass on our traditions of celebrating Christmas."*

- **Beware of creating myths that are an excuse for not dealing with reality.** Telling your six-year-old that the "switch witch" is going to come to trade her Halloween candy for money or a toy postpones a child's learning to deal with reality. The six-year-old can learn to tolerate your family's rule of picking out a few pieces of candy to save, while the rest goes to Daddy's office for grown-ups who love candy and don't get to trick-or-treat. The "pacifier fairy" falls into this category, too. These are not cultural myths. Rather, they are parental crutches that help parents ease a child's pain. But that's just what I believe . . .

Honesty is a character trait that is a reflection not only of the home life and circumstances in which a child is raised but also of the many variables in a child's development. It is intertwined with the child's sense of herself, her self-esteem, her place in the family and in her expanding world. But without question, the families in which honesty is practiced, honored, and stressed lay the necessary foundation for this trait's manifestation in the child's life forever.

❖

CHAPTER SEVEN

"I'm Bored."

Building a Self-Reliant Child

It's a curious thing about having a self-reliant child: You love that he can take care of himself, and you hate that he doesn't need you. Having a child who doesn't require your attention 24/7 might sound pretty darn good to the parent whose child doesn't give her a moment to herself. But to the mom who single-mindedly wants to be the best parent possible and who hasn't reached that tipping point where she's desperate for some alone time, the notion of self-reliance can be downright painful. *If he doesn't need me, then what is my role?* The essential lesson for this parent to learn is that in order to cultivate self-reliance in your child, you need to back off. As long as you, dear parent, are hovering (remember the helicopter parent) and insinuating yourself into so much of your child's daily existence, he is not likely to develop the skills that signal self-reliance. And he certainly will not get the message that you think he is a capable person.

Self-reliance and independence are similar traits. By definition, a child who is self-reliant is also independent. But a child who is independent is not necessarily self-reliant. The independent four-year-old runs off to his room to find the clothes he wants to wear, and because he is self-reliant, he gives putting them on his best shot, all by himself. His twin brother, also independent but not self-reliant, will follow his sibling into the bedroom but call out to you repeatedly to help him undo the buttons of the shirt he's chosen to wear, not even giving it a try. The independent nine-year-old goes off to do his homework in his room and gets it done because he is self-reliant and figures out what he is supposed to do. Self-reliance lives under the umbrella of independence and encourages the development of self-confidence. The self-reliant child is able to function independently because he knows how to think for himself. He is self-confident in certain areas but not necessarily in all areas. He is able to be self-sufficient where that ability is a reasonable expectation. The self-reliant child also tends to be creative (not necessarily "artsy"), resourceful, competent, and spontaneous.

The self-reliant child is one who has faith in himself. He trusts his own judgment and doesn't always find it necessary to seek the advice of others, including his parents, teachers, and even his peers. He is a risk taker who doesn't see the problems he encountered along the way as showstoppers. In fact, many children who are considered self-reliant can also be characterized as problem solvers. The self-reliant child grows into an adult who knows what to do when life throws him a curve ball. While he cannot control the circumstances he encounters, he can control his responses to them, he can formulate what to do next and therefore feel powerful and competent. Having faith in one's own capabilities is a crucial element of being a satisfied adult. It is also a characteristic of children who are not brats. Now, don't you want your child to be self-reliant?

Tips and Scripts for Teaching Self-Reliance

- **Be aware of your tone when you are encouraging your child to be self-reliant.** Your job is to be supportive and encouraging, so use a voice that is not judgmental or threatening. Put away that wagging index finger that your father used on you (as so memorably reenacted by Robin Williams when he pondered, "When did I grow my father's finger?"), and mildly ask, *"Do you feel you are ready to go to school? I think the bus will be here in five minutes."* Or, *"Kids whose teeth are brushed will have time for stories. I hope you are one of them."* And then let the chips fall where they may.

- **Mind your cautionary warnings.** Telling the child, *"Don't do that; you aren't big enough"* gives the child the message that you don't have confidence in him. In addition, such admonitions will limit his willingness to take a risk and try new things. It would be better if you say, *"Give it a try, if you feel safe."* Most children have built in brakes when it comes to risk. If your child doesn't seem to exercise those brakes on his own, you can say, *"I will stand next to you while you try that."*

- **Don't be a saboteur of self-reliance by telling your child what to do.** In their book *Raising Self-Reliant Children in a Self-Indulgent World*, Stephen Glenn and Jane Nelsen discuss the four ways that parents build barriers to self-reliance.

  ○ Directing: *"Don't just sit there and cry. Get up and take your tricycle out of the mud."* Your child would have figured that out for himself.
  ○ Explaining: *"When you don't watch where you are going, you ride into the mud."* This doesn't help your child to analyze a situation and figure it out for himself.
  ○ Rescuing: *"Bring it to Mommy. I'll fix it for you. Don't worry."* This gives the child the clear message that she is incapable of taking care of himself.
  ○ Assuming: *"If you don't keep your eye on the path, your bike will go in the mud."* This comment assumes the child is going to blow it. Not a great message of faith.

  These kinds of comments not only put up barriers to your child's doing so, but can also cause humiliation. That is never a healthy way to learn. Remember, the idea is to help your child to think for and rely on himself.

- **Assume the role of a consultant.** Of course it is easier and faster just to tell your child what to do, how to do it, and when to do it, but what is the lesson? Constant directing sabotages not only your child's trust in himself but also his taking initiative and learning to make decisions. Instead, present yourself as a consultant or an advisor. Some children just need a jump-start in order to get headed in the right direction. *"You have lots of choices about where to put that toy. Which one are you going to choose?"* Or, *"It's so great to play outside on a sunny day. You have so many choices of things to do out there."*

  Sometimes the child will actually do the opposite of what you are asking just so he can assert himself and be independent. Instead of directing, try saying, *"Your carpool will be here in ten minutes, do you remember what you need to do before they come?"* And when the carpool comes and he is not ready (or his teeth aren't brushed when it's bedtime, or he doesn't take a sweatshirt with him on a chilly day), you have choices aplenty—he can go to school in his pj's or just half-dressed, lose sweet foods for the day because he didn't brush his teeth, or go without a sweatshirt and be really cold all day, etc.

- **Allow your child to struggle.** Refrain from offering the quick fix when your child is having trouble. Sit on your hands and zip up your lips! Saying *"Here, let me do that for you"* or *"Let me show you how to do it"* may assuage your own inability to tolerate the struggle, but it won't teach your child perseverance and self-reliance. Instead, support him in his efforts by saying, *"Wow, you really are working hard on that. You amaze me."*

- **Create systems that encourage self-reliance.** With your child's help, make a chart or pictograph of the things he needs to do before he goes to bed or leaves for school. Hang it right next to the front door. All you will need to say is *"Check your list to make sure you are ready for school."* Put some hooks by the back door for sweaters and backpacks so he will always know where they are. Make getting ready for the next day part of your child's evening routine.

- **Develop rituals of daily life that do not change.** Knowing the way you always do it enables the child to do things for himself. "I forgot" just won't work. If packing the next day's lunch before he takes a shower is always part of the nighttime ritual, he will always remember. Funny how children never seem to forget that they can turn on the television and watch cartoons on Saturday mornings all by themselves.

- **Teach your child how to make decisions for himself.** Children need to be taught how we make decisions. For example, instead of telling your child to wear a long-sleeve shirt, suggest, *"Why don't you go out onto the front porch and see how it feels outside? Then you can decide if you need to wear long sleeves or not."* Or, *"Let's look in the weather section of the paper (or online) to check what the temperature will be today. Then you can decide what you want to wear."* Remember to go with his decision based on the information he gathered. When your child comes home complaining how cold he was in school, all the better. He has learned that you honor the decisions he makes for himself and allow for the consequence of those decisions.

- **Allow your child to make choices for himself.** When he does, follow through on his choices and refrain from judging those choices unnecessarily. Saying *"You don't really want that, do you?"* after he has made his decision only teaches the child not to trust himself. For example, if he chooses cereal for breakfast and then asks for the eggs everyone else is having, you can say, *"Today you chose cereal. I will remember tomorrow that you want eggs. Shall I write a note to remind us?"* Should he complain, simply suffer through his protests or tolerate his breakfast boycott. He won't starve.

- **Facilitate your child's successes by allowing him to do things for himself.** Buy a child-size pitcher that you fill with milk so your child can pour it himself. If he spills it, you can remind him how to clean up his own messes, too. Divide snacks into portion-size containers in a basket in the pantry. Allow your child to choose a snack for himself.

- **Experience really is the best teacher.** Repeated directions and warnings fall on deaf ears. In fact, we say the same things so much that we have taught our children to ignore us! That's called "learned deafness." Allow your child to suffer the consequences, positive and negative, of his choices and decisions. It is in the experience—yielding a positive or negative result—that learning happens and the child takes responsibility for himself. He can't blame you if he didn't wear long pants and was cold all day. And don't muddy the experience by throwing in a little guilt. *"I told you that you would be cold. See? I was right, wasn't I?"* That little twist of the knife will undermine the whole lesson. (See chapter 4, p. 75, on consequences.)

- **Give your child feedback about what went right.** It is so tempting always to emphasize what went wrong. But pointing out what went right also shows the child what went wrong. Instead of saying *"You really fought with me about taking a jacket this morning, and I was right, wasn't I?,"* try saying, *"You chose to put your jacket in your backpack today.*

That was a great decision, wasn't it? Who knew it would get so cold that it would snow!"

- **Teach your child self-assessment.** Accessing and getting in touch with feelings—big emotions like anger, frustration, sadness—help the child to assess what is going on, to learn to channel his feelings appropriately, and to trust himself. When a parent says *"Don't you be angry with me, young man"* or sends a child to his room if he can't stop crying, he is being given the message that expressing feelings is not okay. It teaches him that it is better not to express his feelings, to mask them, or worse, not even to have them. Have you ever been really upset and had someone tell you to "calm down?" When you are upset, you need to be upset. The feeling needs to run its course. Being told to calm down is a clear message that your feelings are not acceptable and that you can't trust yourself to feel what you feel. To heck with that! And what about when a parent is really angry with a child? Why is it okay for the parent to explode and not for the child to do the same?

  To teach self-assessment and acceptance, children need to have their feelings acknowledged and validated: *"You are really angry that your brother knocked over your building again. I don't blame you at all. When you are ready, we can talk about what we can do about it. But I cannot let you kick the blocks at him."* This script gives your child the message that you honor his feelings and imposes the limits on the behavior that he clearly needs. It also gives him time to let the emotion run its course and then assess what happened and what could happen next time. That's self-reliance for you. (For an in-depth discussion on the topic of feelings, see the section on emotional literacy in chapter 2, p. 31.)

Thinking for Himself

Being able to think for oneself is part and parcel of being self-reliant. A parent's comments along the lines of "Oh, c'mon, you know better than that," give children the message that their ideas and thoughts aren't good enough. Thinking for oneself grows out of learning that one's own ideas have value, that they are worthwhile and effective.

Tips and Scripts for Encouraging Your Child to Think for Himself

- **Encourage curiosity and observation.** The beginning of thinking for oneself is to notice things. You can model this behavior by observing the everyday occurrences in his life. *"That snail's trail made an S on the sidewalk."* Or, *"I love the feel of the air this morning."* Or, *"Those trees are starting to turn. It's getting to be fall."* When your child makes observations, no matter how small, receive and honor them. He will learn that his thoughts matter.

- **Wonder out loud.** Questioning leads to finding answers. Whether you are wondering about your environment *("I wonder where that car is going so fast?"),* or about parts of stories you are reading *("I wonder why the boy didn't want to play with his friend?"),* you encourage your child to wonder for himself. Honor the response, even the silliest idea, as it is an independent thought. Self-generated inquiry leads to independent problem solving.

- **Ask questions instead of giving answers.** When your young child comes to you and asks, *"Where does this go?"* or *"Where is my airplane?"* instead of giving the answer, help him to think for himself by reframing the question and giving it back: *"Why don't you show me where that goes?"* Or, *"Where do you think is the right place for that?"* I am reminded of the child who thrusts his jacket into his Daddy's arms as he runs off to play or hands his mother the dirty tissue he has just used. Those are missed opportunities for the child to think about (and act on) where the jacket or the tissue should go, to be self-reliant.

  When the older child is stumped by a homework problem or comes to a difficult part of a project, thinking is encouraged when the parent says *"What have you tried already?"* or *"What did the teacher explain about that problem in school?"* or *"What are your ideas for working that out?"* All of these encourage the child to rethink his problem rather than giving up and relying on you for the answer. Sometimes just having you as a sounding board allows him to rethink the problem and find his own solution.

- **Ignore the nasty response.** Be prepared to withstand a whiney or crabby response when you don't give your child the answer he's looking for. Know that he will be disappointed and frustrated when you don't jump in and help him out. (*"You never help me do anything!"*) Take pains to stay on track and not be derailed by his reaction. I am reminded of the time that my four-year-old son Ben was not happy with something I had asked him to do, and he let loose with, *"Mommy, I am going to* be-not-haaave!*"* Here Ben was drawing me away from the issue at hand. Admittedly, it took all that I had not to be distracted by his clever mispronunciation of the word *behave*. Remember, the goal is to get the child to think for himself. Drawing you into a fight will be a great distraction for him, so steer clear. *"I'll be in the kitchen, so let me know when you are done"* sends the right message.

- **Praise the outcome.** Regardless of the quality of the child's solution, praise him for solving the problem or finding an answer all by himself: *"Looks like you are happy with your work. That's feels good, doesn't it?"* If the quality doesn't meet your standards, let the teacher do the dirty work. If the child doesn't like the way his project came out, he'll need to find a different solution.

- **Be deliberate in determining where your child does homework.** Being too available to answer questions about homework (and other projects) discourages self-reliance. The young child—kindergarten through second grade—is the exception, as he usually needs you close by for support as he learns the ropes of doing homework. Not so with your third-grader and older. The child who has to put in some effort to ask you a question (say, coming all the way downstairs) is more likely to think for himself first before giving up and running to you for help. If your child is sitting next to you as he does his homework, and you are able to resist the temptation to immediately help, then good for you. Most parents can't.

- **Ask opinions.** Asking the opinions of older children not only encourages them to think for themselves but also sends the message that you value their thoughts. The young child tends to say whatever he thinks you want to hear or repeat what his parents have said. (Ask your five-year-old who he supported in the last election, and he will enthusiastically shout out the name of your candidate of choice.) The older child likes to show you how he has his own taste, opinion, and thoughts. Make sure that your questions are not obviously rhetorical. And don't let your opinions show. He will see right through you. Take time to explore the ideas he has shared.

Sometimes focusing your questions on the opinions of others—peers, for instance—takes your child off the hot seat, and he will be more willing to share his thoughts. *"What do your friends think about Mr. Madoff going to jail? Do you all agree?"* Or, *"What did your history teacher say about the inauguration? Do you agree with him?"* Doing so is a good lesson in thinking independently.

- **With older children, vary the topic and the focus of discussions.** Most children don't like being put on the spot, so find neutral topics for discussion. Sports, entertainment, and politics are all good subject areas as long as your child doesn't feel he is under the magnifying glass. Listen to his ideas. Remember, he is thinking for himself.

- **Play games whose answers are never the same.** Asking "What if?" encourages the child to key into his own ideas and not repeat what he has heard: *"What would happen if cars only had three wheels?"* or *"What if we had hands attached to our ears?"* Not only do these judgment-free questions encourage independent thinking, but they also encourage a child's resourcefulness as well as creativity.

- **Create your own endings to stories.** Although a young child will protest (as he likes everything to be the same, always!), a child aged four and up can successfully ponder what would happen if there were a new ending to one of his favorite stories. *"Let's say Mama Bear drops Little Bear's birthday cake. Then how would this story end?"* Not only will the child think for himself, but he will have a great laugh in the process.

  For older children, try having them create their own ending. *"So, let's change the end of Goldilocks. How would your ending go?"* And be sure to marvel at his creativity.

- **Encourage brain stretching.** Especially when captive in the car or before a movie begins, pose mental challenges. With your four-year-old, try making up your own knock-knock jokes (and don't they love them!). With your elementary-school child, offer greater challenges: *"How many foods that start with the letter D can you think of?"* And for the even older child, *"What do a dog and an iPod have in common?"* These kinds of questions not only encourage thinking for oneself, but they promote creativity and resourcefulness as well.

Leave Your Child Alone

This sounds a whole lot easier than it actually is, but leaving your child alone while he plays is the first step in cultivating self-reliance. By being alone, your child is left with his own thoughts. And children have really busy brains! Not only is there a lot to think about, but left to his own resources and in the absence of external stimulation, ideas hatch. How great it is when your child runs to find you, joyfully exclaiming, *"Look what I made all by myself!"*

Your second (or third or fourth) child is much more likely to be able to be by himself than your firstborn. Oh, that poor firstborn, your practice child! You still believed that you were supposed to be with him all the time. Then you had another one, and you learned that children who are left to their own devices (safety being considered, of course) cultivate self-reliance. Being with a child all the time gives the clear message that he needs you all the time.

Tips and Scripts for Fostering Your Child's Ability to Be by Himself

- **Enable young babies to be alone for short periods of time.** Always with safety in mind, make sure that your baby is allowed to be by himself for short intervals, absorbed in watching the mobile or entertained by his fingers.

- **Don't interrupt.** When your toddler or preschooler is engaged in an activity of any kind, resist the temptation to involve yourself. Don't even ask, *"What are you doing over there?"* or *"Is everything okay?"* Such questions give your child the message that he shouldn't be entertaining himself. In fact, the opposite is true. When you see that your child is busy, become involved in an activity of your own. Later you can praise what you saw. *"It looked like you were really busy playing while I* *folded the laundry."* Or say nothing at all. Show that this is the way it's supposed to be.

For the child who is unable to play alone, gradually cultivate this ability by expecting him to entertain himself for short spans of time. (See chapter 3, p. 53, for a detailed description of how to encourage your child to be by himself.)

- **Build free playtime into your child's regular schedule.** These days children are so over-programmed that the most valuable activity of all, free play, gets squeezed out. Free play does not mean playing with you or even having a playdate. Free play happens when your child freely decides what he wants to do and how he is going to do it all by himself. It is the epitome of demonstrating self-reliance. If your child's days are filled with lessons and coaching and other activities, he won't have the time to figure out what he likes and wants to do. He has learned to rely on you for entertainment.

- **Resist the trend of keeping your child busy all the time.** Children need to develop a capacity for being by themselves, alone with their own thoughts. It can't happen if they are always busy.

- **Accept your older child's choices for himself.** It may be hard to believe, but the time will come when your child won't want to be with you. In fact, he'll crave alone time, and much of his free play will be spent behind his closed bedroom door. He is relying on himself for his entertainment. Whether he is listening to his iPod while lying on his bed, or just daydreaming, staring at the ceiling, he is doing what he wants to do. Assuming he has met his responsibilities, leave him alone. (See chapter 4 for a discussion on children and responsibilities.) Self-reliance comes in lots of colors and you can't even imagine the thoughts he is exploring.

Boredom

I feel pretty sure that there isn't a child alive who, at some time or other, hasn't whined, "I'm bored!" to his mom or dad. It drives even the most patient of us nuts. Once, when my triplets were about five years old, Lucas came to me and complained, *"We don't have anyone to play with. We're bored."* Oh, please!

Truth be told, it is your child's task to figure out how to make himself happy, not yours! Parents who make it part of their job description to entertain their child cultivate in the child the crazy notion that life is exciting because someone else makes it that way. Your child needs to discover how to entertain himself and what makes him happy. "I'm bored" is his way of saying, *"I want you to be responsible for entertaining me."*

Most of the children I know have a playroom that resembles Toys "R" Us or a garage that rivals a sporting goods store. So when your child claims he is bored, it takes the parent right to a place of: *"You ungrateful, spoiled child. Don't you know there are some children who have no toys at all?"* While going to that place allows you to let off some steam (and guilt—after all, you bought it all or allowed Granny to buy it), it doesn't teach your child how to make life interesting for himself.

Sometimes saying "I'm bored" is a default. It is the easiest way to express a feeling the child is unable to articulate. Boredom can occasionally be a sign that something is out of balance in the life of an older child (middle school and older); often, the imbalance involves friends or school. Sometimes the child is unable to access his feelings; he isn't even aware of what he is really feeling. Something is eating away at him, and "I'm bored" is the safe, catchall expression. If you suspect that something more serious is going on, if he has been uncharacteristically lethargic, quiet, or even depressed, and all you can get out of him is "I'm bored," it would be a good idea to contact a mental health professional.

I do not believe that young children—preschool and elementary schoolers—are bored. Where do they learn that expression, anyway? Some of the most endearing qualities of the young child are his curiosity, his imagination, and his ability to be interested in the smallest of things. Put a child in an empty field, and he'll find rocks to turn into demons that live in an elaborate kingdom that is filled with dungeons, and there are field mice, and . . . and . . . and . . . When the three- or four-year-old says he is bored, he is really saying "I want you to find something for me to do. I don't want to think for myself." Children who are not allowed to be bored, whose parents rescue them from being bored, will just be bored again another day. Boredom is an opportunity for your child to be resourceful. Being resourceful is one of the most useful attributes of a child who is self-reliant.

Tips and Scripts for Dealing with Boredom

- **Allow boredom to develop.** Rather than scheduling your child's time outside of school, allow him to have empty hours. It is during this unscheduled time when, deprived of external stimulation, the child learns to amuse himself, creating his own entertainment and happiness.

- **Try hard not to get angry with your child because he says he is bored.** Your anger is not likely to foster your child's desire to entertain himself. It actually might not be his fault that he is bored. Has he ever been given the opportunity to cure his own boredom?

- **View boredom as an opportunity.** My first response to my own children's claim of being bored was to say, *"Oh good. That means you are going to find something really great to do. You are always so creative when you are bored."*

- **Resist the urge to make suggestions as to what your child might do to alleviate his boredom.** As annoyed as you are, your child will not learn to be resourceful when he doesn't know what to do. While your fix will ease the problem for the time being, no lesson is learned except that you are the one on whom he can rely when he doesn't know what to do. Not much self-reliance there.

- **Explain to your older child that being bored is a choice.** *"Seems like you are choosing to be bored. You don't have to be bored. I am sure you could find something to do."* Let him know that he chooses how he wants to spend his time; he is the boss of that. This explanation will best be heard if you have the discussion long after the incident. When a child has gone to the dark side, he doesn't hear much of what you say. And be prepared for a lot of put-down comments about what a mean mother you are, that you don't care about him, and a whole host of other lovely claims.

- **Help your child (when he is not bored) to make a list of things to do when he feels bored.** This is an especially good practice if you have a child who is chronically bored. During a non-bored moment say, *"When you tell me you are bored, it seems like you just can't remember all* *the things you like to do. Let's make a list of those now so you can refer to that list when you need an idea."* Allow the child to post the list in his room, so if need be you can say in response to his claim of boredom, *"Now would be a good time for you to look at your list."*

- **Help your child start a long-term project.** Working on a project or activity that is cumulative is the gift that keeps on giving. Jigsaw puzzles, models, ant farms, and even vegetable gardens fall into this category.

- **Encourage your child to have a hobby.** It's a real pity that hobbies are considered kind of old-fashioned. So much learning that would not otherwise occur comes from hobbies. For instance, think about all the things children learn about other countries and people from collecting coins or stamps. You may have to introduce the idea of a pastime like this to your child by infusing it with your own enthusiasm and with fun stories from your own baseball card, doll, seashell, insect, or button-collecting days. Help your child get started by providing the necessary tools and organization. There's so much to be gained, including plain old fun.

- **Choose your child's toys and supplies carefully.** Stanley Greenspan, the well-known child psychologist, said, "The value of a toy is proportional to the degree that it invites imaginative creativity." Seems like most of the things we buy our children today are "ready-to-be-made" kits. No longer do you buy a box of Legos; you buy the Lego rocket ship. Your child puts it together, and it's over, bringing on the refrain, *"Now what can I do? I'm bored."* Children of all ages do amazing things with "loose parts." And while loose parts make for big cleanups, they are boredom killers and encourage creativity. Loose parts can be used over and over; new ideas spring forth. Buying kits ready to make also gives a child the message that he cannot make something that is his own creation. He needs someone else's ideas or direction. Look for unspecified toys, the ones that bring the child's imagination to life. Hardwood building blocks, Erector sets, old-fashioned Lincoln Logs and are just a few of so many. Art supplies like pipe cleaners, sequins, sticky paper, tongue depressors, and colored tape yield hours of amusement.

- **Make sure your child-care plan still works.** As a child gets older, he can outgrow the type of child-care he had when he was younger. What was perfect for the preschool child may no longer work for the elementary schooler. He may have outlived his need for the nurturing, grandmotherly figure and now needs someone who knows how to encourage his initiative and self-reliance.

- **Limit technology and screen time.** Today's children are growing up in a screen-dominated world. They can watch their favorite programs wherever and whenever they want: on cell phones, on the miniature DVD players, on MP3 players, on computers, in the family car. Even at the doctor's office, the gas station, the bank, and in the grocery cart, screens draw their attention. But it's not what's on the screen that is necessarily bad; it's what children are not doing when they are watching a screen that is the problem. Children who have too much tech time do not learn how to entertain themselves. They do not develop the ability to be resourceful. In fact, I know many adults who can't think of anything better to do than watch television or explore the Internet. In today's world, many of our technology-addicted teens grow up to be screen-addicted adults who don't know how to entertain themselves in any other way. By limiting the amount of time your child is permitted to use screens of any kind, he will not fall back on the screen when he is "bored."

  A local high school teacher in Los Angeles undertook an experiment to see what would happen when her students eliminated all technology from their lives for one week. All reported finding things to do that they hadn't done in years (if ever), including playing with siblings, hanging out with the family, going on hikes, even reading an entire book.

Resourcefulness

Being resourceful is certainly an antidote to boredom. Plato was right on the button when he said, "Necessity is the mother of invention." Maybe he should have added, "Boredom is the mother of invention." When a child is bored, he has the opportunity to use his resourcefulness. Children who are resourceful know how to make things happen; they are problem solvers. They trust their instincts and abilities. These children usually have healthy self-esteem, too.

Resourcefulness is what enables you to get the job done when you might not have the right tools, so you figure out another way to do it just as well. It is resourcefulness that gets you out of a pickle, that enables you to finish the project when you don't have the right color paint, that gets you through the assignment when your parents are out for the evening even if that means going back and re-reading the information more carefully than you did the first time.

Every child has the ability to become resourceful. The opposite of learned resourcefulness is learned helplessness. As the parent, you are in the position to teach one or the other.

SELF-ESTEEM

Self-esteem (not to be confused with narcissism) is how a person feels about himself. It is the sense of one's self-worth, the feeling that comes from one's very core, that he is valued and that he makes a difference. Contrary to what was once thought, even criminals and people who do bad things can actually have high self-esteem. They are surely misguided in many ways, but they do have a sense that they are powerful and possess the confidence that they can make things happen, bad though they are.

Self-esteem is something that is constantly evolving, but we know that a child's growing years are profound in creating a foundation for healthy and strong self-worth. Possibly the greatest builders of self-esteem are hard work and accomplishment. It is from his independent effort that the child develops that "I can do it" feeling—the confidence, self-reliance, and independence that make for satisfied adults. Self-esteem is something that grows from within. When a child experiences it in its truest form it is tremendously empowering. By the way, constantly reminding a child how great or how smart he is undermines the development of this trait. Such excessive praise will only lead to doubts about the credibility of the message and the messenger.

Tips and Scripts for Encouraging Resourcefulness

- **Less is more.** Most kids today just have way too much stuff. And sometimes having too much from which to choose gets in the way of making any choice at all. When he doesn't have a lot to choose from, your child is more likely to be creative with the things he has. A shoe makes an excellent cargo ship, filled with cars, on the carpet ocean.

- **Allow your child to be stuck.** Don't be quick to jump in and help your child solve a problem. The child who is never frustrated by a task is not likely to develop his resourcefulness. Allowing him the space and time to try to figure out his solution gives him the message that you have faith in his ability to do so. Supporting him in his efforts to figure it out for himself will sow the seeds of resourcefulness: *"You are working so hard to make that puzzle piece fit. It looks like you've almost got it."* Praise his effort in order to get more of the same: *"You really are patient and working very hard to figure out that math problem. I know you can do it."* (Ignore the *"No, I can't"* response and leave.)

- **Tolerate the protest when you don't jump in to solve the problem.** Yes, you will be called "the meanest mommy in the whole world" and be accused of not caring, but when he figures out how to solve his problem, it will have been worth it. Don't absorb the comment and don't cave! (If you've already been practicing letting the much-dreaded label of "meanest mommy" roll off your back per the advice in several other chapters in this book, then you will find this recommendation easier to enact than most other moms.)

- **Join in your child's curiosity.** When your child comes to you with a question, try saying, *"I don't know. That's a really good question. How do you think we could find the answer?"* Immediately answering your child's questions removes any hope of his being resourceful in finding the answers. It really is okay for a parent not to know things. What is more important is the lesson in how we find the answers.

- **Honor inquisitiveness.** Four- and five-year-old children are full of questions. How great is that? Your child's brain is working overtime! Instead of being annoyed, keep a list of questions posted on the refrigerator. On your weekly trips to the library or the regular time you spend together on Google, refer to that list. Answer the questions and keep that brain wondering.

- **Encourage brainstorming.** Say, *"Let's think about that together"* and then let your child do most of the figuring out. Almost any of his responses should elicit from you, *"That's a new idea. I've never thought of that before."* Or, *"That sure is one way to do it!"* Not only will you encourage more of the same, but you show that you value ideas that might be different from yours or from the norm. Be sure to throw in some reinforcement of his show of resourcefulness by saying, *"Boy, you sure know how to figure things out!"*

- **Avoid negativity of any kind.** Even though it would not be your intention, some comments discourage, embarrass, or even shame the child. Saying *"That's not how you do it; let me show you"* or worse, *"Oh please! What are you thinking? That will never work"* gives the child a clear message about his worthlessness. Why should he try if you can do it better? Instead, saying *"Gee, I guess that didn't work. Maybe you should try a different idea"* encourages him to keep trying, supports him, and shows your faith in him.

- **Facilitate play, but don't direct it.** Children even as old as ten still love playing on the floor. And they can be so inventive. Joining them in their play makes it even better and encourages more of the same. Take pains to follow their lead and give up your usual mommy role of directing the action.

- **Provide a (legal) messy place.** Working with art materials of all kinds provides great opportunities to be resourceful. But if your child is afraid that *Mommy will be mad if I make a mess,* the opportunity will be lost. Teach your child how to use a variety of materials and tools, and then let him go. Protect the floor with a drop cloth, cover the table if need be, but make it work. Don't spoil the moment with your own fears of a mess. You will need to join young ones in the cleanup, but school-age children can be shown how to do a proper cleanup and can be expected to do a reasonably good job. Remember, if your expectations about staying neat and clean are too high, your child will not want to get involved the next time.

- **Encourage the scientist.** I can assure you that the great scientists of the world didn't make their discoveries by doing things the way they had always been done. At the appropriate place and time, allow your child to experiment—make magic potions, mix colors of paint together, embark on various projects involving trial and error. More important than the result, is the excitement that the process generates, and the sheer creativity involved. And do you know that even scientists clean up their own messes?

- **Don't buy Halloween costumes.** Manufacturers and parents (especially the ones who think they aren't creative or who say they don't have the time) won't be happy with this suggestion, but making your own costumes generates incredible resourcefulness in both the parent and the child. Not only will your child have a one-of-a-kind outfit, but he will be tremendously proud. Your younger child will love helping you put his costume together, making suggestions, coloring Daddy's old white T-shirt, tearing rags to use as feathers. Your older child will come up with the plan by himself, using you to help gather the parts. Children whose costumes are homemade from the earliest ages will learn not to be reliant on the costume store for Halloween or for other dramatic play adventures.

- **Build something with your child.** Whether it's a fort using pillows from the sofa, a house made from a refrigerator carton, or a skateboard ramp constructed from purchased lumber, children need to see how things can be made. If everything is store-bought, how can they learn to create things for themselves, using their own great ideas? Who knows, one of the world's next great inventors may be experimenting in your own home!

- **It's the process, not the product that counts.** Let your child do his own work, his own way. Adults (including parents and teachers) make a big mistake by touching a child's work. Of course you can do it better, faster, and neater, but that isn't the point. The learning takes place in the process of creation.

Perfectionism

It can be difficult for the child who has perfectionist tendencies to be self-reliant. It's tough to count on himself when he has a critical inner voice. While your child may be able to think for himself, often the voice in his head screaming *it's not good enough* or *mine won't be good, so you do it* is drowning out the voice that's telling him to give it a try. A child with this propensity might be unwilling to take a risk or embark upon anything new because he might worry that he'll never be good enough with that particular activity, or that he's just not any good at all. Another child might feel that he is supposed to be good at an activity or skill right from the start, and therefore he won't allow himself the experience of learning. And then there is the child who spends an inordinate amount of time on a project or assignment because he has unrealistic standards for his product; it is never good enough to be considered finished, so he keeps on working to perfect it. There are many ways that a child's perfectionism stops him from being self-reliant as he feels his work can't cut it. Have you seen the child who erases and erases so hard on his page that he makes a hole in his homework? Then you know what I am talking about.

Children (and adults) who are perfectionists often possess some of the following characteristics. They:

- have exceptionally high expectations and goals for themselves.
- are self-conscious and embarrass easily.
- have anxiety about making mistakes.
- are highly sensitive to criticism.
- have a hard time making decisions.

All of these characteristics get in the way of a child's ability to happily get through the business of daily life. There are many reasons for perfectionism, and one of them could well be a genetic predisposition. As a result of nature or nurture, my daughter Jessie began to exhibit her mommy's perfectionist tendencies when she was six, crumpling her art work when it wasn't just as she envisioned. An intervention using many of the tips in the following section got her back on track. But most experts agree that it is a combination of inborn tendencies, temperament, and environmental factors that are at the root of perfectionism. It may well be that a child's perfectionist tendencies result from his need for parental approval. He may see parental love as being conditional and linked to his performance and achievement. He fears disappointing parents or teachers. Another child may have observed his parents' own perfectionism in action for years: *If it's good enough behavior for Dad, it's good enough for me.*

In reality, perfectionism cannot be totally "cured." But it can be tamed enough to allow the child to be self-reliant and not disabled. If you do have a child whose perfectionism is extreme and debilitating, you should contact a mental health professional.

Tips and Scripts for Dealing with Perfectionism

While many of these ideas are good for all children, they are intended specifically for the child who has already demonstrated that his perfectionism is getting in the way of his functioning. By contrast, these tips and scripts do not apply to the child who has to be encouraged to try harder or to work a little more, or for whom a touch of perfectionism wouldn't be all that bad.

- **There is no such thing as perfect.** Say it out loud! There is excellence, there is a job well done, but perfect doesn't exist.

- **It's impossible to complete every task without making a mistake.** Challenge your school-age, perfectionist child to give you an example. You'll be able to prove him wrong because it is the truth. There is always someone who will tell you how to do something better than you have done it. Ask any professional athlete.

- **Teach your child that it is by making mistakes that we learn.** You will have lots of opportunities to teach this lesson, so look out for them. *"Next time I will know that adding the salt before I cook the meat makes it tough. I learned a great cooking lesson by making that mistake."*

- **Tune into your own perfectionism.** Remember that your child is watching you all of the time. If you tell him it's okay to make a mistake and then berate yourself when you blow it, your message will not be received. Children can spot hypocrisy a mile away.

- **Remove the word "perfect" from your vocabulary.** When you pay attention, you will be astounded at how often you use this word.

Whether you're being sarcastic, *"Oh, that's just perfect!"* or making a judgment, *"That's perfect!"* your child hears you saying it. Change the habit.

- **Make mistakes in front of your child.** This tip may really go against your grain, but get your priorities in order; it's for your child's well-being and growth. Children need to see their parents making mistakes, spilling, breaking, and dropping things, doing things incorrectly—and then recovering—in order to accept such mistakes when they make them.

- **Don't berate yourself for making mistakes.** Instead, cut yourself some slack whenever your child is present. When you bake something that doesn't quite look like the delectable photo in your cookbook, for instance, try saying, *"I didn't do so well on this recipe. The piecrust is crooked and I cooked it too long. Oh well, I'll do better next time."* Or, *"It's good enough because it sure tastes good!"* And then add, *"See, I told you that nobody's perfect!"*

- **Model recovery.** While your child watches you do things well, most children don't get to see how their parents recover from their missteps. Of course he sees you cleaning up your messes, but he doesn't get to see you fix them. For example: *"I don't like how I drew this picture. Wait! I'll just turn it around and draw it this way!"* Doing so gives the child permission to make a mistake and offers a possible solution at the same time.

- **Share your own stories of perfectionism.** Let your child know that he is not alone in his struggles with needing to be perfect. Children love to hear tales of their parents, good stuff and bad. You being less than perfect allows him to be the same. Tell funny stories of mistakes you made when you were a child or current ones that you have made and what you did about it.

- **Laugh at yourself.** Have a sense of humor about mistakes that are made, yours especially. Without being cruel, laugh at mistakes that others have made, ones that they might laugh at, too. Watching shows like *America's Funniest Home Videos* goes a long way toward accepting others' foibles as well as your own.

- **Try something new with your child.** Take a class that allows your child to see you not be good at something. Taking a knitting class, piano lessons, or tennis lessons—especially something that you find daunting—are all good ideas. Even if you're not the best at these skills, your child will see you learning and enjoying yourself just the same.

- **Practice what you are learning.** Children need to practice practicing, especially those who have unreasonable expectations for themselves. I have heard from adult clients that taking up piano fit that bill well. The whole house was subjected to their practicing, as well as to the proud concert performance in the end. This allows your child to see that "practice makes better." Note that the old expression "practice makes perfect" is not useful. Just ask Peyton Manning or anyone who has good days and bad.

- **Teach your child about valuing process over product.** Some children are so focused on the destination that they fail to enjoy or see the value in the journey. When you are playing a game with your child, for example, stop and say, *"I really love playing with you. This is really fun for me."* When you have cooked a meal together, the result of which was less than divine, say, *"Well, I don't much like what we made, but I sure loved making it with you. That was the best part!"*

- **Teach your child to break a task down into baby steps.** The enormity of a task is magnified if you only have your eye on the end product. Creating small goals enables a child to have some success along the way. Each achievement builds confidence and the ability to move forward to the next goal. *"Writing a report is a huge task. Why don't you break it up so you can do a little bit every day? What are the parts that need to be done?"* (For example, reading and note taking, writing an outline, first draft, final draft.) *"Let's make a calendar so you will know on what day you will complete each part."*

- **Beware of "Do your best."** In the competitive world in which we live, this small phrase has become a mantra. I think it's a mistake, an unrealistic expectation, and not very motivating. No one does his best all the time. In fact, I don't know anyone who is good at and/or tries his best in everything. While we want to encourage our children to focus, to try hard, think twice about always asking your child to do his best.

Too often, "Do your best" hides your real admonition, "Do well." Remember, the perfectionist child is his own worst enemy. He always tries his best, and he thinks it isn't good enough. Instead of asking, *"Did you do your best?"* try, *"Were you happy with the effort you put in?"* or *"Is there something you think you would do differently next time?"* These nonjudgmental questions give the child some breathing room. If you are of the opinion that your child's work was not really up to snuff, allow the teacher or the coach to be the critic. The child is likely to hear anyone else's comments more than yours.

- **Teach "good enough."** Help your child to learn that there will be many times when good enough is just that. *"You have worked really hard and really long on that project. It really is good enough. I know your teacher will appreciate how much effort you put into it."* You will not be sacrificing quality; you will be allowing your child to let go. Good enough certainly doesn't mean bad.

- **Teach your child "self-talk."** Self-talk happens when a child speaks the words he hears in his head. Many times in the school setting I have heard a child tell himself, *"That's okay. I can clean it up,"* when he has spilled something. The child who can't tolerate dirty clothing assures himself by saying, *"It doesn't matter. My mommy will wash it."* That is self-talk that soothes. Often, having a script to fall back on when the perfectionist child has made a mistake or is being hard on himself helps calm the waters. Tell him: *"When you're not happy with your work, you can remind yourself, 'That's okay. It doesn't have to be perfect.'"*

- **Practice losing.** Children in the five- and six-year-old range are really poor sports, and they just hate losing. It's not just your child, I promise. Find small games to play that are not dependent upon skill, such as Rock, Paper, Scissors, or the card game War, which are games of chance. Play them over and over so your child can see that sometimes you win and sometimes you lose.

- **Keep a tally.** For the older child who is a sore loser, keep an ongoing tally of game results. Find an easy, quick game, like Tic-Tac-Toe. Or rolling dice. Some nights you will be ahead and other times he'll be in the lead. That way, it's never really over and his tolerance for losing will grow.

• **Decrease your own emphasis on winning.** Most young children evaluate a sport based on winning or losing. Help to change that importance by not asking who won and by not discussing the score. Place the emphasis on the contribution your child or other players made. *"Who gave the assist for that goal in the soccer game (or assisted that basket in the basketball game)? Were you happy with how you played today?"* You can add, *"It sure looked like you were having fun."*

Never compare siblings' abilities or performance. Do I really need to remind you of this?

As with some of the other positive traits you hope to instill in your child, being self-reliant includes having self-awareness and good judgment. While a parent wants her child to be able to take care of himself, she also needs to teach the child that there are times when he should ask for help. For the parent, an important skill in raising a self-reliant child is learning to act as a "spotter," allowing and expecting the risk while walking right alongside of him. Children need to know that adults will catch them if they fall.

CHAPTER EIGHT

❖

"Is This the Only Present I Get?"

Making a Gratitude Adjustment in Your Child

You've taken a whole day off to spend with your child. It's all about her—from the park visit, to lunch out, to Color Me Mine, to Build-A-Bear, to the ice cream store, and finally a bike ride at the beach—and when it's time to go home and cook dinner, your four-year-old lets loose with, *"It's not fair. I never get to do anything. I don't want to go home. I hate dinner!"* And you think, *Why, you ungrateful little twit. I gave you my whole day. Where is my thank you? How dare you complain?!*

Gratitude is a difficult topic because sitting right next to it are feelings of deprecation and worry about yourself as a parent. *Is my child spoiled? Entitled? Did I do something wrong?* It takes you right to that guilty, blaming place. *Maybe I have given my child too much (stuff, toys, clothes, attention, privileges). Maybe I have let her do too much. Now what should I do?*

We expect our children to feel gratitude, yet we're not really sure how such gratitude is fostered. Does it just appear magically? Is it like learning to walk, the child just starts doing it? There isn't a parent alive who doesn't want her child to feel grateful and to appreciate all that she has, literally and figuratively. We all know that our children are more fortunate than most of the world's population. Why don't they feel it?

Why Cultivate Gratitude?

There are reasons beyond the obvious. Of course, it is part of good manners, a social skill that helps you to get along in the world. On a deeper level, feeling and expressing gratitude actually contribute to a person's well-being, aside from the fact that your child will be in big trouble if she doesn't learn to say thank you! We teach our children to consider the feelings of others in encouraging their expressions of gratitude. But in reality, gratitude is a favor that we do for ourselves. There are studies that show that not only are grateful people happier, more optimistic, physically healthier, and more resilient, but they also have a higher self-esteem and are able to have more fulfilling relationships throughout their lives.

Religions and different philosophers have long encouraged people to feel and express appreciation for their bounty, whatever size or form it may come in. There is a good reason for the old adage "Count your blessings." Doing so is actually good for you.

The Components of Gratitude

Gratitude is difficult to define because it has different meanings for different people. Commonly, it is seen as a character trait and, by some, a moral value. It is part of a person's core and is crucial to the foundation of one's sense of self. Gratitude can be seen as an aspect of personality. It is an attitude, a perception, and a way of viewing the world, and a habit to be cultivated. Gratitude is also viewed as a social skill, a demonstration of manners, and a tool that aids in navigating daily life. And most will agree, gratitude is an emotion, as it is something that one must feel.

Expressing appreciation and feeling appreciation are the two parallel paths that lead to genuine gratitude. The manners of gratitude have to be taught, like teaching a baby bird to fly. The feelings of gratitude, on the other hand, have to be nurtured.

In twelve-step programs, participants are encouraged to behave themselves into right thinking. So it is with gratitude. When children practice acts of gratitude (saying thank you, demonstrating appreciation, writing thank-you notes, etc.), they will begin to feel it. Gratitude becomes a habit motivated by the feeling.

To feel gratitude a child needs to be developmentally capable of thinking about it. In order to build a framework for understanding gratitude, the child must recognize that something good has even happened to her. Then she needs to be able to realize that the good stuff is not of her making, that it came from someone else, somewhere separate from her. Expressing, feeling, and understanding gratitude grows with the child's development in these areas.

Milestones in a Child's Development of Gratitude

- **The toddler is unable to understand that other people have feelings.** She is accustomed to having everything done for her. (And she expects that you will spend all day with her.)
- **The preschool child is beginning to understand that other people have feelings.** She has power over and choice in the way she treats people and the way they treat her. But the child is not yet able to understand time and quantity. (From her perspective, spending a whole hour with her is the same as spending just ten minutes with her.)
- **The elementary-school child has the capacity for empathy.** She can share in another's joy and sorrow. She knows the concepts of time and effort and can appreciate both.
- **The preteen is busy practicing her independence.** While she is capable of empathy, she is self-absorbed and focused on her task of growing up and growing away.

Where Gratitude Begins

Remember your infant, fresh from the womb? She was all about receiving (and boy, wasn't she!). She cried from hunger, she got the breast; she cried with a wet diaper, she got a diaper change; she cried from fatigue, she got rocked to sleep. Basically, she cried and you ran and met all her needs. The payoff? All that love oozing from every pore of your body. With these actions you were building a trusting relationship that will last forever. You are doing what every parent in the animal world instinctively does: meets every need of her young. Was your infant grateful? Nah. She expected it. She didn't know any other way. But that is the foundation for gratitude: the parent gives and the child receives. That's the way it's supposed to be at the beginning.

But the child grows, and things change. One day you wake up and wonder when the appreciation is supposed to kick in. You give and give and give. Where's the thank you? Why doesn't your child appreciate what she is getting? Now your precious little lamb is an ungrateful four-year-old, assuming she will get whatever she wants, whenever she wants it, and screaming bloody murder when she doesn't. Not an ounce of appreciation. What happened? How did you give birth to the ungrateful child you swore you would never raise?

The first lesson of showing gratitude begins with Mommy instructing her toddler, "Say thank you," upon receiving her cup of water or a gift from Grandma. And the child learns that these are the words that make Mommy happy and proud. But it is shortsighted to think that saying thank you is necessarily a genuine show of gratitude. In reality, it is a rote and imperative response, kind of a get-out-of-jail-free card that children learn to parrot. It is a manners lesson, well learned, and an important one, too. It is the beginning of the journey down the path called "expressing gratitude." Implicit in knowing to say thank you is the acknowledgement that someone else's feelings and needs are important. To reiterate: The behavior—expressing gratitude—comes first; the understanding and feeling come later.

That understanding grows in concert with your child's growing empathy. (See chapter 2 on empathy.) It requires a child's understanding that gratitude involves both receiving and giving at the same time. When your child says *"thank you,"* showing gratitude, it is part of learning to share in another person's thoughts and feelings; it is the beginning of empathy. Saying *"thank you"* acknowledges that someone else did something for you, and your words make that person feel good. As the child grows in her ability to know that someone else has feelings, otherwise known as empathy, so grows her ability to say *"thank you"* unprompted.

Feeling gratitude is a whole different story. Children cannot be taught to feel gratitude, any more than they can be taught to feel anything. Feelings are things that have to grow from within. Seeds of genuine gratitude need to be sown. And, as stated earlier, often the feelings of gratitude can grow from acting grateful.

The Parent's Contribution

Children are not born with a gratitude gene that kicks in at a certain point of development. Many of the variables that affect the degree of gratitude that a child feels have more to do with you than her, including:

- Your personal history and upbringing, which shaped your attitudes and fed your values, the ones you practice and that your child is observing day in and day out
- The particular culture in which you are raising your children
- The competition and pressure that you feel in your world every day
- Your temperament and the degree to which it fits with your child's, as well as your ability to withstand your child's reactions

If you are entitled, then you learn to measure and evaluate everything you receive. The nature and the value of what you receive trumps the fact that you were given something at all, and it casts a dark shadow on feeling gratitude. For the entitled adult, many things are not good enough. You might focus more on what you don't have rather than on what you do have. How can there be gratitude?

Some adults have a hard time demonstrating and feeling gratitude because they were raised to feel that it is most important to take care of themselves. You're not supposed to need anyone. Accepting help from someone else is seen as a flaw because you appear to be weak. Saying *"thank you"* indicates that you are needy and not good enough.

Raising children who lack gratitude, who may be entitled or enabled, hits you in that place of parental insecurity and uncertainty. You question yourself, your motives, and your priorities. Are you a "bad" parent? Are you spoiling your child?

It may help to realize that, in giving so much to your child, you are reacting to your own experiences of growing up and what you did or didn't get from your parents. You may think, *Am I depriving my kid?* when you say no to her. Or, *I will give her just what I didn't get but wanted so much.* Giving in or giving stuff to your child also speaks from that competitive place. *Is mine the only kid who doesn't have an iPod? Is mine the only four-year-old who won't be taking soccer skills classes?* And it speaks from that guilty place. *Since I couldn't make it home all week, I'll just buy her that American Girl doll she's been wanting to make up for it.* So many excuses for giving giving giving.

It is impossible to escape our culture, which whets our kids' appetites for material possessions, regardless of one's place in the socioeconomic stratosphere. Your kid sees it, and she wants it.

Not only does our culture of "gimme, gimme, gimme" undermine the cultivation of gratitude in our children, but our language supports it, too. In his article, "The Gift of Gratitude," Rabbi Harold Kushner points out the way in which our language leads us to believe that life is mostly about taking. We take a vacation, take a trip, take a drive, take an exam, take a drink, and when we are wiped out, we take a nap. Where is the giving part?

The Importance of Longing

I can't think of a parent who isn't driven to make her child happy. There's nothing quite as satisfying and heartwarming as seeing your child's face light up when she gets just exactly what she wants. We also know that not giving your child what she wants will make her unhappy, really unhappy. We're the ones who will have to suffer through the expression of that unhappiness. Because it's so easy to give in when our children are that disappointed, my advice is to just cover your ears! Kids today have a seemingly endless lust for stuff. We get mad at them for this, thinking that they don't appreciate what they already have. Just her wanting something more seems to set us off. We see her as ungrateful and unappreciative of what she does have.

Children are egocentric. Remember that infant, then the baby, whose needs were immediately met? That's the way it's supposed to be. It is natural for a child to long for things. From the developmental perspective, the young child doesn't have the capacity to see the big picture, to know how much she has; she just sees it, she likes it, and she wants it. The child doesn't yet have the concept of time and lacks the ability to conceptualize how many glass figurines she will have if you buy her just one more. She doesn't understand that there won't be enough cherries for Daddy if she eats them all up now. And finally, your child likely doesn't have very much experience in not getting what she wants. Why blame her for longing? It isn't her fault; she doesn't know any better.

While your older child is developmentally able to understand your reasons for saying no, she just may not like it. If her complaining usually leads to your giving in, she sure is going to keep on doing it. It just may work again!

In reality, it isn't the longing that is bad. It's how you deal with the longing that creates the problem. How can you expect a child to be appreciative of all she has when she has never known another way? If a child gets everything, she will miss out on one of life's great teachers—the feeling of longing. It is longing that waters the seeds of gratitude.

The energy invested in wanting is really powerful stuff. It is a great motivator. (That's why bribes usually work with children.) It's what propels a toddler to get up on those tiny little paddles and start to walk. It's the longing that motivates her to keep trying to say the word that will bring the cracker when you have no idea what she is saying. Longing propels effort, and next comes the growth. The trick is not to eliminate the longing by giving in. Longing is a good thing and needs to be seen that way.

The child's feeling of gratitude will be encouraged to grow in direct proportion to the amount of time and effort involved in attaining or obtaining what she wants. A child who is taught to wait, to work, to save for what she wants, who is allowed to long for something before getting it, and sometimes doesn't even get it at all, will surely feel appreciation when her desire is satisfied eventually. And at the same time, you will be teaching your child the crucial life skill of delaying gratification. Either she learns to live with the reality that you don't always get what you want, her desire is satisfied by something else, or she waits and works and finally gets the object of her desire. It's a valuable life lesson for sure.

Appreciation

Gratitude grows out of appreciation. Children whose desires are satisfied right away are deprived of the chance to cultivate an appreciation for what they do have. Getting one's wishes granted immediately doesn't make your child more grateful; often the converse is true. The sooner the child gets what she wants, the sooner she'll be done with it. That's the reason why the souvenir from the circus—a revolving flashlight that makes sparkles on the ceiling that your child couldn't live without—is relegated to the junk drawer even before the circus leaves town.

Not giving things or giving in, as previously stated, is often accompanied by an intolerable reaction. No one likes to see her child unhappy, to say nothing of having to deal with those outrageous outbursts. Dad walks into the house, exhausted and too late for dinner. Molly's joyful greeting is punctuated by her plea to stay up and watch the Westminster Dog Show with Dad. Reading Mom's fierce look that says, "Absolutely not," Dad says no, and Molly collapses to the floor, hurling accusations at Dad. "I hate you.

You always say no. I hate this family." Dad wonders if it just wouldn't have been easier to give in and have a pleasant night at home. Faulty thinking, to be sure. The learning has to begin somewhere. The lesson of the meltdown that doesn't lead to satisfaction is a good one. And it fuels the growth of appreciation when she does get what she wants. The added benefit is the lesson that meltdowns don't work. Molly will be especially thankful when Dad does invite her to watch the dog show on some future occasion.

A client once shared with me the story of her two young girls who were seldom allowed to eat sugary foods. On their first trip to a local amusement park, her husband encouraged her to let the girls have ice cream as part of their special outing. (She was a bit over the top in her restrictiveness, and Daddy knew it.) When Mommy suggested that they begin their visit with an ice cream cone, the girls were giddy with excitement. The touching part of her story (good or bad) was that the girls fell all over themselves thanking Mommy and expressing their appreciation. They ate their ice cream, relishing every lick and drip, and continued to thank their mommy throughout the whole day, recalling the yummy ice cream. While there are many lessons in her story, the point is that these girls definitely felt appreciation and gratitude. Given something they wanted but were seldom granted led to an explosion of genuine thankfulness felt and expressed.

Tips and Scripts for Allowing Appreciation to Grow

- **Allow your child to long for . . . something.** Whether it is a toy, getting her ears pierced, or being able to watch a particular movie, the longing will lead to appreciation when it finally comes to fruition. Tell her: *"It is really hard to wait when you want something so badly. I know you are going to love having pierced ears when you are twelve. You're just going to have to wait."* And say it like you have been there, done that yourself.

- **Consider giving your child less.** Instead of giving her the complete Miley Cyrus DVD set, give her just one or two. Children who have too much do not appreciate what they have—and it's not their fault that they have it all.

- **It is not reasonable to expect a child to feel appreciative of something she is accustomed always to having.** Things that come to your child via work will yield much greater appreciation. Remember Thomas Paine's famous quote, "That which we obtain too easily, we esteem too lightly." To that I add a big *Amen*!

- **Don't be quick to replace the broken toy.** Whether it's a battery-powered fire truck or an iPod, living without it or waiting for it to be fixed adds to the appreciation of having it when it is repaired or replaced.

- **Allow your child to not get something . . . ever.** This may sound heretical, but none of us gets everything we want, always. The disappointment in not getting something will lead to appreciation in getting something else. In addition, the lesson of learning to tolerate disappointment will be reinforced.

For the three-year-old:

"You really want that Thomas engine. I'm sorry, but I am not going to buy it for you. Let's go see if Daddy is ready to go to the park." Distraction still frequently works for the young child.

For the five-year-old:

"I know you are really disappointed that I won't buy you that spaceship Lego set. Learning that you don't always get what you want sure does sting, doesn't it?" Then share a story from your youth, and feel free to embellish!

For the eight-year-old:

"I know how much you want to see that movie, but Daddy and I feel strongly that this type of show is for older children. This is a decision that parents get to make, and I know it makes you really angry. Maybe I can help you find a different movie." Be prepared for an explosion of *"You are the meanest mom on the planet!"* Ignore the comment, knowing it will pass and that you have imparted an important lesson.

- **Allow your older child (at least six years of age) to work to get something—an item, a privilege, or an experience.** Hard work in order to get what you want leads to a feeling of appreciation. Working toward a goal not only increases the appreciation of its attainment, but it certainly demonstrates the positive power of work. *"I told you that I would spend $35 on your athletic shoes. The ones you want cost $15 more than that. Shall we figure out a way for you to earn that extra money so you can get the shoes you want?"*

- **It's okay to say no to your younger child.** Allowing your older child the privilege of going out on a school night, receiving a longed-for electronic gadget, or having an age-appropriate experience, and not doing the same for her younger brother is a good thing. You know that life is not fair, so stop trying to make it fair and stop sabotaging your younger child's experience of longing.

- **"When you are older . . . " is good for children of all ages to hear.** Changing your mind and adjusting the previously stated goal-age just to make your child happy not only cheapens the goal but erodes your credibility. Stick to your guns.

- **Teach your child to be gracious.** The child who receives a sweater from her grandma for her birthday that she would NEVER wear needs to be taught to show appreciation, even though she is really disappointed. It is a life lesson that sometimes we get gifts that we just don't like, but we still have to show our appreciation for the gift giver's effort. Tell your child, *"Grandma heard me say that you could use another sweater, so she thought she was being helpful by buying it for you for your birthday. Then she drove all the way across town to bring it to you. You need to tell her that you appreciate that she did that."*

Tips and Scripts for Cultivating the Expression of Gratitude

At some point in a child's life, the two paths of gratitude—expressing gratitude and feeling gratitude—will intersect. When this happens, the true feeling of gratitude is spontaneously expressed without your coaching. It is then that a parent knows she is on the right track. It takes conscious and deliberate work to get to that point.

You are your child's primary teacher. You must model, teach, and expect your child (from the age of one) to express appreciation. My husband tried his best with our children. The three twelve-year-olds, not very adventurous eaters, were admonished by him not to say one word of complaint and to eat and appear to enjoy the homemade vegetable lasagna I had slaved over, including the homemade pasta. At the end of dinner, Lucas piped up, *"Mom, thanks for making this dinner. You don't ever have to make it again."* Now that's a lesson in expressing gratitude!

- **Expect gratitude.** You are not likely to cultivate gratitude if you don't expect it. Teaching your child to say *"thank you"* starting when she is eighteen months old is the first step. *"Mommy gave you your cracker. This is where you say 'thank you' because I helped you. That makes me feel good."* It's a first lesson in expressing gratitude and a beginning lesson about empathy. (For an in-depth discussion of empathy, see chapter 2.) But if the "thank you" doesn't spring forth, let it go. Don't withhold and insist upon it. The lesson is still learned, and it will come one day soon.

- **Model expressing gratitude.** As with cultivating all character traits, modeling is the most potent way to teach an attitude of gratitude. Children are born copycats, and gratitude rubs off. Audibly, give thanks throughout your daily life, and let your child see you doing so. Say *"thank you"* at every opportunity to anyone who deserves it—the grocery checker, the mail carrier, your child's bus driver. Be animated in your appreciation. Send your own mother flowers on *your* birthday. Children internalize their parent models.

- **Don't forget family members.** Familiarity can breed inattention. Studies show that people, in general, are more likely to express gratitude to mere acquaintances and even strangers than they are to their own family and their peers. Even if she always clears the table, your child needs to hear you sharing your appreciation for what she is doing. *"Every time you clear the table, I feel lucky that you are my daughter. It really is a big help to our family."*

My mother shared with us children how her elderly British friend, Janet, always thanked her husband for a dinner out, finishing the meal with, *"Thank you, John, darling."* It became a family joke and a ritual that drove the point home. I still say, *"Thank you, John, darling"* to my husband, Ray, even when it was my credit card we used.

- **Pass on compliments to your child from someone else.** It is a subtle way of expressing gratitude and appreciation to your child. *"I ran into Mrs. Keith in the grocery store, and she mentioned what a polite guest you had been at her house last week. That made me proud."*

- **Be specific in your gratitude.** It isn't enough to simply say thanks. Let your child hear you describe not only what you are grateful to her for, but also why you are appreciative. It will begin to make sense to her. *"Thank you for folding the laundry. You really helped me get through my chores today."*

- **Enthusiastically accept gratitude when it is shown to you.** On those occasions that your child or anyone in front of your child thanks you, receive the words graciously, audibly saying, *"You are so welcome,"* and mean it.

- **Demonstrate being grateful through play-acting.** For younger kids, role-playing using puppets or stuffed animals can bring your message to life. When Elephant is grateful to Monkey for sharing her food, you can make her "ham it up" to show how grateful he is. And Monkey can share how good she feels to have been thanked. Even negative examples can drive home the point, too.

- **Count your blessings out loud and use the word "grateful."** Start your day with a show of appreciation about even the smallest things. *"It is such a beautiful day. I am so grateful that we have a bright sun shining."* Say it; don't just think it!

- **Express gratitude when it is not expected.** *"I am so grateful that I have you for a daughter"* or *"Every day you get yourself up and all dressed for school without any prodding from me. I really appreciate that."* It is these comments that have the greatest impact, especially on children.

- **Catch your child showing gratitude and praise it to the hills.** *"I heard you say thank you to Mrs. Bava when she dropped you off after school. That made me so proud of you."*

- **Notice and praise little acts of service.** Share your appreciation where most people normally would not. *"It was such a big help when you carried your own sweater in from the car."*

- **Do not demand thanks from your child.** Rather, show appreciation when it is given, or say, *"Grandma spent a long time looking for that sweater for you. It would make her feel so good if you were to thank her."* Demanding a verbal "thank you" should not become a war between you and your child. If it does, saying *"thank you"* will move from an expression of gratitude to a battlefield of control. The gratitude will be lost.

- **Write thank-you notes and expect your child to do the same.** Expressing appreciation for a gift or a kindness is the direct route to feeling grateful. Children who see their parents writing thank-you notes will know that it is not only a kind act but also a necessary chore. Part of receiving is giving thanks.

  Your expectation for an appropriate thank-you note will be based on your child's age and development. Children as young as three can scribble a thank-you picture. Four-year-olds can create a design above their dictated thank-you words. Five-year-olds can sign their names and maybe write a word or two. And so on. In order to receive and keep a gift, the note must be written and put in the mail.

- **Let your child give the gift of thanks.** Whether it's giving the birthday gift or carrying the hostess gift, your child can feel the pride and warmth that comes from being the giver.

- **Let your child see you showing appreciation for the small stuff and encourage her to do the same.** When your child says the spaghetti is yummy, Mommy can say, *"You can thank your dad for making it. I really love Dad's spaghetti, too."*

Tips and Scripts for Cultivating the Feelings of Gratitude

While behaving gratefully will lead to feeling grateful, sharing your own feelings of gratitude will spark your child's feelings of appreciation.

- **Stop. Pay attention. Look around you. Be grateful.** Let your child know it's in the small stuff that gratitude can be felt. So often it is in the pausing that we are able to breathe in all we appreciate. Your child will learn to pay closer attention to the small stuff, too. *"Oh my gosh, can you believe the color of the turning leaves today? They are the most gorgeous yellows and reds I have ever seen. I sure do love getting to see fall colors each year."*

- **Talk out loud about the things you appreciate.** Your children don't get to hear all that you are grateful for. Start sharing. When a driver lets you into her lane, take the time to say, *"That was so nice of that woman to let me in. I really appreciate her doing that during rush hour."*

- **Always express the reason for your gratitude.** Saying *"thank you"* is the first step. Describing why you feel the gratitude expands the child's awareness of the impact of her behavior on others. *"Thank you so much for cleaning up the family room. I am really tired today, and you saved me from having to do one more thing."*

- **Describe rather than demand a "thank you."** Tell your child what you did to make the goodness happen. *"Do you know what I did to make sure you had just the kind of jeans you wanted? First I called five different stores, and then I drove all the way to Cloverfield to buy them. It took me a long time, but I was glad to do it for you."* It is likely that your four-year-old will let loose with a genuine *"thank you,"* and your point will have been made without inducing any guilt or dishing out blame.

- **Create an atmosphere of gratitude in your home.** Put photos of your favorite vacation spots, special cards, and mementos on your refrigerator or family bulletin board. Remember them out loud! These will remind you and your children of things for which you are grateful.

- **Share your special loves.** My children grew up with a mom who openly adored Mother Nature's fireworks, often driving all over Los Angeles to find a magnificent Liquid Amber tree or a fully purple Jacaranda in the late spring. Now, each autumn I can anticipate a call from at least one of my children wanting to share tales of a beautiful fall scene he has just witnessed, knowing that I would have loved it, too. Not only are they pausing to appreciate the sight, but they are also sharing their gratitude with me, and that makes me so grateful for them. The phone call is an added bonus!

- **See the good in the not so good.** Try to look for the "silver lining," as the saying goes. There are those days when you'd just like to crawl back into bed, but your child is watching: *"It's raining so we can't go to the park. But we can watch old family videos. Yippee!"* Or, *"The power went out so you can't watch your favorite TV show. But now we have time to play an extra game of Old Maid."* There is always something good to appreciate. Find it!

- **Practice retrospective gratitude.** The good in things that don't feel so good at the moment can best be appreciated retrospectively. The power of the feeling (fear, anger, disappointment) blinds the child from seeing any good at that time. The practice of seeing the good after the fact will carry over to the moment in the future.

  Getting a shot from the doctor is a prime example. I've never met a child who exclaims, *"Oh goodie, I get to have a shot"* upon hearing the news of her upcoming physical examination that will include an inoculation. But explaining to her afterwards that, as much as it hurts, *"We are actually lucky that our doctors can give us shots with the medicine that keep us from getting really really sick"* will eventually sink in. The next shot may still elicit screams of protest, but your gentle reminder will likely lessen its intensity.

- **Create ritualized opportunities for saying thanks.** Around the family dinner table on Friday nights, before bed, on birthdays, and of course at the Thanksgiving table, create regular times when you each express your feelings of gratitude. A ritual of gratitude will reinforce its importance. Remember, behaving gratefully leads to feeling gratitude. It is an attitude.

  A client shared with me her idea for expressing appreciation as a build-up to Thanksgiving. Much like an Advent calendar, every day beginning November 1, each member of the family writes down on a strip of paper something for which she is grateful. It doesn't matter how small or silly. On Thanksgiving, the strips of gratitude are read. It is fun, often funny, and always meaningful as everyone's thanks are shared and discussed.

- **Create a system of surprise acknowledgement, aka "The Red Plate."** When my children were young, we had a ceramic red plate on which was written, "You Are Special Today." On any day and always unexpectedly, one of them would find her meal being served on the Red Plate. With great ceremony her dad or I got to describe why the child had gotten the Red Plate. It was a great way to offer praise and acknowledgment, and to "catch him/her doing the right thing."

You can use the Red Plate idea to "catch" your child expressing gratitude in a special way or to just invite her to for look on the sunny side of things. You can even call it your Sunny Side Plate, and have fun creating it at one of the ceramic painting studios that are all over the country.

- **Create a "Lucky List."** Let your child dictate this list to you, or, if she is old enough, encourage her to create her own list of things she feels lucky to have. You need to have a list, too. Don't be frustrated if your child's list begins with a long recitation of her favorite possessions. That is a start. With experience, as she grows, and in hearing other people's lists, hers will expand to include the more abstract and bigger things for which she is grateful. Be sure to have a regular time for making list entries as well as for list sharing. This is a good example of behaving yourself into feeling.

- **Help your child learn to delay gratification.** One of the peaks that must be scaled in order to grow up is tolerating not getting what you want at the moment of wanting. This lesson can begin with a child as young as six months. When a parent immediately meets the child's needs, the child doesn't learn to wait. Whether she needs to wait two minutes, an hour, or until Christmas, it is a crucial lesson of growing up. *"You really want that Princess Leia action figure. It is so hard to wait to get something. Let's put it on your 'wish list' and maybe you will get it for your birthday."* Just think how grateful she will be when she finally gets what she wants. Or maybe she will have changed her mind by then. Not getting what you want right away feeds the feeling of appreciation if and when you do get it.

- **Find ways to satisfy a material desire other than by owning the object.** Young children are taught by your example that they get to have what they want. Instead, visit your friend who has the trampoline your daughter may want to own. Tell her, *"We can enjoy the trampoline at*

Elizabeth's house whenever we want." Or say, *"I heard about a great new book you might enjoy. Let's go to the library and see if we can find it to borrow."*

- **Emphasize the having and move your child's focus away from the not having.** This is very much like maintaining an attitude that the glass is half full as opposed to half empty. It is necessary to validate and acknowledge the child's sad feelings but important not to dwell on them. Repeatedly pointing out what she does have trains the mind's eye to look for the good. Model doing the same in your daily life: *"I sure am disappointed that I didn't get to go to that movie last night, but I had a fun time at home watching the DVD."*

- **Try going without.** Gratitude for what you have springs forth from not having. Unplug the computer for a week and see how grateful your child feels when she gets it back. A little sacrifice helps her to appreciate what she has and takes for granted. Not only will she be grateful but she might become a little humble too, and she might even learn that she doesn't need quite as much as she thought she did!

- **Discuss with your child (age five and up) the difference between wanting and needing.** Wanting is okay, but it's important to note that we don't always get what we want. In fact, we don't need everything we want. Model her reality yourself. *"I really like those shoes, but I just don't need another pair of red flats."*

- **Explore different points of view.** With your four-year-old or older child, look at situations that require gratitude from the different players' points of view—the giver, the receiver, the sibling who didn't receive, and the like. The ability to understand how it feels to receive gratitude grows along with the development of empathy.

"Did you see how pleased Auntie Barbara looked when you thanked her for the sweater? I know it wasn't your favorite gift, but you made her feel so good by thanking her as if it were."

"It is so hard not to be the birthday girl. You could see how sad your sister was that you were getting all the gifts. That's a tough lesson to learn, isn't it? She will really be happy when it's her birthday."

How We Sabotage the Cultivation of Gratitude

Some of the ways in which parents respond to children's desire for stuff actually sabotages the child's expression and feeling of gratitude. Chewing out your seemingly unappreciative child, berating her, or putting her down always backfires. It leaves a child feeling angry and defensive. The whole point is lost, as your child's energy will go into defending herself against what she perceives as an attack on her character. Here are some of the ways that we are unwitting saboteurs of gratitude:

- **Meeting all her needs.** Instead of jumping at the chance to meet your child's every request (which is seldom followed by a "thank you"), don't automatically or always comply. Inform your child that she is able to get her own water or blanket. You can add, *"Showing appreciation for my help makes me want to help you."*
- **Negative associations.** Sometimes a parent yells at the child who is not showing the gratitude she feels she is owed. When a parent says, *"You ought to be grateful for all the time I spent with you,"* the child might easily grow to associate expressing gratitude with being yelled at.
- **Reverse envy.** Guilting a child into feeling grateful usually backfires. *"You ought to be grateful. There are children who have no toys at all."* Remember, the child who always gets doesn't know any better. She has never had to go without, so how should she know what that feels like?
- **Rhetorical questions.** My parents used to say, *"Don't you know there are children who are starving in Africa?"* when we balked at eating our meals. The answer: *"No. I don't really know about starving children."*

"That American Girl doll costs $80. Do you have any idea how much money that is?" The answer: *"No. I am just learning the value of money, and cognitively I am just beginning to understand quantity. Is $80 a lot?"*

"You have already seen two movies this month. Do you know that some children don't even see one movie in a year?" The answer: *"No. All of my friends see more than one movie in a year."*

"Don't you think you have enough Legos?" The answer: *"You can never have enough Legos."* And you hope that your rhetorical question will lead to your child's epiphany. *"Gee, Mom, you're right. I have more than enough Legos, and they are really expensive. And some poor kids probably have no Legos at all because their parents are spending all their money on food and rent and clothing. Whatever was I thinking? I really should be grateful for all I have."* (Dream on!)

- **Misusing logic and reason.** Of course we all think our child is "gifted," and so we explain our logic, as if she is going to get it:

  "You have so many action figures, more than any one child can possibly use. Why don't you just give your brother one or two?" The child's answer: *"No, I don't! I need every one of these figures, and I am not going to share one of them."*

  "If you stay up and watch this DVD, you'll be really tired in the morning and you won't be able to concentrate at school, you'll lose focus and you won't learn anything all day." The child's answer: *"No, I won't!"* A child's desire usually overrides her ability to listen to logic or reason. She wants what she wants, and she is going to try her best to get it.

- **Imposing guilt.** *"I work my fingers to the bone for you every day, and where's my thanks?"* Humiliation isn't a particularly powerful or healthy form of teaching. Genuine gratitude grows out of genuine expressions of feeling.
- **Lecturing.** Your child will turn a deaf ear to your lectures in the same way you tuned out your parents' lectures. Not only will your child ignore you, but your apparent lack of understanding for her position will drive you two apart. Save your breath.

Sowing the Seeds of Gratitude by Giving

Many of the character traits parents hope to cultivate in their children go together, kind of like peas and carrots (to quote *Forrest Gump*). So it is with kindness and gratitude. Behaving in considerate ways, sharing with others, practicing those random acts of kindness—being "other oriented"—feeds a person's feelings of gratitude. (See chapter 9, p. 199, for a discussion of other-orientation.) Conversely, it is easier to be kind and to share if you live a life that is filled with gratitude.

- **Share with others.** Make sharing with others a regular habit. Children need to learn that there is a world out there beyond themselves and their immediate family.

  ○ When you are baking, make an extra loaf of banana bread and share it with your local fire fighters.
  ○ Model regularly cleaning out your closets and drawers (bedrooms, kitchens, linens closets) to share with others.
  ○ Buy extra food items to give to your local food banks.
  ○ Drop coins into the containers at your local grocery store and other businesses.

  Giving to others, demonstrating kindness, when it isn't required is a powerful experience. Let your child begin to feel it. Sometimes it is better than receiving. And the good feeling lasts a lot longer.
- **Share with others for no reason at all.** Giving those extra fresh vegetables from your garden to a neighbor "just because" is the ultimate form of giving. There is no expectation for anything in return.

  My mother-in-law used to show up with a gift for me "just for instance," she would say. That act taught me to do the same for others, and it gave me tremendous pleasure too. How much I appreciate her kindness, especially now that she is gone.
- **Help your child to remember relatives' and friends' birthdays and other occasions.** Children need to learn to think about occasions celebrated by others. While the effort to make the call or create the card may elicit some complaints and whining, the recipients' gratitude easily extinguishes those flames. There is goodness in remembering and in giving.
- **Share the joy you get by giving.** The thrill derived from giving a gift, and seeing the recipient's face light up, is something that

grows in time. As your child opens a gift say, *"I love to watch you open a gift. It feels so good to give something I think you will like."*

- **In the face of your child's disappointment, focus on others.** When your her cancels her playdate because of illness, most parents will assuage the disappointment with a replacement activity. Instead, help your child to make the sick friend a get-well card or bake her some cookies. Kindness is powerful medicine.
- **Let your child see you practicing random acts of kindness.** Allow a car to cut in front of you in line, put a quarter in someone else's parking meter, hold the door for a man with an armful of groceries. Then share the good feeling you have in doing so and express your gratitude for being able to help someone else. *"It feels so good to do a good deed for someone else when he doesn't even expect it!"* And, *"Can you imagine how surprised she will be when she finds the cake on her doorstep? I love being the 'good fairy.'"*

Gratitude is one of those traits that grow slowly, right along with your child. All that you do to cultivate appreciation will certainly serve as the fertilizer that helps it to blossom. But the true bounty of your work will come when your child is an adult—when she has to fend for herself, pay her own bills, keep her own house, and work to make things happen. In fact, many a parent will agree that it wasn't until she became a parent herself that she truly appreciated all that her parents did for her. Be patient. The gratitude is developing.

❖

CHAPTER NINE

"Gimme, Gimme, Gimme!"

Eliminating Spoilage in Your Child

At some point, most parents feel that their child is a bottomless pit—often that happens when he is around six or seven years old. He is insatiable, wants everything he sees or hears about and anything that someone else has. He's the nightmare child, the brat, the one that's spoiled to the core—the one you vowed you would never have. But having a spoiled child isn't the only problem you worry about when this trait rears its ugly head. You worry about what kind of adult this child will grow up to be. You fear that he will:

- not know the value of money
- be grossly materialistic
- act as if he is entitled
- lack motivation
- be unappreciative
- lack gratitude

You're not wrong to worry that your spoiled child will possess these characteristics long term. A caring parent should worry. These are some of the traits of a full-blown brat. And we are living in the midst of an entitlement epidemic, characterized by a "gimme, gimme, gimme" philosophy, so it's not unrealistic to think the problem will get bigger if it goes unchecked.

It is not just a problem of the rich, nor is it just about money. These worries plague parents across a wide range of incomes. Solidly middle-class families struggle with many of the same issues as more affluent families do. All are equally vulnerable to the causes and ills of spoilage.

Here's the truth of the matter: Spoiling your child has more to do with parents than with children. After all, your child wasn't born spoiled, was he? It's not his fault. The good news is that while you may be the root of the problem, you also hold the key to the cure.

Parenting Today

While the biology of parenting hasn't changed over the years, despite advanced reproductive technologies (1 ovum + 1 sperm still = baby) the sociology and the act of parenting certainly have changed. Thirty years ago, people had babies, asked their parents what to do, flew by the seat of their pants, and voila! Soon they had grown children.

Not anymore. These days, many men and women are becoming parents at much older ages. Often they begin having children well after they have spent years advancing their careers. They have had plenty of time to shape their dreams and their ideas about family, too. When the time comes, they take the same measured, deliberate, well-researched approach to parenting as they did with their professional lives. They know what they want for themselves, and they know what they want for their children. Anyone standing in their path should look out because they are on a path to get it! Parenting is the new arena in which these accomplished adults are prepared to compete as aggressively as they do in the workforce. They are determined to make sure that their offspring stay on top of the heap. They view this as their job.

As someone who guides parents through the school placement process, I all too often meet parents who say, "I want my child to go to the preschool that will get him into the best elementary school and then into the best high school, and into the best college." Talk about having goals!

Can you imagine what it is like for that firstborn child? That "practice child" is the recipient of the accumulated aspirations of his two parents plus the aspirations of his parents' parents (i.e. his grandparents). All want the absolute best for this child, whatever that is. Observing what their friends are doing with their children just feeds the frenzy, as does being the target of advertisers who overwhelm them with an endless barrage of products and possibilities. Soon they want it all. They have drunk the Kool Aid and in so doing have watered the seeds from which spoilage sprouts.

The More Things Change . . .

Every generation of parents thinks its kids are spoiled. The "Gimmes" isn't a new problem. But it does seem as if the spoilage has intensified with this generation. More people have more money than ever before. Remember when having a million dollars was newsworthy? Inflation and the state of the economy aside, there sure are more millionaires—even billionaires— today than there were when I was a child. And there is a new acceptance of showing one's wealth. Thanks to the media and the Internet, we are plugged into what everyone is doing, buying, wearing, and spending. Adults and children now see privilege in ways that were previously never possible. Who knew? Naturally, the goals we set for ourselves and our children are shaped by all this information.

Two and three generations ago children didn't receive luxury cars from their parents, let alone on their sixteenth birthdays. They hadn't been to Ha- waii, the Caribbean, or Mexico before the age of five, either. Parents didn't outsource the role of teaching their kids to pitch a baseball, or hire help to get lice out of their children's hair, or to choose a Christmas tree for their living room, or to do the holiday shopping. Three generations ago, young parents actually worked hard to make ends meet. Every penny really did count.

The media is creating a younger and younger consumer culture as well, which only adds to the "Gimme Factor." (That's what advertisers love!) Not only do your children hound you to have what they see on TV, but they are made to believe they are entitled to have it: "Go tell Mommy and Daddy that you want the Glow-in-the Dark Devil Pen Set." Our children are getting the message that what is important in life is the accumulation of stuff. They are being led to believe that life is about the possession of things, not necessarily about experiences, feelings, and interactions.

To top it off, nothing that one buys lasts very long anymore. Styles and fads come and go quickly, necessitating the continual purchase of new and improved items. This applies to everything from electronic equipment, appliances, and clothes to sporting goods, lotions, and potions. The day after you pay for your new digital camera you can no longer buy a battery for that model because it's obsolete. Such impermanence breeds further need and greed.

Values

The last time I looked, there were still twenty-four hours in a day. But another of the differences in today's world is that there just doesn't seem to be enough time for anything, but especially for families to be together. Children are so programmed and scheduled, parents are juggling so many balls, that it's a race to get to bed in order to wake up and start all over again the next day. And with so little time to spend with their children, parents make up for their absence by giving them whatever it is that will make them happy. The thinking is: *I have so little time with my son. I want the time we have together to be pleasant, not spent listening to him whine or cry. So I'll give him what he wants.* They give presents instead of their presence.

When time is of the essence, the first thing to go is family time. You have to take one more phone call; you must go into the office on Saturday morning; you are called into a last-minute meeting that makes you late for dinner, if you can even get home at all. Children are seeing less of their parents, the very people from whom they receive the values they will take into adulthood.

Many parents aren't certain about the values that they most want to instill in their children. Some haven't even initiated this important discussion. Much like a last will and testament for your physical belongings, an ethical will describes the legacy you want to leave your children—the values that you cherish, the lessons you have learned, the insights gleaned by life experience. If early on you and your spouse take the time together to articulate the specific values you intend to impart to your children as they grow, you will have a head start in achieving that goal.

THE BEST INHERITANCE OF ALL

An "ethical will," also known as a legacy statement, dates back to the Old Testament story of Jacob who was said to have bestowed a blessing on each of his twelve children before he died. It is not a legal document that is officially recorded. Rather, an ethical will is a text of the values you want to pass on to your progeny, written in any way you choose, from creating a list to writing descriptive prose. Not just for those who anticipate death, the writing of an ethical will is used by young and old adults alike to focus on what matters to them, the result of which can be living one's life more deliberately. (See the website www.ethicalwill.com for more information and examples of ethical wills.)

Values aren't passed on in just one sitting. They are transmitted through repeated interactions over many years. In the absence of family time, children end up developing their own values, ones they have absorbed from the activities in which they regularly participate and which are based on those of other children, the media, the Internet—and often related to material objects as opposed to meaningful ideas.

While materialism is certainly not a new phenomenon, it used to be accompanied by a strong value system. Children were able to see that value system in action when they interacted with their parents daily and participated in an exchange of thoughts around the dinner table. It then became their own value system. Even some of the world's wealthiest people managed to raise children who were not spoiled, who had a strong work ethic because of this routine and sustained interaction. But the combination of family values and religious beliefs that used to influence children has since been diluted, if not eliminated, in many families. Extended families are no longer living together. Gone are the "old, wise ones" who reminded us of our roots and of the things that are truly important. And where are these wise ones now? They're in rest homes and retirement communities, segregated from our children and robbed of the valuable role they once played in all of our lives.

In the absence of family time and the influence of our elders, most children spend a tremendous amount of time in front of screens of all kinds: TV and movie screens, computer screens, phone and BlackBerry screens, iPod screens, car DVD screens, video game screens, and more! While it is tempt-ing to review the content children are being exposed to on such screens, it is not the content that worries me. It is what watching these screens prevents your children from experiencing that concerns me. Edward Hallowell of the Harvard Medical Schools said, "Face to face communication is the key to what counts in life, from a happy family to physical health and longev-ity." Screen time tends to deny your children the conversations, interactions, and activities that shape the kind of people they will become. It takes them away from absorbing the values that you believe are essential to model and reinforce.

What About Money?

Money alone is not at the root of spoilage, but it certainly plays a role. I am often asked how children learn the value of money. The most direct answer is that children take their cues in this regard from observing you and your money habits, and from listening to what you say to others (both in person and on the phone). Often you are not even aware of how you're influencing your child's money values.

Each of us has our own ideas on the subject. Those attitudes were shaped by a variety of experiences, the most dominant of which was our own parents' attitudes and habits with money. Your father's voice may echo in your head as you ponder a purchase: "What do you think, money grows on trees?"

Similarly, your children will adopt or reject your money values, but they will not ignore them. Your behavior around money is that important. If you admonish your child for wanting another Lego set, and you come home with yet another purse or golf club, he will be hard pressed to accept your reasoning as valid.

Many people actually feel it is easier to talk to children about sex than about money. That's how uncomfortable it might be for you. In my par-enting groups, when I ask how many people knew while they were in el-ementary school how much their parents had spent on a car or a house, it is surprising how few hands go up. Asked who knew how much their parents earned, almost no hands go up. Parents just don't talk to kids about money and expenses except when they are admonishing them.

I am not advocating that you print your latest tax return and hand it to your child. But I am suggesting that you give some thought to talking to your child about money. The ostrich school of economics just doesn't work. Not talking about money robs your child of the opportunity to learn what things costs, the value of money, and the skills he will need to manage money later on.

Tips and Scripts for Talking About Money

- **Explore and examine your own money attitudes.** Make sure that the money values you are communicating to your child match your own behavior. Hypocrisy undermines your credibility.

- **Be prepared to teach and talk about money.** The following is a quote my husband gave me from an airline magazine, author unknown: "The best time to start talking to your kids about money is when they will no longer eat it." I agree!

- **Don't confuse talking about money with lecturing about money.** Your child will tune out your money sermons just as fast as you tuned out your father's. *"What do you think I am made of? Money?"* won't work for your child, either.

- **Real conversations and explanations with your children build trust.** Inclusive conversations show your child that you respect his ability to learn. You are setting the stage for future valuable discussions in which you want your child to ask your sage advice.

- **Let your child sort money.** The more familiarity your child has with real money, the more he will understand it. Let your child put your penny collection into paper rolls to take to the bank, be the banker in Monopoly, and count the change on your dresser or line it up according to size. It's all useful experience.

- **Use real money for your transactions.** Children today rarely see a parent using green money; they seldom see checks anymore, either. Today we use credit cards for everything. In order to learn about money, kids need to see it, all the denominations, the counting, the change received.

- **Include your child in your bill paying beginning when he is seven years old.** Children this age understand quantity; younger children just hear numbers big and small. How will your child have a context for understanding about cost unless he starts hearing how much things cost? Tell him: *"I am paying the water and power bills. Did you know that we spent $150 on water over the last two months? We pay for the water we use in the bathroom and kitchen and to water the garden."* And *"That tank of gas cost us $52,"* or *"My grocery bill was $120, Each month I send the building owner a check for $2,000 to pay for our house."*

- **Explain your request for privacy.** Parents fear that their child will run out and exclaim to the first available listener how much you pay each month for the car. You are not wrong to worry! For this reason it is a good idea to say: *"I am sharing with you the cost of our car payment because I want you to learn about money and what things cost. But that information is private, just for our family. I trust you not to talk about it with anyone outside our family. It is our private business."*

- **Show your child that you put money into your savings.** To encourage him to do the same, explain that each month you put what you can, no matter how small, into your savings account. Then take the time to explain what it might be used for: a house repair, a vacation, his education, a "rainy day."

- **Children need to know that you make choices about how you spend your money.** Avoid saying, *We can't afford that.* In reality, most of the things that your child requests you actually can afford. You just don't choose to spend your money on them. Rather than saying, *"That's too expensive"* try: *"I don't choose to spend money on that."* Or, *"That is more money than I want to spend on a squirt gun."* You do have a choice and so will he when it's his money to spend. As the child gets older and has his own spending money, offering him the chance to buy what he wants with his own money brings the lesson home. It's easy to spend someone else's hard-earned cash but not so easy to spend your own. It is a choice.

- **Show how you make your choices.** When in the grocery store, narrate why you are choosing to buy a particular brand or size item. Children can learn that the cereal with the toy in the box costs more than the one without (and the toy is a piece of junk!). Organic food costs more because more effort went into producing it. The bigger size costs only a bit more but has way more product, or it has a lot more than you need and it's a waste.

- **Teach your child about budgets.** Share with your child the balance you create between the luxuries your budget affords and unnecessary excess. The child learns this lesson and others about budgets from you. Take the time to talk about it with specific examples: *"Every month I make sure I set aside some money from my check for special things we all can enjoy. That is a part of savings."* My children have copied the lesson they learned from my husband and me. We were dirt-poor when we were first married and we lived not far from the ocean, so we had a "Vacation Account." Every time we had a day at the beach (which cost us nothing), we each put a certain (rather small) amount into that account, until we had saved enough to go on a weekend vacation.

Allowances

When children are old enough to understand quantity (around the age of seven), they ought to have an allowance. It is through having his own money that the child learns three valuable lessons: how to be responsible, how to manage money, and the value of money.

There are many different systems for allowances, and everyone has something to say about which is good and which isn't. The only thing about which most people agree is the value in having an allowance.

The three allowance systems among which most families choose are as follows:

Allowance: The parents as the breadwinners share a certain amount of money with their child each week. Hence the word "allowance." He is allowed to have this money. No jobs or responsibilities are attached. Allowance cannot be withheld.

Wages (allowance for work): The child has certain specific daily and/or weekly jobs for each of which he is paid a predetermined amount every week when the chore is completed. (See chapter 4, p. 84, for a discussion about personal and community responsibilities.) These chores are not personal responsibilities, the ones that everyone does for himself. Rather, they are chores that contribute to the smooth running of the family and the household that someone has to do. The amount of the total wage is determined by the number of jobs completed each week. It can vary. The child keeps track of his jobs/wages earned with a chart hung in a public place.

If your goal in having an allowance is to teach about work and earnings, then you have to pay the child for something you would like him to do for the whole family. There are those who believe children should not be paid for their family work contributions; they should do it because everyone does something. This system would not be for them.

CHORE	Monday	Tuesday	Wednesday	Thursday	Friday	Saturday	Sunday
Set the table $0.50							
Empty Dishwasher $0.50							
Sort Laundry $0.50							
Empty All Small Trash Cans $0.50							
Clean Craft Area $0.25							
Total Earned: $ _____							

Chore Chart for Delia
Week of December 7, 2009

Allowance Plus Wages: The child receives a very small allowance as a base pay. It is small enough that he will want more money ($2 per week, for example) and will, therefore, subscribe to work for wages to augment his allowance, through his weekly assigned chores.

I am a fan of either **Wages** or **Allowance Plus Wages**. The child learns the value of real work when he is paid real money for doing it, and it can be a very satisfying and fulfilling experience for him. After all, that is how our economy works.

Tips for Implementing an Allowance System

- **Your child has to want to have money in order for an allow-ance system to work.** You will know when it is time. He will start asking about money and about how much things cost. If you are too quick to grant requests for things or for cash to buy things he wants, you will impede the growth of the desire.

- **Do not be quick to hand out money.** For an allowance to have meaning, the child ought not to be handed money by each relative as he walks through the door. Nor should he be able to pick up loose change all over the house and call it his own.

- **Be committed to following through consistently on the system, week after week.** If you are not prepared, your system will fail.

- **The allowance belongs to the child.** It cannot be removed as pun-ishment. Once it is his, it is his.

- **The amount of allowance is determined by the amount of money parents want their child to have at the end of the month.** This amount will change as your child gets older and needs/wants more money. Remember, the child might have three chores, each of which he completes five (or maybe seven) days a week. If he earns $.25 per job, that's $3.75 per week. That might be a lot of money for a seven-year-old.

It will not surprise you to learn that there are differing opinions on how much a child should earn per week. And with the ups and downs in the economy, what once worked may no longer be ap-propriate for your family. Some say one dollar per year of age, giv-ing the six-year-old $6 a week. To my mind, that is too much for children under twelve, the age at which desire and spending often kick up a notch. As there are no rules about this, it will depend upon your child, his needs, wants, and habits, and yours, too. The child who is a serious baseball card collector might need to have more. Remember, it is also about learning to handle money, working for what you want, and making choices. Here are some rough guide-lines:

- For six- and seven-year-olds: base pay of $2; total of $5 a week
- For eight- and nine-year-olds: base pay of $3; total of $7 a week
- For ten- and eleven-year-olds: base pay of $4; total of $8 a week

- **Pay your children (the younger ones) in coins.** Coinage makes it feel like you have more and encourages counting (good math practice).

- **Help your child as young as six to open a bank account.** Experiences with real bank accounts are life lessons that teach responsibility and follow-through. Be prepared to drive your child to make deposits. It is his job to make the deposit; it is yours to be the taxi. A few banks (but not many, unfortunately) still offer bankbooks, a great way to keep track of one's deposits and balance.

- **Debit cards are good ideas for middle/high school children; credit cards are not.** It is too easy to spend money with a credit card. The first step is the debit card. Your child will need to watch the balance and pay for overdraft charges. Lost cards lead to bye-bye debit cards.

- **As the child gets older, suggest possible expenditures.** *"Your father's birthday is coming up. Would you like me to take you to the 99 Cent Store to look for a gift?"* (Then prepare dad for the new car window squeegee he is about to get that Michael paid for with his own money!) Your child will be so proud.

- **Suggest that your child fulfill his desires with his own money.** When your child wants expensive athletic shoes, tell him what you will spend and that he can use his own money to cover the rest. It's his choice.

- **Your younger child can look forward to receiving an allowance when he is old enough.** Just because the older child receives an allowance doesn't mean the younger sibling gets to have one, too. Looking forward to things you get when you are older is a good thing.

- **Create jobs for your child to do.** Doing so will require that you not do particular chores, or you will need to ask the household help not to do that job. The chore has to have true meaning. And once accomplished, the parent cannot "do it over" If it isn't up to your reasonable standard, help your child to do it better.

- **Limit your funding.** As your child gets older, he must begin to pay for things you have funded in the past. Being able to afford a movie with his friends is motivation to do his jobs. This will require you stepping back and tolerating a tremendous protest when you are no longer funding all of his activities and treats.

- **Allowance money (and all money that comes in) gets divided into three banks: Spending, Saving, and Sharing.** You and your child can decide for what he is saving (or agree it is "to be determined"). Explain to your child how you try to put money in savings so that you can afford things as they come up.

- **Have some limits on spending.** If it is not okay for your child to spend his money on candy, that can be your rule. Your child has freedom within your license. Beware of too many rules, however. It is through irresponsible spending that your child learns to be responsible and make meaningful choices.

- **Decide with your child to what charity he will give his sharing money.** Hopefully, your child has seen how you share with various charities some of the money you earn. It is incumbent upon all of us to help take care of others and support causes that are meaningful to us.

- **Allow your child to suffer the consequences of his misspending.** *"Yes, I know you wish you hadn't spent all your money on that flashlight at the circus. Next time you will think twice before making your decision."*

What's a Parent to Do?

It is a heady responsibility indeed to be the single most important influence in a child's life as he passes through his elementary-school years. In accepting that role, there is much you can do to avoid and even eliminate the spoilage in your child. I didn't say it was easy, because it isn't. But it can be done.

Tips and Scripts for Eliminating Spoilage

- **Be with your child.** Your values will rub off on your child if you spend time with him. Just being in the same room doesn't count. Being with your child meanings interacting, talking, and experiencing life together.

- **Deliberate, conscious interactions create a trusting, respectful relationship.** Make sure they happen.

- **Don't let shopping or a visit to the mall be the time you spend with your child.** The association with getting you and getting stuff is obvious.

- **You are not your child's friend.** Your job is to be your child's parent. Sometimes that means making unpopular decisions and your child will "hate" you. It will pass—within the hour or the day.

- **Set clear, firm, consistent boundaries and limits for your child.** Parents help children to develop self-management skills, to learn to tolerate frustration and disappointment, and to tolerate inevitable unhappiness by setting limits and sticking to them. Spoiled children lack these skills.

- **Implement logical consequences for limit violations.** Be sure to follow through; don't issue hollow threats. Teaching a child that in choosing his behavior (a limit violation) he also chooses a consequence is good medicine for spoilage and for eliminating bratty behavior.

- **Say no.** Your child is not deprived. Whether it is a purchase or a permission, he can live without it. Children who are spoiled think they cannot.

- **Be cognizant of the difference between pleasing and loving your child.** Often, loving your child means not pleasing him. Ask yourself if you love your child enough to tolerate his often-outrageous expressions of unhappiness. *"I know you are really angry that I won't let you stay up and watch that program. Let me know when you are done being angry and we can talk about it."*

- **Giving things or giving in do not equate with loving your child.** Love is not measured in material ways. In response to your child's claim that you don't love him when you won't buy him the Wii, say, *"I always love you, even when you say mean things to me when I won't buy you what you want."*

- **Learn to distinguish between what your child wants and what he needs.** To a child who really wants something, all his desires become needs. He is desperate. Ignore it. He'll get over it. Hours from now you can remind him that it wasn't such an immediate need. *"Remember this morning when you thought you couldn't live without going to the game? Looks like you did just fine. I am glad you're learning that you really can live without the things you thought you would die without."*

  Children to whom things come too readily or too easily grow to believe that the world owes them.

- **Allow your child to learn to delay gratification.** When a desire develops, it has a crazy immediacy for the child. A crucial life lesson is learning to wait, to postpone, or even not to get it at all. Take every opportunity to delay fulfilling a need, be it lunch, a trip to the baseball card store, or a craved acquisition. (The appropriate responses to the above are: *"I'll be happy to make you lunch in ten minutes, when I am done with my work,"* and *"Yes, we will go to the card store. I will take you this afternoon, after I have finished helping your brother,"* and *"That's a great item to put on your birthday list. Please write it down for me and leave it on my desk."*)

- **Allow your child to struggle.** True growth and learning come from hard work and lead to self-reliance. (For more information on self-reliance, see chapter 7.) Children who are spoiled are unable to help themselves. Refrain from quickly stepping in when your child is struggling with a project, an assignment, or a task of any kind. If you must, help him to help himself. *"Hmmm. That looks really hard. Tell me what your idea was for doing the edge of the puzzle."* Often just showing an interest or being there for support is all the encouragement your child may need to keep trying.

- **Encourage your child to work for something that he wants.** When things come too easily to a child, he develops a feeling of entitlement. Instead of giving in or saying no, try *"Let's see how you might make the money to buy that video game."*

- **Teach the power of work.** Model, insist, and allow your child to work. Children need work experiences in order to develop the sense that achievement is a function of their own efforts. Some work is for plain old accomplishment and some is for gain (allowance).

- **Demonstrate gratitude often.** The child who lives with people who practice gratitude in action will have a head start on being grateful himself. (See chapter 8.)

- **Model taking initiative yourself.** Instead of calling for your spouse to change the light bulb, open the wine, or take out the trash, do it yourself. Children need to see their parents doing real housework. In an age of privilege, too many children see their parents directing others to do their work. How will your child learn to clean up his messes if he never sees you taking care of yours? He will grow up to expect that others should do his work. That is the height of spoilage.

- **Beware of bribery.** It is not a healthy form of child rearing. Bribery makes it difficult for a child to cultivate intrinsic motivation or even to make the "right" decisions in the absence of external direction. It also teaches a child to associate achievement with getting paid as opposed to self-satisfaction. *"I'll give you $10 for every A you earn"* and *"I'll pay you for every goal you get in the soccer game"* are promises the spoiled child has heard.

- **Be careful not to give a lot of "freebies."** It is the direct route to spoilage. When the occasional surprise gift becomes the expectation—*"What did you bring me?"*—that's when you know it's time to stop the freebies. The only exceptions may be for essentials, such as clothing.

- **Don't assuage your guilt by giving gifts.** If you haven't spent the time you would like to spend with your child, give yourself to your child (instead of some other gift) by carving out some special time with him. When you come home from a trip, you are the present your child seeks. The object you bring may soothe your guilt, but it also spoils your child and teaches him to expect a gift every time you go out of town.

- **Give gifts on gift-giving occasions.** After the age of four, children need to learn that getting stuff doesn't just happen continually. There are certain times when gifts are given; the days of *"I bought this for you because I knew you would like it"* need to stop or else the child will continue to expect and feel he is owed presents.

- **Experiences make the most memorable gifts.** A fishing trip, tickets to a live performance, a camp-out in the backyard make especially wonderful gifts. Giving isn't just about stuff.

- **Encourage grandparents and family members to give the gift of an experience.** Your child will remember the excursion to the county fair with Grandpa long after he has forgotten what toy he received for his birthday.

- **Give "choosements."** Zachary, the son of a client, created the name for this category of gift when his mother gave him the choice of a Chanukah gift or a coupon for an experience with her. I had shared with her parenting class the idea of creating a treasure chest of coupons for special experiences with a parent: a cuddle with Mommy in her bed while watching a movie together; a special cooking day with Daddy; a hike in the hills with just Mom and Dad (no sibling), and the like. The child can dip into the Choosements Chest as a gift or even as a reward. A cure for spoilage is learning that intangibles can be the most special gifts.

- **Your child is part of a team.** Your child is part of the family, no matter what the configuration. The spoiled child—the brat—puts himself first—or at least he has been led to assume that position. Make the well-being of the whole family (the whole class, the whole team) more important than the happiness of one member.

- **Emphasize and praise cooperation.** Choosing a "choosement" is a perfect reward for an unusual show of cooperation.

- **Don't fall prey to the plea "But everyone has one."** This approach feeds into your own feelings of competition and wanting to make sure your child is keeping up with the pack. You are the parent; you get to do what you think is right for your family.

Other-Orientation

Spoiled children see themselves at the center of your universe. In reality, at one point they really were, especially if they're the firstborn. But as soon as your child turns two, he needs to be plucked out of the center and put along the side to take his place with everyone else. Providing a value structure that takes your child out of the center of the universe teaches him the sad truth that the world doesn't revolve around him.

Research has shown that children who grow up in households where other-orientation (consideration of others) and philanthropy are habits will take these same values with them into adulthood. As discussed in the chapter on cultivating gratitude, parents are put off by their child's selfishness and his lack of awareness that there are people in the world who are far less fortunate than he. But your child knows only the world he knows. It is your job as a parent not only to expose your child (in an age-appropriate manner) to the different ways that people live but also to cultivate the habit of sharing with others, regardless of their circumstance. Sooner or later your child will be old enough to understand that the vast majority of the world does not enjoy the privileges that we do. Children need to be taught philanthropy. It is unquestionably an antidote to spoilage. Sharing what you have and giving your time to help others need to be a part of your daily lives.

Tips and Scripts for Cultivating Other-Orientation

- **Considering others begins with allowing your child to be disappointed when a family decision doesn't go his way.** This is the beginning of simply thinking of others. The happiness of the whole is more important than the happiness of just one.

- **Make thinking of and sharing with others a habit in your daily life.**

  "Let's make an extra loaf of banana bread to bring to Mrs. Dallmeyer next door."

  "As long as we are going to the grocery store, let's see if Mrs. Grossman needs anything."

"I made so much soup, I am going to share some with our neighbors."

"Let's buy some extra cans of food to donate to the food pantry."

- **On birthdays, make it a ritual and a habit to donate to charity or a gift to your school.**

- **For birthdays celebrated with big parties and an abundance of gift-giving guests, suggest to the guests that they bring a gift to be donated or name a charity to whom they can donate in your child's honor.** While there will always be those people who will donate and still bring a gift, it is a solid lesson for your child and for the gift giver that you are thinking about and sharing with those who are less fortunate. (And no child needs to receive twenty-five gifts on his birthday!)

- **Turn part of a gift-receiving occasion into a time for gift giving.** For example, celebrate one of the eight nights of Chanukah by making cookies to give to the local firefighters. During Christmas vacation, dedicate a day to making Cranberry Bread to bring to your neighbors.

- **Allow your child to choose some of his gifts to donate to a worthy cause.** Praise him to the hills and let the world know what he has done!

- **Help your child regularly to clean out his belongings (toys, clothes, books) and donate the harvest to children who can use them.** While most schools have charity programs that include "drives" of various kinds, your children need to see these actions reinforced at home. Knowing that young children often see their possessions as extensions of themselves, it may be very hard for them to give up anything at all. So when your child hands you that Barbie arm, don't turn it down. It is the beginning of learning at least to share something of what you have.

- **Let your child see you regularly cleaning out—and not just once a year.** It is not only your clothing but also your kitchen and household items, linens, and overstock of cleaning supplies and the like that can be sorted through and donated regularly.

- **Allow your child to see you writing checks or making your cash donations to the charities you support.** Explain to him what you are doing and why. Habits are learned over time, and children are copycats.

- **Have a regular ritual of making charitable donations.** Many religions make donating money a part of regular worship services. Whatever your orientation, include your child in the act of giving to raise his consciousness about our obligation to donate and share.

- **Be a volunteer.** Children will do just what they have watched their parents do as they grow up. My husband always coached our children's sports teams. We felt no end of pride when we heard that our son Ben was volunteering to coach a basketball team.

- **Involve your child in volunteer activities when possible.** Look for opportunities for your child to join you in such activities. Be it picking up trash in the park, doing maintenance or repair work at school, decorating for a school festival, or packing food to be distributed to the needy, it is all about giving your time for a cause and being helpful. Countless websites such as the Acme Sharing Company offer ideas and opportunities for sharing with others as a family activity.

- **Show that grown-ups are helpful.** Your actions will teach your child that one of the responsibilities of being an adult is assisting others in many different ways. Whether participating in organized volunteering or assisting a neighbor, you are modeling helping others. Point out human interest stories of strangers helping people in need or even in trouble, such as the article about the woman who called 911 for someone in trouble and waited with her until help arrived.

- **The idea of being homeless or needy can be frightening.** While the young child can understand that some children don't have as many toys or clothes as he does, he will be frightened at the idea of being homeless and in need. Consider your child's age and development before exposing him to some of life's harsh realities, like homelessness. He is likely to become worried that he will be homeless or won't have enough food or clothing. You will need to reassure the young ones, *"Daddy and I make enough money for us to have the things we need to live."*

Taking a child to distribute food to the homeless before he is able to make sense of that sad reality may cause unwanted anxiety. You know your child best.

While the ups and downs of the economy certainly play a role in the degree to which a child has a case of "affluenza," they are only one of the contributors to the spoiled child who screams "Gimme, gimme, gimme!" Recognizing all of the different ways in which we entitle and enable our children is the first step toward fighting off their spoilage. The effects will be long term, too.

❖

CHAPTER TEN

"Knock, Knock. Who's There?"

Bringing Humor into Your Child's Life

Isn't it funny how many commonly used expressions and retorts reference humor when they aren't about humor at all, like "Isn't it *funny*?" How about when we say, "Oh, don't be silly!" or "That's ridiculous!" None of these is necessarily being used in a positive vein, either. But they do indicate our collective need and desire for humor. It is, after all, an important ingredient in a life happily lived.

Someone once said, "The best thing a person can have up his sleeve is a funny bone." Having a sense of humor is an integral part of being human. In fact, it's hard to imagine living without laughing. Everyone has heard the expression, "Laughter is the best medicine." And who can deny the great feeling of laughing until you cry? Research has pointed to the quantifiable physical benefits of laughter. A belly laugh signals the excretion of "feel good" neurochemicals in the brain. It increases blood flow to the heart. Some studies have shown that humor and laughter can actually boost the immune system. And certainly humor has emotional benefits. In fact, humor is a way of managing emotions. Being able to escape to the lighter side, if just for a chuckle, is undeniably a good thing; it brings hope and helps us get through some of the darkest times. A good sense of humor can inform your overall outlook on life. Poor Eeyore could have used a dose of humor, couldn't he?

Everyone has the capacity to be funny. But it does seem that some people have cornered the market on humor. They see it in everything, especially in the things that others might miss. *Why is that?* I wondered, so I conducted an informal survey and asked the funny people I know such questions as, "Were you always funny?" or "Did your parents do anything specific to en- courage your humor?" The answers were varied, but the one constant was that all of my subjects were also the youngest in their families. I've heard that many professional comedians are the youngest in their families, too. When I stopped to think about it, this finding really didn't surprise me, as humor can be a useful way to get attention, especially if you're the baby.

Play is the language of childhood. In fact, play is the business and the work of childhood; it is how children learn. And it is out of playfulness that humor grows. While we accept that young children play and laugh, we also expect them to "get serious" as they grow older. But can't seriousness coexist with humor? The answer to that question may lie tucked away in the fact that the adolescent brain begins to "prune" away the cells that are not used for play, according to Dr. Shirah Vollmer, a UCLA child psychiatrist. Surely the survival of such cells tells us something about the importance of humor to our well-being. Dr. Vollmer also says, "If you don't play in childhood, you won't play in adulthood." Imagine a life without playfulness. Clearly, humor is a trait that parents need to encourage and cultivate in their children, as it will serve them well throughout their lives.

The Development of Humor

Ever try telling a three-year-old a knock-knock joke? Talk about a comedian laying an egg! In the young child, the development of a sense of humor is usually dependent upon the most recently achieved milestone. As he masters each new stage and idea, the child plays with them. At first it is experimental, then he becomes a regular old jokester. The two-year-old learns that shoes go on feet, so it's really funny when you put your shoe on your ear. A light bulb switches on in the five-year-old's mind when he suddenly "gets" the concept of a pun: A word can mean two different things, and when you interchange them it's really funny.

Infancy

A baby's first smiles arise spontaneously from his nervous system, some- times when he is as young as two weeks. Thereafter, they pour forth in response to your voice. And by the fourth month, baby is giving away those smiles almost for free, just at the sight of you. By six or seven months, it is the unusual behavior that cracks him up. Motorboat noises, tummy tickles, and games of peek-a-boo bring about a divine laughter from your baby. These actions are funny to him because the child now recognizes the behaviors as different from what you usually do. Nothing induces a case of the giggles from your one-year-old like flying him through the air as if he were an airplane. It's all about the things that he observes. In fact, the things children at this age find most amusing usually come from an outside source. The seeds of humor have been sown.

The Toddler Stage: Eighteen Months to Two Years old

By the second year it is through play activities of all kinds that a genuine sense of humor surfaces and begins to grow in your toddler. Around the age of two, a child first begins to dabble in fantasy play. Nothing throws your two-year-old into fits of laughter like pretending to feed you make-believe pizza, or when you pretend to nibble his toes. Because he is just beginning to engage in make-believe behavior, it may not seem so funny at first; *What's going on here?* he wonders. Then he gets it and shouts *"More!"* or *"Again!"* laughing harder and harder with each silly thing that you or he does. What a sucker you are for that infectious laugh.

Toddlers like to make you laugh, and they like to laugh at what you do. But they also like to be in control of the play; otherwise, it doesn't seem as funny to them. It is a reflection of their mastery, remember? The toddler's own glee grows from physical activity; wildly, he runs in circles and falls down, then looks up to see if you are laughing along with him. He tries to rope his playmates into his play, or he follows them. Group playfulness has begun. There's nothing quite as hysterical as falling down in Ring Around the Rosie. And a scream at the end is just about as funny as it gets.

The two-year-old is making sense of his world. He knows that pots and pans are for cooking, so when he puts one on his head, he gets that that's not the way it's supposed to be. He's shaking up the order. It's hilarious!

The Preschool Stage: Three to Five Years old

The preschooler is learning to distinguish fantasy from reality. His comprehension and facility with language expand the bounds of his humor as he plays with words and their meaning. "Look at the bananas on your feet" is pretty darn silly. Misnaming objects, distorting and making up words, and creating nonsensical rhymes are the source of contagious laughter. "The Name Game" song (*"Greg Greg bo beg, banana fanna fo feg . . . "*) is much loved for just that reason.

Playing with what he has mastered is the source of great humor to the growing child. And so it is with potty talk to three and four-year-olds who have just acquired toilet skills. "Pass the pee-pee juice" is a hoot, but not quite as side-splitting as "You tushie head!" Truth be told, body parts and everything that comes out of the body is endlessly entertaining to this child. Add to the mix the five-year-old's favorite knock-knock joke and now you get it: *Knock, knock. Who's there? Mickey Mouse's underwear.* Underwear? Is there anything funnier?

But as witty as your four-year-old may be, he is also self-conscious. He can laugh uproariously at you, but you dare not laugh at him, unless he is trying to induce your laughter.

The Elementary School Stage: Six to Ten Years Old

This child's humor is reflective of his intellectual development, especially his command of language and words. Puns, double entendres, and riddles are fodder for joke after joke, usually followed by a "Get it?" and a desire to explain why it's funny. Many an eight-year-old falls asleep pouring over his riddle books.

As the child gets close to the middle-school years, his humor gets racy and even gross, as he flirts with danger. It doesn't matter whether the audience offers an "Eeewwwww" or a laugh, as long as he has gotten some attention. In addition, humor can often help the middle-school child relieve anxiety by taking the attention off of him and putting it anywhere else.

Bodily functions continue to be an unending source of humor, especially for boys. The poor child who allows a noisy fart to slip out in school will have satisfied the whole class's laughter quotient for the day. And it will be long remembered. As the kids double over, they'll also think, *Thank goodness it wasn't me.*

Middle School

Real life provides plenty of fuel for this child's humor. The mistakes and faux pas of others are the fodder they need. Although being the butt of the jokes can be painful, it is also a lesson that has to be learned, because everyone has a turn. Sarcasm is big, starting in middle school, and walks hand-in-hand with the testing of boundaries that surfaces with this age child. (See section on sarcasm, p. 215.) Sarcasm can morph readily into teasing, and that's not always a good thing. Teasing reaches new heights at this age, as the middle schooler sees it as his job to figure out who's in and who's out and where he fits in. He also figures out that the best defense is a good offense. He will do anything to get out of the spotlight, even if it means "dissing" a friend by teasing him. However, when teasing becomes bullying, that's where the humor ends. (For more on teasing, see p. 216.)

The Benefits of Humor

Humor brings a broad range of benefits to children, just as it does to adults. It enhances a child's intellect, and builds emotional and social connections and development, helping him to better negotiate his world as it unfolds before him. Simply put, kids who have a sense of humor have an easier time growing up than those who don't.

Intellectual Development

Humor is a form of intellectual play, and language is its vehicle, as it is how many people express their thoughts. Discovering that the same word can have two meanings, exemplified in puns and some riddles, is a great "ah-ha" experience for a child. He is off and running, as he notices and finds more of the same. It is an intellectual exercise in that it leads to expanded and enriched vocabulary.

Seeing the humor in things takes the child to a new level of thinking, that of abstract thinking. When he has reached that level of intellectual development, after the preschool stage and early elementary age to be sure, the child moves beyond the words and goes for the ideas. To understand jokes, a child needs to progress from concrete to abstract thinking, which is a sign of his growing intellect.

Looking for humor is an exercise in thinking creatively. Some also label this as "thinking outside the box," which certainly is at the root of some forms of humor. It is one of the things that makes Jerry Seinfeld so funny; he takes the ordinary and looks at it differently, twisting the audience's perspective so as to offer a new way of seeing things. Thinking innovatively, something that humor requires, is a direct path to problem solving.

Emotional Development

Managing one's emotional state is not a skill with which children are born; yet it is crucial to healthy development. In the course of their emotional development, children learn all the "legal" ways of dealing with their big feelings. (Clearly, the high school student who throws his cell phone at the wall hasn't learned enough about these ways.) Often, humor as a coping mechanism is overlooked. Being playful, looking at the lighter side, and laughing at yourself are all ways children can be taught to deal with some of their feelings and, as they get older, with their anxieties. Humor can lighten the bluest funk, taking the child to a different place by allowing him to let go. Paul McGhee, humor educator and comedian, points out that children who are helped to build strong humor skills as they grow have a clear advantage over their "terminally serious peers" in dealing with their daily stressors. As proof of the value of humor, he points to the trend in big business of hiring play consultants to teach their employees how to bring humor and playfulness into the work place. Making a whole bunch of people laugh is not only an intoxicating experience, but it can be a real esteem booster. (Of course, we have all heard of the class clown, the child who grows dependent upon his humor to nourish his sense of himself, and he doesn't seem to get it from anywhere else. In this case, humor is more of an avoidance mechanism and is not necessarily a good thing.)

Social Development

Humor can actually be a social skill. It is a common language, an icebreaker, and an antidote to a room full of tension. Telling a joke can be like giving a gift. Sharing a good laugh is a bonding experience. As such, humor serves all human creatures well in their interpersonal relationships. Even the young child appreciates the way humor connects him to his peers, as he discovers the contagion of laughter and doing silly stuff. As long as it doesn't cross the bounds of what is acceptable—breaking rules or being unkind—it is a safe way to join in the fun, even for the introverted child. The shy child, too, can be one of the gang, laughing along with the others, without having to put himself in an uncomfortable position.

It is interesting to note that the child who is able to be funny is the one who is more likely to participate in social activities and, therefore, build his own confidence. He is the funny one whom others want to befriend. This child tends to be likable and popular, as others gravitate to him. It is that child who can put all the others at ease, using humor as the link and common ground. This is true for adults, too.

Tips for Cultivating (Appropriate) Humor in Your Child

Developing humor in your child is for his well-being and for yours—and for your sanity, too! Children who start young will have honed the skills of humor and experienced all its usefulness by the time they become adults.

- **Recognize that the desire to play and laugh is part of a human being's hardwiring.** Your child will be interested in play, playfulness, and humor even if you do nothing at all. Don't squelch it! And if you respond positively when you catch glimpses of that budding humor, you will boost the odds of your child developing a beneficial sense of humor that will last a lifetime.

- **Not everyone laughs in the same way.** Some children give it up more easily or more readily than others. Perhaps they are quieter by nature, more introverted by temperament. But even these children need to laugh and learn to see the humorous side of things. While your expectations should be adjusted, don't give up. Find the things that make this child laugh and keep them coming. Laughter and humor in any degree can be freeing.

- **Make sure that the humor you use matches the child's development at the time.** Not "getting" the joke when everyone else is laughing feels bad. In addition to using age-appropriate humor, clue your child in by explaining what's funny. It will honor him, expand his understanding of humor, and save him from embarrassment.

- **Laugh at yourself.** Being able to do so is critical to getting through all the inevitable mistakes, faux pas, and embarrassing moments all people encounter. Laughing at yourself yields a much more positive response from those around you than does your negativity. And laughing at yourself teaches your child to do the same.

- **Beware of discounting your child's feelings.** Saying, *"Aw, c'mon, that didn't really hurt your feelings, did it?"* after someone has joked with your child isn't a good idea. Shame and embarrassment are powerful feelings, even for the very young child who can be self-conscious. Rather, wait a while until after the moment has passed, then in private you can explain, *"Uncle John was trying to be funny; he wasn't trying to hurt your feelings. But that wasn't funny to you. You can tell him that it made you feel bad."* You can add, *"As you get older, you will learn to laugh with him. Sometimes laughing at yourself is the best way not to feel bad."*

- **Be playful.** Humor springs forth from play, and play offers opportunities to use or recognize humor, which can take many forms: laughter, funny games, wordplays, incongruity, absurdity, ridiculousness, amusing stories, physical play, joke telling. Try them all.

- **Be silly.** This may be more difficult for the adult who never learned to be silly, but it's worth the effort. Your young child, in particular, will be the best audience. Doing anything out of the ordinary will tickle his funny bone—call things by their wrong names, use nonsense words, walk into doors, put a sock on your nose, be inept at something. Making a fool of yourself lets your child see that even Daddy can be ridiculous.

Billy Crystal tells the story of being a little boy, dressing up, and sticking pennies on his forehead for his family. That was his start as a comedian. My friend Barney Saltzberg, who is a children's book author, says that the sillier he is, the larger the crowd of children he attracts. Kids (of all ages) love an adult who can be silly and who can laugh at himself right along with them. Physical humor, the clown who trips on purpose, for example, is the height of silliness, and it is harmless humor, too.

- **Experience humor as a family.** A home that is very serious will yield a child who is very serious. Be a family who honors and has a place for humor. Children are much more likely to laugh and take pleasure in a trusting, comfortable, safe environment, one that is free of pervasive conflict and bickering. Whether that means watching comedies together, reading the comics out loud, or telling riddles and jokes at the dinner table, bring humor into your family in a deliberate way. This puts into practice the social nature of humor. Family participation sends a strong message about the importance of humor in one's life, and it encourages a good sense of humor. Be sure your humor selection is appropriate to all members of the family, using the youngest child as your gauge. Even the most introverted child will eventually join in the fun.

- **Use humor throughout your day.** Whether you're waiting in line at the grocery store, driving in the car, on the subway, or waiting for a doctor's visit, humor will brighten a boring time. Turn your regular word games (*"I'm thinking of something that is blue . . . "*) into more humorous ones (*"I'm thinking of something that is blue, has four legs, big horns, and wears a bathing suit . . . "*). Take the opportunity to be silly and joke around.

- **Over dinner or at bedtime, ask your child what made him laugh that day.** Take the time patiently to listen to his long-winded, funny tales, as he hones his storytelling skills.

- **Share something from your day that made you laugh.** Funny stories or ideas increase his awareness of what is funny and underscore how you value humor.

- **Read funny stories to your child and laugh out loud with him.** Enjoying humor together gives it the added association of warmth and closeness. Talk about what is funny in the story. It will expand his understanding of humor.

- **Appreciate the child's own attempts at humor.** Refrain from the groan, acknowledge the humor, and support your child's efforts. Remember that his humor reflects his stage of cognitive development. I am reminded of Dustin Hoffman's character, Ray, in the movie *Rain Man*, when he finally learned to make a joke, and said with pride, *"I made a joke."* He got it.

- **Don't laugh at "cute."** It is typical for adults to laugh at the cute things children do or say. It's almost an automatic response. The four-year-old has his shoes on the wrong feet and you laugh. Until he learns to laugh at himself, save the chuckle. It feels disrespectful to the child and embarrasses him.

- **If it isn't meant to be funny, don't laugh!** When your three-year-old does exactly what you have just told him not to do, don't laugh. That laugh is more out of amazement, and it certainly doesn't reinforce the limits you have set. In addition, it is confusing to the child. *Is that how I make Daddy laugh? Is that what humor is for, to get me out of taking responsibility for my behavior?*

- **Don't mistake nervous laughter for humor.** Often the young child, the two-year-old outlaw in particular, will laugh as he does something wrong, knowing that he is crossing the line. This is not humor; it is anxiety at its finest. That laugh says, *I am trying to figure out if this is a game or not, and I am not sure what to do.* In this case, the laugh must not work.

- **Expand your young child's circle of friends.** Parents tend to have their child associate with friends who are just like him. Expose your child to all kinds of youngsters—serious ones, physical ones, artistic ones, and silly ones. It will expand his horizons as well as desensitize him to the kinds of behaviors that might have previously made him uncomfortable

- **Be cognizant of the difference in laughing with your child and laughing at him.** No one likes to be laughed at, especially not the four- or five-year-old who is so self-conscious. The young child likes to be the one to make you laugh; he feels powerful and in charge. When you laugh at him, he feels ashamed, as if he has done something wrong.

- **Make your standards for humor known.** Of course, you don't want to take the fun out of funny, so you need to have a broad tolerance for different styles of humor. But it is from you that your children will learn what is and isn't acceptable humor. Sometimes just a raised eyebrow will give the message loud and clear. Other times you might need to comment on the acceptability of the humor without putting down the funny guy. *"It is not okay to hurt anyone's feelings, even if you are just kidding. Kidding can hurt."* Or, *"In this family we don't make fun of anyone. Let's find another way to be funny."* Or, *"The jokes we tell in this family don't use bad language."*

- **Sarcasm and teasing are illegal humor.** Someone is always the target or victim, and that's never good.

- **Know when to draw the line.** Your child needs to learn from experience when something is funny and when it really isn't. Take the time to explain the difference between a good joke and a bad joke when the opportunity arises. Jokes that put down others, that are mean spirited or cruel, are bad jokes. There is a fine line between having fun with someone and doing so at his expense. (See Teasing, p. 216.) If your child has crossed that line, take him aside to explain this. Telling him in front of others will embarrass him, and then he will definitely not hear your message. He'll only feel humiliated. *"I think you didn't realize that calling Terry a klutz was hurting his feelings. I could tell from his face that he hurt himself and felt bad when he tripped, so it wasn't a joke to him."* And be sure to suppress your own giggle at how incredibly klutzy Terry was.

- **Take pains not to overreact to unacceptable humor.** The bigger your reaction, the more likely you are to fuel more of the same. Shocking Mom or Dad can be a real thrill. You can disapprove without allowing steam to come out of your ears.

- **Eliminate "off-color" humor.** When I was a child, "moron" jokes were popular. "Why did the moron . . . ?" And we would howl at the answer. People today are much gutsier and crueler, and "moron" is replaced by almost anything that you are not. Jokes that are misogynistic, racist, ageist, and those that belittle others should be removed from everyone's repertoire. Remember, the walls have ears and children are listening when you are on the phone. Just your repeating the joke with the caveat, *"I know this is terrible, but . . . "* gives acceptability to that brand of humor.

- **Don't tell a joke about someone that you wouldn't tell to his face.** This is a good guideline for all kinds of communications, including humor, jokes, and gossip.

- **Monitor your child's dosage of mean-spirited or inappropriate media humor.** This is easy to do with your young child. Just turn it off! It's not so easy with your older child. Your best defense is letting your child know why you disapprove. While he may not agree, the message will sink in. Then mind your own intake of the same kinds of humor.

Illegal Humor

Sarcasm

Sarcasm is a form of illegal humor. Why? Because it is often delivered at the expense of another and can be hurtful. Sarcasm seems like it is playful, even witty and clever, but it is not as innocent as it may seem. Underneath that sugar-coating of a joke is an insult or a put-down. The person trying to be funny usually means just the opposite of what he is saying, and it is belittling. Knowing that it isn't okay to say what he means, the person couches it in sarcasm to cover his true feelings. He may not be brave enough to express the thought directly or he knows that it is unacceptable, so instead he throws in a splash of humor, making it legal. A person I know frequently says "Duh" in response to something I have said. I know that he is agreeing with what I am saying, but what comes across is "Any dummy knows that!" and it makes me feel bad.

The word "sarcasm" comes from the Greek noun, *sarkasmos*, which derives from the Greek verb, *sarkazsein*, which means, "to tear flesh." Doesn't that just say it all? Sarcasm tears into someone's feelings, even though it is disguised as humor.

Many of the television sitcoms that older children and adults enjoy regularly use sarcasm. The characters in these shows are often mean-spirited, even deceitful and conniving. They break the rules of acceptable social interaction, and they get away with it. That's part of what makes it funny. There is a certain one-upmanship to these interactions. One sarcastic comment generates another even more brilliant jibe from his target, and so it goes, a playful kind of verbal jousting. In these shows, the viewer doesn't get to see the real feelings, the hurt that is generated, only the humor. Hearing sarcasm used so much, one becomes immune to it as being harmful. It creeps into the viewer's own social interactions.

The young child just plain doesn't get sarcasm. He is a literal thinker and takes what you say at face value. Learning to process sarcasm is developed over time. While he can detect sarcasm somewhere around the age of six, he doesn't see it as humor until he is much older, around the age of ten.

I am reminded of a kindergartener I once taught. At the end of a long and trying day, she carelessly but nonetheless accidentally knocked over a tray of paint, making a huge mess and a whole lot of work for a very tired teacher. When I said to her, "Way to go, Heather!" she looked up at me and said, "That's the way my mommy always talks to me." How I wanted to crawl into a hole and disappear.

Tips and Scripts for Vaccinating Against Sarcasm

- **Always remember that sarcasm is cruel.** Hopefully, you are not sarcastic. And you certainly don't want to appear that way.

- **Remove sarcasm from your toolbox.** Cultivate different ways to be funny, if that is your intent. Your child learns from your example. If it's okay for you to be sarcastic, it will be okay for him.

- **Say what you mean.** Rather than sweetening your comments with supposed humor, give a clear message. Doing so demonstrates respect for your child and his ability to deal with reality. And it sends the message that you expect him to take responsibility for his actions. In the kindergartener's case, I should have said: *"Heather, I know you didn't mean to bump into that tray filled with paints, but now we have a huge cleanup job. Can you help me, as I am really tired?"*

- **Make a midcourse correction.** If the day is getting the best of you, if you have no energy for saying what you mean and a biting comment just slips out, simply stop and take it back. *"Oh, Heather, that was not a nice way for me to have spoken, and I really am sorry. I guess you can hear in my tone that I am so tired today. But being tired is not a good reason to say something mean to you."*

- **Call it out when your child uses sarcasm.** *"That sounds like something they say on* Sponge Bob *or* iCarly. *In this family and in real life we don't speak to one another using cruel sarcasm."* Giving it a name helps your child to recognize that kind of talk and stop himself from using it in the future. When you recognize the sarcasm as coming from one of your older child's peers, it gets trickier, as you don't want to put down the other child. *"In Andy's family it may be okay to use sarcasm, but in our family it is not. Different families have different rules."* And add, *"Can you rephrase that in a more acceptable way?"*

- **Sarcasm is often a testing of boundaries.** Remember that preadolescents are busy testing boundaries of all kinds. That is part of their process of individuating and of separating from you. Being sarcastic is like testing the water. Sometimes a raised eyebrow is comment enough, but your older child needs to know without exception that your rules cover a lot of ground, including humor, sarcasm, and respectful interactions. *"I know that you guys talk that way among yourselves and you don't find it offensive. I do. Please respect me."*

Teasing

Everyone teases at some time or other. Throughout life people take turns being the teaser and then becoming the one who is being teased. In fact, I think it would be impossible to eliminate teasing from the many ways people interact. Little boys and girls tease one another on the playground as a form of early connection and flirtation. People tease others as a means of cajoling them out of a bad mood. Teasing is used for social bonding, like in harmless hazing and mischief. Much of humor in media today is actually based on some form of teasing. And our reaction to watching teasing—laughter—is a reflection of the relief felt at not being on the receiving end of the tease.

Phew! In fact, teasing can be playful and even good-humored when it causes everyone involved, including the target, to smile or laugh.

Teasing, however, can also be another form of illegal humor when it is at the expense of someone else. Put-downs, name calling, belittling, even ridicule are not humorous at all. They hurt. When teasing crosses the line, when it becomes repetitive, hostile, even tormenting and harassing, then it is bullying. There is no humor in bullying. If teasing is bullying disguised, it is unacceptable and must not be tolerated. It is imperative that the child involved seeks the help of an adult, as bullying will require adult intervention.

Children need to have experience with teasing in order to learn the difference between good and bad teasing. And, as it is an inevitability, they also need to be taught skills for coping with teasing.

Tips and Scripts for Legal Teasing

- **Think twice before teasing your child.** Children count on their parents to accept them with all their warts. Your teasing (about almost anything) says that he is not acceptable to you. The same holds true for cruel teasing (even in jest) by older children in the family. Just because he is family doesn't make it okay. The child who fears being the target will not let go enough to experience the family humor. The child needs to feel protected by his parents from all kinds of harm, and that includes mean-spirited humor.

- **Mind the way you respond to teasing.** Do you slough it off? Ignore it? Use a clever comeback? Get mad? Whatever it is you do, your child is watching and absorbing. You are his model and first teacher.

- **Legal teasing happens between two people of equal personal power.** When the two are on equal footing, there is less chance for teasing to get out of hand and become hurtful. Teasing between different-age siblings is often hurtful because the power is unequally distributed. The target in an equally matched pair can be taught the responses that will make him feel powerful and not a helpless victim of teasing.

- **Teasing your child will not thicken his skin.** Teasing to encourage playfulness is one thing; both people are taking pleasure. Teasing about a misstep or mistake causes embarrassment or shame. Teasing about a physical challenge or an emotional situation is never okay. Rather than thickening his skin, the opposite can occur. The child will be sensitized to your teasing and look out for it, and perhaps even misinterpret innocent comments in order to protect himself.

- **Teasing that is playful and has no underlying hostility is legal.** The child can be taught to detect the difference by paying attention to how a tease makes him feel. When a child feels put down or hurt, when he fails to see a tease as being in jest, then it is no longer okay. Otherwise, it is just having "a little fun." Ask him: *"Do you think that Simon really thinks your shoes look like submarines? He really is your good pal. Does it really hurt your feelings when he says that? If it isn't a big deal to you, you can just laugh with him. He's just teasing."*

- **Do not overreact to stories of teasing.** As awful as teasing can be, your child's reaction to teasing will be flavored by yours. Temper your response without ignoring your child's feelings. Life will be peppered with lots of bad stuff, like teasing. Your child needs to learn to weather it.

- **Teasing cannot be stopped.** This is an unfortunate reality. We cannot control what other people say, but we can control how we react. While teasing cannot be prevented, the child can be taught how to handle it. *"Here is something I have learned. Sometimes if I just laugh it off and don't show a reaction, the teasing stops. Some kids are just trying to get you to react. So don't let it work."*

- **Acknowledge your child's feelings.** Knowing that you understand how he feels will enable him to listen to your suggested solution. *"That really hurt your feelings when Warren teased you for being the last in line. I know how that feels. Bad!"*

- **Give the message, "You can handle it," and teach him how at the same time.** The saying goes, "You prepare the child for the path, not the path for the child." While conveying understanding and concern, also let your child know that you have faith in his ability to weather the teasing and that you are going to teach him how. If, however, you see that the teasing is harmful and crosses the line to bullying, it is imperative that you seek the help of the powers that be—teachers, school administrators, or coaches.

- **Create scripts for particular situations.** Having a script at the ready is one of many coping skills that helps a child tolerate harmless teasing. *"Let's figure out what you could have said to Warren when he teased you."* When he comes up blank, you can add, *"What did you want to tell him?"* and listen to him say where he wants Warren to go. It will be cathartic for him, too. Then offer, *"Maybe next time you can tell him 'Last in line is best because you can see what everyone in front of you is doing.'"*

  The more practice he has scripting his responses, the more spontaneous he will become in saying them in the moment.

- **Teach your child about "self-talk."** It is a way of being your own cheerleader. A child can think, *I don't like what he is saying, but I know what to do.* He can tell himself, *That's not really true. I am not a frecklefaced fish.* And he can remind himself of his good qualities. *My Dad says that my freckles are power spots and I am lucky to have so many.*

- **Teach your child to slough it off.** You can teach your child the following one-word response that will take away the power from the teaser. It's what you used to say when you were a child: "So?" It shows a kind of indifference, and it's a great response because no one really knows how to respond to it. Your child will feel powerful to have that tool at the ready, and it's easy to remember.

- **Agree with the tease.** Older children (upper elementary/middle school) can be taught the power in agreeing with the teaser. It is another way of taking the power out of the words, and it leaves the teaser nonplussed. *"It's true, I am really tall. At least no one can block my view. Lucky me!"* Such a comment puts the victim in the power position, as he appears confident and unflappable. Three cheers for him! The same holds true when the victim replies with a simple, *"Oh, thank you,"* showing that he isn't phased. Using humor tells the teaser that the tease didn't sink in and therefore isn't important.

- **Ignoring, giving no response at all, can be the best response.** This is a hard lesson, but your child needs to learn the power of not responding or ignoring mean teasing. Often teasers do so in order to get a response, making them feel superior.

  Tell your child: *"The kid who teases wants to be powerful. Teasing someone else makes him feel big. If you say nothing at all, he doesn't feel anything, except maybe frustrated!"* The child can be told to ignore the teaser, not even to look his way, as if he hasn't said anything at all. The perpetrator will likely seek out another target if he doesn't get satisfaction. This response will best be taught by role-playing with your child. *"So, let's practice. I'm going to be Ricky the teaser and really try to get you to react. Now remember, don't you react to me at all. Don't even look at me!"* Then play it up, lay it on, and walk away, mumbling, *"Wow, I better find someone else to tease. That wasn't any fun at all."* Big kudos for practicing are given to your child.

- **Encourage your child to be with the friends who make him feel good.** Remind your child that he doesn't need to hang around with kids who make him feel bad. Real friends make you feel good, and he has a choice of who his friends are. You might need to help facilitate new friendships by helping to arrange playdates with other kids and suggest things he can do with them.

- **Teach your child that teasing is usually not his problem; it's the other guy's problem.** Even children as young as five can understand that sometimes people who use mean teasing are not happy with themselves. *"When Adam teased you about being short, I think he is showing that he is worried about his own size. Or maybe something else is bothering him about himself."* And continue, *"It's usually the people who feel bad about themselves who tease other people. That's how they get their bad feelings off of themselves and put them on someone else."*

- **Your child can be taught to look at why the teaser needs to tease.** *"I'll bet you that someone is teasing Adam at his home. He is copying just what someone else does to him. That's really too bad, isn't it?"*

When Your Child Is the Teaser

Everyone takes a turn at being the teaser at some point. Those children who are teased at school, for example, are liable to give it a try on a younger sibling at home or in the neighborhood. Children need to be taught some guidelines about when teasing is legal and when it isn't, without putting a hex on humor and being playful.

Tips and Scripts for Taming the Teaser

- **Put yourself in his shoes.** A child should be taught to ask himself when he is about to tease, *How would I feel if someone said that to me?* Admittedly, this may not always work, as the teaser's need to be big may trump his ability to be empathetic at that time. You can let your child know your feelings about people who tease. *"It is disappointing to think that I have a child who likes to make other people feel bad. I want to help you learn how important kindness is in our family."*

- **Know when to stop.** If the person your child is teasing doesn't see what is fun or funny about what he is saying, it needs to stop right away. If the laughter becomes tears, the game is over. *"You know when you have gone too far. Pay attention to that. It is never okay to hurt someone else's feelings."*

- **There is a difference between having fun with someone and making fun of someone**. If both parties are laughing, then it's having fun. If not, then it's unkind teasing and is not okay. *"It is never okay to hurt someone's feelings intentionally. Hurting feelings is as bad as hurting bodies."*

- **Clean up your mess.** When a child crosses the line with his teases and knows it, he can be reminded of the power of an apology. *"If you didn't mean to hurt Matt's feelings, you can tell him so. I know it will make him feel better."* However, being forced to say you are sorry when you are not is teaching a child to lie. (See the tip about saying "I'm Sorry" on p. 116 in chapter 6.)

- **There should be a consequence for intentional teasing.** While the best consequence comes from the victim's own declaration of not wanting to be friends or to play, sometimes a parent needs to step in, if all else fails. Harmful teasing is unacceptable. *"Since you are not able to be kind to your friends, you lose the privilege of being with them on playdates after school for the rest of the week. We'll try again next week and see if you can have fun with your friends without teasing them."* (Consequences are always crafted with the child's age and development in mind. For more information, see chapter 4, p. 75.)

Humor will serve your child well in so many different areas of his life. While it may not be a trait that all parents feel is imperative to cultivate in their child, I hope you now understand how it can help to enrich his life as well as get him through some of the rough spots. But it is one of those traits that needs to be nourished, as it can be easily extinguished. Engaging your child in wordplay, telling knock-knock jokes or riddles, or just being silly together can actually be time well spent. These activities are not only useful in cultivating humor but are icing on the cake when it comes to raising your children.

Fifty-Two Cures for *AFFLUENZA*—
One for Every Week of the Year

.   ❖   .

1. Be present for your child, physically and emotionally. Your children need your *presence*, not your *presents*.
2. Make your children your top priority; then *behave* as if they are.
3. Practice saying no to your children. Provide them with clear, firm, consistent limits.
4. Have appropriate consequences for limit violations and follow through.
5. Be the person you want your child to be. Children are apprenticed to parents in the business of growing up. They develop their values by observing the way you behave as a person.
6. After you and your co-parent have clarified the values you wish to impart to your family, model and live the values you have chosen. Actions are more powerful than words.
7. Always be mindful of the messages you are sending when you forget that your child is watching.
8. Make sure that your actions are consistent with your values.
9. Allow your child to struggle. It is the lesson learned from a struggle that he will remember.
10. Teach your child to delay gratification. Wanting and not getting is a good thing. Remember Mick Jagger's famous words: "You can't always get what you want. But if you try sometime, you just might find, you get what you need."
11. Help your child to learn to tolerate disappointment. Don't "fix" everything, whether it is replacing a broken toy or offering a substitute activity.

12. Share with your children that it is your choice not to buy something.
13. Help your child not to become entitled by giving her whatever she may ask for, dream for, yearn for. (To an entitled child, all wants are needs.)
14. Don't use the word "need" when you really mean "want."
15. Notice how much attention you give to other people's acquisitions and material possessions within earshot of your children.
16. Steer your conversation away from talk of what you have bought, what you want to buy, what your friends have bought.
17. Pay attention to your own feelings of competition.
18. Explain your choice not to compete on the playing field of acquisitions.
19. Use every opportunity to demonstrate to your child that you value the kind of person someone is over the things that he accumulates.
20. Value, praise, reward, and emphasize kindness and caring, above all else.
21. Make the good and the well-being of the whole family (the whole class, the whole team) more important than the happiness of one member.
22. Reward and praise cooperation (but don't reward with "things").
23. Model gratitude.
24. Make sharing with others who are less fortunate a regular part of your life and an expectation.
25. On gift-giving occasions, make a ritual and a habit of giving a "toy for a tot."
26. Help your child regularly to clean out her belongings and give them to children who can use them.
27. Be a volunteer.
28. Expect that your children will be volunteers and find opportunities for them to do so.
29. Talk with, but don't lecture, your children about money.
30. Be honest; don't tell your child you can't afford something if you really can afford it. Rather, explain why you don't choose to buy it.
31. Help your child to understand that there are limits on spending; don't allow her to spend freely without limits or conditions. Having money doesn't mean you spend it.
32. Strive to create and model a balance between the luxuries that your bank account affords you and unnecessary excess.
33. Talk with your child about the values you see exhibited in the TV shows and advertisements that she watches.

34. Try not to let a visit to a mall or to your favorite store become your most frequent family outing.

35. Reward your child in non-monetary ways. Time with you is more valuable than any material object.

36. Never use money or things to control your child's behavior.

37. Spend your time with your child doing something besides shopping or purchasing. Go the library, the museum, the beach, play cards, do things together. Experience things together.

38. Make people more important than things.

39. Create family rituals. Make family experiences more important than things. It is out of these experiences, time together, that a "family soul" is created.

40. Refuse to "keep up with the Joneses." Tone down the birthday parties, the birthday gifts, First Communion celebrations, the Bar Mitzvahs, Quinciñeras. Instead, let your celebrations reflect your values, and verbalize your choice to do so.

41. Allow your child to earn real money for real work.

42. Instigate an Allowance System for your age-appropriate child (seven years and older).

43. Allow your child to save for something she wants "so badly." Have her pay for the whole thing.

44. Encourage your children to use their money to buy gifts for others. Take them to affordable stores.

45. Don't rescue your child from her money problems. Help her find her own solution.

46. Help your child to open a savings account. (Seven years old is a good age for this.)

47. Discuss with your child how she will use monetary gifts she will receive.

48. Consider having three categories of savings: Spending, Saving, Sharing (charity).

49. Allow your child to experience the joy that comes from making other people happy through helping and sharing.

50. Help your child to see that happiness is transitory and that affluence doesn't necessarily lead to happiness.

51. Model for your child the reality that a happy life always includes disappointments, limitations, mistakes, obstacles, pain, loss, and suffering,

as well as all the good stuff. Verbalize your own experience with these realities as they happen; they will be seen as a part of everyone's lives.

52. Find every opportunity to show your child that the best things in life aren't things.

100 Ways to Say "Good Job!"

❖

1. You're on the right track now.
2. You're working so hard.
3. Your project is first rate.
4. You've outdone yourself!
5. That's much better.
6. That's the best you've ever done.
7. Now you've figured it out.
8. Now you have it.
9. What an imagination!
10. The time you put in really shows.
11. Keep working on it; you're getting better.
12. You make it look easy.
13. That's the way to do it.
14. You're really going to town.
15. You've just about mastered that.
16. You're really improving.
17. Keep it up.
18. You've got that down pat.
19. Keep on trying.
20. You've got it made!
21. You must be so proud of yourself.
22. You made the difference.
23. You're sensational!

24. You're amazing!
25. You're work is super!
26. You're learning fast.
27. How thoughtful of you.
28. You've got what it takes.
29. You're a shining star.
30. You're right on target.
31. You're a winner.
32. You've really grown up.
33. You came through.
34. Your help counts.
35. You tried really hard.
36. You've earned my respect.
37. Clever!
38. Amazing effort!
39. Unbelievable work!
40. Incredible!
41. Superb!
42. Terrific!
43. Dynamite!
44. Exceptional!
45. Top rate!
46. How extraordinary!
47. Thumbs up!
48. Way to go!
49. Hip-hip, hooray!
50. Take a bow!
51. Now you have the hang of it.
52. You figured that out fast.
53. That's it!
54. You're really working hard today.
55. Congratulations, you got (name the behavior) just right.
56. That's quite an improvement.
57. Couldn't have done it better myself.
58. You really make being a parent fun.
59. One more time and you'll have it.

60. What a genius!
61. You're so kind.
62. You're so thoughtful.
63. You're so helpful.
64. You're so patient.
65. Great answers!
66. You deserve a hug.
67. Great discovery!
68. You're a champ!
69. You're a great friend.
70. You're a pleasure to know.
71. That was a great effort.
72. What a careful listener.
73. Great idea!
74. You did it that time.
75. That's the way!
76. Now you've figured it out.
77. You haven't missed a thing.
78. Nothing can stop you now.
79. You must have been practicing.
80. Right on the button!
81. Great remembering!
82. Great listening!
83. You did so much work today.
84. You certainly gave it your all.
85. You're really trying.
86. You're doing just fine.
87. You're really learning a lot today.
88. You're doing the best you can.
89. You remembered!
90. That gives me such a happy feeling.
91. Well, look at you!
92. That's really _____ (fill in the blank with a descriptive adjective).
93. You used all your might.
94. Your (name the behavior) amazes me!
95. That's my boy (girl).

96. You're the best, _____ (fill in the blank with your child's name).

97. You made it happen.

98. You've earned my respect.

99. You fill me with pride.

100. You're just the son (daughter) I dreamed I would have.

The Ethical Will of a Grandfather
to His Grandson

❖

1. When there is a job to do—do a good job, never a sloppy one.
2. Work hard when you work. But play hard, too.
3. When your time is free, explore the things you think might be interesting. Follow your curiosities.
4. Be active with your hands and mind, but find plenty of time to observe how beautiful and strange the world is.
5. Respect your body. Keep it clean and healthy.
6. Never live too far away from the outdoors, from trees and birds and animals and plants and mountains and blue water.
7. Never load yourself down with too many things. Have only such property as you really love and use. Have those few things as fine as possible, and then cherish them and care for them lovingly.
8. Never start a fight. But if someone else does, give 'em back what they asked for.
9. Never make excuses for yourself. Own up to your mistakes and don't repeat them if you can help it.
10. Think for yourself. Don't believe what you read or what other people say, unless it seems true to you.
11. Make plenty of friends. But learn to enjoy being alone, too. Don't ever count on anyone but yourself.

Sigmund Hirshorn to his nine-year-old grandson, Mitchell Koff

Selected Sources

❖

Listed below are some of the sources that were particularly valuable, influential, and helpful in writing this book.

Ames, Louise Bates, Frances L. Ilg, and Sidney Baker. *Your Ten- to Fourteen-Year-Old.* New York: Dell Publishing, 1988.

Brennen, Mark L. *When "No" Gets You Nowhere.* New York: Prima Publishing, 1977.

Biddulph, Steve. *Raising Boys.* Berkeley, California: Celestial Arts, 1998.

Coles, Robert. *The Moral Intelligence of Children.* New York: Random House, 1997.

Davis, Laura, and Janie Keyser. *Becoming the Parent You Want to Be.* New York: Broadway Books, 1977.

Elkind, David. *All Dressed Up with No Place to Go.* Reading, Mass.: Addison-Wesley Publishing, 1984.

———. *The Hurried Child.* Reading, Mass.: Addison-Wesley Publishing. 1981.

Emmons, Robert, and Michael McCullough. *The Psychology of Gratitude.* Oxford: Oxford University Press, 2004.

Faber, Adele, and Elaine Mazlish. *How to Talk So Kids Will Listen; How to Listen So Kids Will Talk.* New York: Avon Books, 1980.

Gallo, Eileen, and Jon Gallo. *Silver Spoon Kids.* New York: McGraw-Hill, 2002.

Gardner, Howard. *Multiple Intelligences.* New York: Bantam Books, 1995.

Gesell, Arnold, Frances L. Ilg, and Louise Bates. *The Child from Five to Ten.* New York: Harper and Row, 1977.

Ginsberg, Herbert, and Sylvia Opper. *Piaget's Theory of Intellectual Development.* Englewood Cliffs, NJ: Prentice Hall, Inc., 1969.

Glen, Stephen H., and Jane Nelson, Ed.D. *Raising Self-Reliant Children in a Self-Indulgent World.* Roseville, Calif.: Prima Publishing, 1989.

Goleman, Daniel. *Emotional Intelligence.* New York: Bantam Books, 1995.

———. *Social Intelligence.* New York: Bantam Books, 2006.

Hallowell, Edward M. *The Childhood Roots of Adult Happiness.* New York: Ballantine Books, 2002.

Kindlon, Daniel. *Raising Cain.* New York: Ballantine Books, 1999.

———. *Too Much of a Good Thing.* New York: Miramax Books, 2001.

Kohn, Alfie. "Five Reasons to Stop Saying 'Good Job!'" *Young Children,* September 2001.

———. *Punished by Rewards.* Houghton Mifflin Company: Boston, 1993.

Kushner, Rabbi Harold. "The Gift of Gratitude: Lessons from the 23rd Psalm." *Family Circle Magazine,* September 2, 2003.

Levine, Madeline. *The Price of Privilege.* New York: HarperCollins, 2006.

Levine, Mel. *A Mind at a Time.* New York: Simon and Schuster, 2002.

Martin, William. *The Parents' Tao Te Ching.* New York: Marlow and Company, 1999.

Milgram, Stanley. "Behavioral Study of Obedience." *Journal of Abnormal and Social Psychology* 67: 371–78.

Mogel, Wendy. *The Blessing of a Skinned Knee: Using Jewish Teachings to Raise Self-Reliant Children.* New York: Scribner, 2001.

Murphy, Lois Barclay. "Sympathetic Behavior in Very Young Children." *Bulletin of the National Center for Clinical Infant Progress.* 12, No. 4: April 1992.

Unell, Barbara C., and Jerry L. Wyckoff. *20 Teachable Virtues.* New York: Berkeley Publishing Group, 1995.

Wareken, F., and M. Tomsell. "Helping and Cooperation at 14 Months of Age." *Infancy* 3 (2007): 271–94.

Wolf, Anthony E. *It's Not Fair, Jeremy Spencer's Parents Let Him Stay Up All Night!* New York: Farrar, Straus and Giroux, 1995.

———. *The Secret of Parenting.* New York: Farrar, Straus and Giroux, 2000.

Websites

www.aacap.org American Academy of Child and Adolescent Psychiatry.

www.aboutourkids.org New York University Child Study Center.

www.acmesharingcompany.com Online resource for finding activities that teach families about giving back.

www.apa.org/topics/kidscare American Psychological Association.

www.connectionparenting.com Useful website for parents and teachers.

www.empoweringparents.com Useful website for parents and teachers.

www.eqtoday.com A website that offers practical tools for emotional intelligence.

www.naspcenter.org National Mental Health and Education Center.

www.parenting.com Website for *Parents* magazine.

www.parentcenter.babycenter.com Online resource for parents of children two to eight years old.

www.parents-choice.org Parents' Choice reviews children's media.

www.parentingscience.com Evidence-based information for the thinking parent.

www.zerotothree.org Zero to Three is an organization that addresses the needs and development of infants, toddlers, and families.

Index

❖

ALSO BY
BETSY BROWN BRAUN

JUST TELL ME WHAT TO SAY
Sensible Tips and Scripts for Perplexed Parents

ISBN 978-0-06-145297-0 (paperback)

Parents are often perplexed by their children's typical behaviors and inevitable questions. This down-to-earth guide provides "Tips and Scripts" for handling everything from sibling rivalry and the food wars to questions about death, divorce, sex, and, of course, the universal and all-encompassing question, "whyyyy?" Betsy Brown Braun blends humor with her expertise as a child development specialist, popular parent educator, and mother of triplets. Whatever your dilemma or child's question—from "How did the baby get in your tummy?" to "What does 'dead' mean?"—Betsy offers the tools and confidence you need to explain the world to your growing child.

"Betsy Brown Braun is a master teacher and one of the wisest parenting experts I have ever known."
—Steven Carr Reuben, Ph.D., author of *Children of Character: Leading Your Children to Ethical Choices in Everyday Life*

"Raising a healthy child to become a self-sufficient, satisfied adult is the aim of this well-written book. Betsy Brown Braun is a fine observer of children and has the remarkable ability to offer practical solutions to the everyday task of child-rearing in a readable, informative, and careful text."
—Robert M. Landaw, M.D., Pediatrician and Assistant Clinical Professor of Pediatrics, UCLA